PROCESS AND PERFORMANCE OF GRAM PANCHAYAT WOMEN AND DALIT PRESIDENTS

By the Same Author

- Building Skill and Capability among Gram Panchayat *(In Press)*
- Dynamics of New Panchayati Raj System in India (in 15 volumes series)
- Emerging Dimensions in Decentralisation *(In Press)*
- Ethnic Identity and National Loyalty of Ethnic Group (A Case Study of Tamil Nadu) *(In Press)*
- Functional Efficiency of Gram Sabha in Tamil Nadu *(In Press)*
- Grassroot Democracy in Indian Society
- New Panchayati Raj System at Work : An Evolution
- New Panchayati Raj in Tamil Nadu (with Act in Original)
- Capacity Building for Local Body Leaders
- Rural Transformation and People's Entitlement

About the Author

Ganapathy Palanithurai, Professor in Rajiv Gandhi Chair, Gandhigram Rural Institute is an academic activist working with the people in rural areas for building the capacity of the leaders and people to reinvent sustainable grassroots democracy. He is heading the Department of Political Science and Development Administration, in Gandhigram Rural University, Tamil Nadu. His policy advocacy role at the governmental level is increasingly felt at present in all the three levels, namely, sub-regional, regional and national as he does more field work than theorization. He has been associating himself with State Planning Commission of Tamil Nadu, Population Foundation of India, Rajiv Gandhi Foundation, CAPART, Ministry of Rural Areas and Employment and DANIDA (Danish-Indo Development Agency) in specific areas of activities in connection with empowerment of people. He is in the network of the Non-Governmental Organisations for Panchayat activities. He involves himself in capacity building exercise for local body leaders. He has evolved training module and manual for local body leaders. He has to his credit twenty-four books, seventy-five articles in reputed journals, ten working papers, seven monographs, seven review articles on three major areas, namely, Legislative Behaviour, Ethnicity and Panchayati Raj System. He was a recipient of Fellowship from Sastri Indo-Canadian Institute, New Delhi and World Academy of Art and Science, USA. He has visited the US and Canada, on academic assignments. He was a visiting fellow in the MiGill University, Canada in 1989. He is a life member of Indian Institute of Public Administration, Indian Association of Public Administration, Indian Association of Political Science, Indian Association of American Studies, and Indian Association of Canadian Studies. He is a member of the expert committee constituted by the Government of Tamil Nadu, to monitor the training programme for local body leaders.

PROCESS AND PERFORMANCE OF GRAM PANCHAYAT WOMEN AND DALIT PRESIDENTS

(With 38 Case Studies of Tamil Nadu Panchayats)

By

G. PALANITHURAI

CONCEPT PUBLISHING COMPANY, NEW DELHI-110059

Cataloging in Publication Data—DK
Courtesy: D.K. Agencies (P) Ltd. <docinfo@dkagencies.com>

Palanithurai, G. (Ganapathy), 1953-
Process and performance of gram panchayat women and dalit presidents : with 38 case studies of Tamil Nadu panchayats / by G. Palanithurai.
p. cm.
Includes bibliographical references (p.)
Includes index.
ISBN 8180692035

1. Panchayat—India—Tamil Nadu—Citizen participation—Case studies. 2. Women in politics—India—Tamil Nadu—Case studies. 3. Dalits— India—Tamil Nadu—Political activity—Case studies. I. Title.

DDC 320.840 954 82 21

IISBN-81-8069-203-5

First Published 2005

Published and Printed by
Ashok Kumar Mittal
Concept Publishing Company
A/15-16, Commercial Block, Mohan Garden
NEW DELHI-110059 (India)

Phones : 25351460, 25351794
Fax : +91-11-25357103
Email : publishing@conceptpub.com

PREFACE

In India there are several paradoxes in the functioning of the political system. The British Government took a short time to transfer powers to Indians. But both the Centre and State governments took more time to transfer power to the people through the Panchayats. Finally Rajiv Gandhi started the exercise of devolving powers to the people through the concrete measure of enacting a legislation. Of course he was forced to fail, but his successor, P.V. Narasimha Rao, succeeded in the attempt. Basically it is an attempt to democratize Indian society. Indian society still maintains a feudal character and it is in the grip of patriarchy. To capture power the poor and the socially underprivileged have to struggle in the political system since the social obstacles are enormous. In order to attain a respectable status women and Dalits have to struggle hard. Right from the adoption of the Constitution to the recent 73rd Amendment, an array of steps had been initiated by the state to provide equal status to women and Dalits. Constitutional provisions have provided due status and role to the underprivileged but the communities do not allow them to enjoy the equal status and opportunities provided by the Constitution. A remarkable transformation is going on in the rural areas as women and Dalits have moved over to institutions of governance and struggled to establish themselves as leaders. Despite their handicaps they perform their roles and responsibilities. It is interesting to look into how they discharge their roles and responsibilities.

Of the three Governments, the Panchayat Raj System is the first government and the most complicated one when compared to the Central and State Govenments as the Central and State Governments have clear cut lists of powers whereas the task of giving powers to the Panchayat Raj System to make it an institution of self government has been entrusted to the State Government. Perceptions of the Panchayat Raj System vary according to the perspective one develops for operationaliza-tion.

Yet, the system has been created, elections have been conducted, leaders have been positioned in different offices, powers have been devolved, however limited they are, finances have been devolved, however meager they are, functionaries have been attached to the system, however inadequate they are, and activities have been carried out by the Panchayats. The results are coming out from the Panchayat institutions, patterns are emerging in Panchayat administration and struggles are on to capture power. All these developments have to be captured and put in proper perspective to identify the obstacles and barriers in the process of devolution of powers. To look at the issues in Panchayats, one should keep in mind the fact that the basis developed by the late Rajiv Gandhi for constitutionalizing Panchayats through amendments is the basic framework for the Panchayat Raj System and the issues have to be analyzed against the backdrop of the framework.

To speak about the issues, one has to start from the experience of the Panchayats and in that respect the exercise has to be started from the functioning of Gram Panchayats, that too under the leadership of women and Dalit representatives. Basically this document presents cases with their socio-economic background, their recruitment process, their perception and their performance. It is more of a compilation rather than an analysis of all those issues. Basically it provides information for theorization. It is full of narrations. Though the possibility for theorization is less, one can deduce propositions out of these cases. This study brings out the achievements of the elected women and Dalit representatives along with their struggle.

PRIA, New Delhi, extended financial support to carry out this study. The staff of the Rajiv Gandhi Chair devoted their time and energy with a sense of commitment to collect data from the field. Panchayat leaders responded to our request and spared their valuable time with the research team and provided the needed information. Gandhigram Rural Institute provided the needed ambience to carry out this kind of activities as it is one of the basic objectives of the Gandhigram Rural Institute. The teaching staff of the Department of Political Scinece and Development Administration extended all possible cooperation to complete this task. I, as Coordinator, extend my heartfelt thanks to those institutions and individuals who extended whole hearted support to me to complete this project successfully.

Gandhigram
23.07.2004

G. PALANITHURAI

CONTENTS

ABBREVIATIONS

ABDO	-	Assistant Block Development Officer
AYC	-	Ambedkar Youth Committee
ASSEFA	-	Association of Sarva Seva Farms
AMT	-	Anna Marumalarchi Thittam
CENTEC	-	Centre for Development and Communication Trust
CRSP	-	Central Rural Sanitation Programme
CPR	-	Common Property Resources
DWCRA	-	Development of Women & Children in Rural Areas
DANIDA	-	Danish International Development Agency
DRDA	-	District Rural Development Agency
DYFI	-	Democratic Youth Federation in India
EAS	-	Employment Assurance Scheme
IAY	-	Indira Awas Yojana
JFM	-	Joint Forest Management
JGSY	-	Jawahar Grama Samridhi Yojana
JVVT	-	Jawahar Velaivaipu Thittam
IAY	-	Indira Awas Yojana
NABARD	-	National Bank for Agriculture and Rural Development
NYK	-	Nehru Yuva Kendra
OAP	-	Old Age Pension
OHT	-	Over Head Tank
RETC	-	Regional Extension Training Centre
SIRD	-	State Institute of Rural Development
SGSY	-	Sampoorna Grama Samridhi Yojana

SSLC	-	Secondary School Learning Certificate
SFC	-	Social Forestry Scheme
SHG	-	Self Help Group
TANWA	-	Tamil Nadu Women in Agriculture
THADCO	-	Tamil Nadu Adi Dravida Housing and Development Corporation Limited
TNSWB	-	Tamil Nadu Social Welfare Board
TWAD	-	Tamil Nadu Water & Drainage Board
TRYSEM	-	Training of Rural Youth in Self-Employment
VHN	-	Village Health Nurse
VAO	-	Village Administrative Officer

1

INTRODUCTION

The present conditions, particularly in the developing countries, demonstrate that the state and the government are no longer effective and capable of serving the people and ensuring good governance. One finds a wide gap between the citizens and the government. Governments, by their unlimited expansion and growth, have come to take away a major chunk of the revenues as management cost to deliver services. In the process of expansion people have been driven away from governance and participation in the development process. To stem the flight attempts have been made to connect the citizenry with the government. To perform the above task steps have been taken to devolve powers from the federal government to the lowest unit of administration in the society. It is not a limited exercise done in a country or two but is spread over around sixty to seventy countries in the world. Such initiatives have broad objectives and expectations. They are :

1. Deepening of democracy,
2. Protecting the self-respect of the people,
3. Ensuring basic facilities to the people,
4. Delivering better quality of service to the people,
5. Securing the entitlements of the people,
6. Ensuring livelihood security,
7. Ensuring participation of the people in governance,
8. Administering economic activities,
9. Delivering social justice,
10. Maintaining efficiency in administration,

11. Establishing transparency in administration,
12. Reducing corruption in governance and administration,
13. Reducing government establishments,
14. Increasing the responsibilities of the citizens,
15. Building partnership between citizens' organizations and institutions of the state or the government,
16. Providing more employment opportunity for human energy,
17. Initiating planning exercises from below,
18. Giving due consideration to reducing gender disparity,
19. Protecting the environment, and
20. Working for the upliftment of the poor.

Objectives of Decentralization

The objectives vary from country to country, depending on their needs and conditions. In India, the objectives are broad and deep as they have to achieve far reaching changes in the attitude, behaviour, performance and the lifestyle of the people who live in the rural areas. The objectives are:

Deepening of Democracy

The democracy confined within the framework of the parliament and state legislatures has to be broadened to percolate to the last rung of the society. Collectivities who have been hitherto marginalised and deprived have to be brought into the fold of democracy. More numbers from women and *Dalit* groups have to be brought into the system of governance. This should be an affirmative action by which the marginalised and the depressed are given an exclusive space through reservation of seats in the local bodies. Thus it is a process by which democracy will be widened and deepened.

Ensuring People's Participation

People's participation is the *sine qua non* for development. Development initiatives are to come from the people. People are the initiators and the government is the facilitator. To shift the government to a facilitator's role from the role of a provider, people have to take the initiative and accept new responsibilities. Their participation in the development activities will bring about accountability on the part of the government. People have to assess their requirements and chalk out schemes and programmes according to their needs. They should be people's programmes and the government has to participate in the programmes by enabling the people to carry out the programmes on their own.

More Responsibilities to People

In the past fifty years, all the responsibilities of the people and the community have been taken away from them and vested with government departments. Communities had enormous responsibilities to manage their affairs on their own and they have their own management system. In the name of nation-state, governments have expanded their departments. The expansion of the government has increased only the management cost and not the efficiency in delivery. To deliver service worth one rupee, the government spends six rupees as delivery charges. Moreover, the quality of the service is poor. In this structural expansion of the government, people have lost their orientation towards the responsibilities that have to be discharged by themselves as citizens. Ultimately what we find in the society is that people have a voter's orientation and they do not have a citizen's orientation. In order to make the people responsible citizens, more responsibilities have to be given to them. Hence development works could be allowed to be carried out with the involvement of the people.

Reduction of Government Structure

Many of the countries in the world are facing crises as a result of the expansion of the departments of the governments. The bigness of the government is a burden on the society. It will pave the way for the disintegration of the nation. The unwieldy expansion of government departments becomes a threat to the elected representatives. Moreover, people are terrorized by the government through its procedures, rules and regulations. The larger the size of the government the lesser the contact with the people. Hence there will be a gap between the people and the government. In order to resolve this complication caused by the bigness of the government, it is felt that the structure of the government should be reduced to the minimum level and that this could be done only by giving more responsibilities to the people through the institutions created legitimately.

Harnessing Human Energy

It is a truism that development can be achieved only according to the way in which human energy is being utilized. Human energy has different forms and different levels. The state should find a way to raise the level of the energy of people and more particularly the state should work out a mechanism through which the energy of people could be utilised. The developed nations have demonstrated to the world how far the energy level of the people could be enhanced and how best the enhanced energy could be utilised for activities to accelerate economic growth. To utilise the energy of the people, appropriate space could be created through an institutional arrangement. Local body institutions are one such institutional device or mechanism to make use of human energy for productive functions.

Administering Development and Social Justice

It is a well known fact that countries which are in the process of decentralising powers have different objectives. But, in India, it was a conscious decision of the Central Government that Panchayati Raj institutions have to work for administering development and social justice by evolving their own plan of action. Traditionally, Panchayati Raj has been looked upon as an institution meant for providing services and facilities. But, in the new context, it is meant for not only services and facilities but also growth with equity.

Planning from Below

Traditionally, planning exercise had been done at the central level, which resulted in large scale demands of the people being unmet. In fifty-two years of governance, centralised planning has achieved tremendous results in the macro economics of this country and yet the rural realities have not been changed significantly towards achieving development. Still people are living in sub-human living conditions in the rural and urban areas. In order to provide basic facilities, to make use of the facilities for growth and to initiate economic activities planning has to be done at the micro level. It has been thought of many times in independent India, whether planning institutions could be created at the bottom either at the block level or at the district level. Now this concept has gained currency and planning is sought to be initiated at different levels, starting from the Gram Panchayat.

Building the Capacity of People

It is an imperative in decentralization of power that people should take on more responsibilities and discharge the same effectively and efficiently to deliver services of quality to the people. To perform the new responsibilities, the capacity of the people has to be enhanced. As of date, people have developed the stereotype that the government has to provide everything and people will to receive the same. Now the role has been reversed. People have to manage their affairs on their own. Therefore, the new system envisages a new task of building the capacity of the leaders and the people. In a market driven economy, for every act, people require skills and efficiency. People with skills are to be updated and upgraded to match the requirements of the market. Against this background capacity building assumes significance.

Establishing the Principle of Subsidiarity

The whole exercise has to revolve round the principle of subsidiarity. Activities that could be carried out at the lowest level could be allowed to be carried out at that level and things that could not be carried out at the lowest level could be allowed to be carried out at the next higher level. Activities are to be carried out at the appropriate levels depending on the capacity of the people. Based on the above principle, powers are to be devolved.

Putting the Last First

Fifty years of development in India have demonstrated the postulate that development cannot be achieved without the involvement of the people in the development process as stakeholders. In all these years, development programmes have been the programmes and schemes of the government and not of the people. In the whole development process one would find the people as the last beneficiaries. As a result real development was not achieved as planned. Programmes should not be generated by the government but have to be evolved by the people. Programmes and schemes are to be owned by the people. Governments have to participate in the programmes and schemes of the people. People come first and the government comes next.

Establishing Good Governance

Administration surely alienates the people. Proliferation of administrative procedures, norms and regulations has made the system totally non-transparent. As long as administration is being run non-transparently corruption will continue to spread to every nook and corner of the society. To prevent such malaise, the administration should simplify the procedures, norms and regulations. The whole process has to be initiated from below. Administration should be transparent. Further, it should accommodate every segment of the society, particularly women and the marginalized.

It should be Pro-Nature

The alarming environmental problems and global warming caution our policy makers and administrators that unless a serious action is taken our life will become problematic. The global scenario calls for local action to protect the environment. The activities of the people should be oriented towards protecting the environment and maintaining the natural order. While taking decisions at the micro level and implementing schemes and programmes for rural development adequate care should be taken to protect the flora and the fauna. All the ponds, wells, tanks, channels and lanes are to be protected and maintained properly. All the commons are to be secured and managed well. There is a close link between environmental problems and poverty. The green is the lifeline of the poor. By protecting the green, the poor can be given life.

It should be Pro-Poor

All the activities are to be decided on the basis of equity. While taking decisions and fixing priorities for rural development activities, the Panchayat has to decide whether the benefits will reach the poor. Normally, if basic facilities and amenities are not available, the rich do not bother about it, because they can afford to purchase the same. But the life of the poor will be miserable in the absence of public basic facilities and amenities. Hence priority has to be given to the poor. 'Unto this last' has to be the policy of the Panchayat. The poorest of the poor has to be given priority in determining beneficiaries and benefits.

It should be Pro-Women

Panchayat activities have to be carefully designed so as to provide enough scope for women both in terms of participation and benefits. Hitherto, the neglected section of the society has been women, who should be integrated into the mainstream of economic and political activities. Further, among the problems faced by the rural society, 70 to 80 per cent relate directly to women because of the absence of basic amenities, facilities and services. Hence, the decentralised political institutions nearer to the people should have resilience to accommodate womenfolk in their activities.

To achieve the above stated objectives two historical amendments have been brought into the Constitution of India.

They are the 73rd and the 74th Constitutional Amendment Acts. All the States in India have enacted provincial acts to conform to the basic characteristics of the 73rd and 74th Constitutional Amendment Acts. The operationalization of the principles varies from State to State. The impact of the Constitutional Amendment Acts has to be gauged in course of time. It is not so easy to assess the impact of the devolution of powers. Likewise the process of devolution of powers is also very difficult and painful. Hence, it is necessary to evaluate the process of devolution that takes place at the grassroots before assessing the impact of devolution of powers.

After this decentralization of powers to the institutions of governance at the grassroots, research ventures have been initiated, but not at the global level. Sporadic studies in many of the countries discovered both positive and negative results. Steps are on to evolve an appropriate strategy for viewing this local governance in proper perspective. Close analysis sometimes discovers negative results also.

Against this background, in India, attempts have been made to strengthen the grassroots institutions for which proper evaluation is needed. While evaluating the performance, pioneering studies in the west focused on (1) participation, (2) new styles of leadership, (3) accountability and transparency, (4) capable public management, and (5) respect for law and human rights. These aspects have to be kept in perspective while evaluating the functioning of the grassroots institutions.

In India, contrary to expectations, reports are being highlighted in the press about the negative results of decentralization of power such as misuse of power and corrupt practices. Cases reported in the newspapers are very small in number and yet the opinion gets strengthened in the absence of realistic analysis of the performance of the grassroots level institutions. There is evidence to show that the grassroots level institutions have their own track record of performance, but they are not scientifically documented and analyzed.

Against this background an attempt is made to evaluate the performance of the Panchayat leaders and document it. The present documentation has two main objectives, namely, evaluating the performance of the Panchayats and their leaders, documenting the best practices for larger level emulation and replication, and suggesting ways and means to eliminate the factors which act as deterrents to the success of the Panchayats through policy advocacy.

When performance evaluation is being done, one has to take note of some methodological issues in the context of India. For about three decades since independence, evaluating the performance of the governments was a neglected subject despite several pleas and requests. Economists have evaluated the performance of the governments so far but their analysis is always of growth and development. Comprehensive evaluation of governmental performance has not been carried out in any one of the States or for the Central Government so far. Many reasons are put forward for this neglect. Of these reasons non-availability of a standardized performance scale for such evaluation is important. Social scientists are bound to face many difficulties in evolving a standardized scale for the evaluation of the performance of grassroots institutions. The commitment to decentralization of power being imperative, the evaluation should be based on scientific knowledge. Bearing this in mind, an attempt has been made to evaluate the performance of the grassroots institutions in Tamil Nadu. To theorize the decentralization of power and to eliminate the determinents to the success of decentralization of power, the methodology for evaluation should be subjected to scrutiny before using it for evaluating the performance of the grassroots institution.

The aspects to be taken into consideration while evaluating the performance have to be incorporated in the evaluation scale. The performance of the institutions can be assessed based on the activities carried out and recorded. The recorded performance cannot be evaluated unless the individuals and groups involved in the process of the activities are also studied.

To evaluate the performance of the Panchayat leaders there are certain factors which have to be studied carefully. They are:

(a) Socio-economic background of the leaders.
(b) Political socialization process of the leaders.
(c) Political recruitment process of the leaders.
(d) Role perception of the leaders.

(e) Their perception of development.
(f) Their perception of democracy.
(g) Their perception of gender issues.
(h) Their perception of the marginalized.
(i) Their perception of participation.
(j) Capacity of the leaders in managing the Panchayats.
(k) Interface between leaders and the councils.
(l) Interface between leaders and officials.
(m) Interface between leaders and the people.
(n) Performance of assigned roles.
(o) Performance of assumed roles.

In a democratic polity the above variables do play a significant role in determining the success or failure of leaders in public office. All these aspects have both quantitative and qualitative variables. They are to be assessed.

To conduct this study the quantum of cases has been fixed. It was proposed to select cases from all the districts representing successful and unsuccessful women Panchayat leaders and successful and unsuccessful *Dalit* leaders. In each district two elected representatives are to be studied and the assessment has to be documented. Case study method has been used to do this exercise. In all these cases the process of their management of Panchayats has been assigned.

A note on the limitations of the study will ensure a proper perspective. Some of the Panchayat Presidents were very uncommunicative and a few were too ignorant to be able to communicate anything. A few Panchayat Presidents who were only figurehead Presidents, were very hesitant to provide information. The presence of other villagers during the interviews seemed to restrain some Panchayat Presidents from speaking frankly, particularly about members of communities other than their own. This study has focused its attention on the two segments, namely women and *Dalit* Gram Panchayati leaders. Success and failures of Panchayati Institutions and leaders are analysed. But there are gaps in this analysis as the researchers could not get enough data from the respondents owing to the reason that they have many inherent weaknesses in their system. Although this work is not for generalization and theory building, it captures the vital elements and factors for the success of the institutions and also indicates the barriers and obstacles in performing the assigned roles and responsibilities. In this study cases have been drawn from the first tier of the Panchayat system, namely Gram Panchayat. The reasons for selecting the Gram Panchayat are many. Primarily Gram Panchayats are freed from the party clutches in the whole of the Panchayati Raj system. Secondly, it is working with the participation of the people. Thirdly, the Gram Panchayat Presidents are performing their functions both as elected leaders and executive heads in the system. Thus this study focuses its attention on the process of devolution of powers at the lowest level.

CASE ANALYSIS

2

CASE ANALYSIS

CASE – 1

BALAMUTHUR GRAM PANCHAYAT
ORATHANADU BLOCK, THANJAVUR DISTRICT

Socio-Economic Background

Ms. Eswari is the President of Balamuthur Village Panchayat. Her age is 28. She belongs to the Kallar community. Her schooling in a Christian convent made her move close to Christian understanding and she is now a firm believer of Jesus. She does not believe in conversion. But she discontinued the practice of visiting Hindu temples. She is now attending the prayer meetings of the Pentecostal sect of Christians.

Recollecting her early childhood days, Ms. Eswari stated that her father was an alcoholic, lost his property, and went to a foreign country for earning. Due to unexpected circumstances, her schooling in the English medium convent became a problem. The Christian missionaries helped her to continue her education. With the limited money sent by her father, her mother managed the family. Apart from her, her parents have two children. As she was a mature girl, the sisters in the convent entrusted responsibilities to her. She used to look after young children and helped the teachers in their several activities. The poverty experienced by her taught a lesson to her. She decided to help poor children, particularly in their studies. Her father returned to the native village and led a simple life, cultivating 2.5 acres of dry land with borewell facility. Coconut trees were planted. And he took on lease one acre of land for paddy cultivation.

Ms. Eswari, in the meantime, completed her higher secondary school education. She helped her brother and sister in their studies. She started service to the community and to the neighbours in several ways. She realized the problems of the poor families belonging to other castes including the Scheduled Caste. Her father is a member of the Village Committee in which local issues are settled peacefully. When the election to the New Panchayati Raj institutions was declared, her father was an active member of the Tamil Manila Congress. As the post of President was reserved for general women, the villagers of Balamuthur proposed Ms. Eswari's name. But her father did not take it seriously.

The Recruitment Process

Even though her father did not encourage her candidature, Ms. Eswari thought that it was an opportunity to serve the villagers, that too the poor and the women. Hence she expressed her willingness to her parents and her determination to contest in the election. There are four hamlets including Balamuthur in her Village Panchayat. A candidate from the hamlet Kudikadu was fielded against Ms. Eswari by the villagers of Kudikadu. This candidate was also from the same Kallar caste. She was a married woman and her husband was an activist in the local unit of DMK Party. She spent a lot of money to defeat Ms. Eswari. But Ms. Eswari won by two votes and these too were disputed by the opponent. Hence, the election officials declared that both the candidates got equal votes. Confident of winning in a lot, the other candidate agreed to the suggestion for a lot system from the election officials while Ms. Eswari disagreed. Despite this the election officials, with the concurrence of the elders, decided to select the winners by lot. It happened to be Ms. Eswari. The other candidate accepted the verdict. Ms. Eswari became the fortunate President of Balamuthur.

The villagers of Balamuthur helped Ms. Eswari in canvassing. Her father accompanied her during canvassing at Balamuthur. Her relatives and friends of her father joined her when visiting the other three hamlets for canvassing. Ms. Eswari assured the people that she would provide basic facilities to the people, particularly drinking water. Wall posters were printed and pasted and notices were distributed assuring that necessary welfare facilities would be provided to the villagers by this candidate. The overall expenditure was below Rs.10,000. The canvassing was smooth but the defeated candidate took it as a serious challenge. Hence, even after the election, she maintained a feeling of enmity with Ms. Eswari. Her faction resorted to disturbing the Panchayat activities. They disputed the identification of a site for the construction of a *balwadi* and a ration shop in their village.

But Ms. Eswari, with a sense of responsibility as President, did not do any injustice to the villagers of Kudikadu. She carried out the necessary work in Kudikadu village also. She said that she patiently maintained calmness instead of reacting to the anti-Panchayat activities of the opponent. After a period of two years, the villagers of Kudikadu dropped their enmity with the President. But the opponent did not completely change.

The major contributory factors for her success, according to Ms. Eswari, were her educational background, her character and her Christian faith; her sociability with all communities; and, her father's social leadership.

Her Perception

On the concept of Panchayati Raj, Ms. Eswari had no knowledge except that reservation was provided for women in the Panchayati Raj institutions. But, after becoming the President, she attended the training programmes, meetings and other programmes convened by officials. Slowly she was able to make out from the deliberations of the officials what Panchayats were.

Regarding awareness of the Tamil Nadu Panchayat Act, she does not know the provisions of the Act and the rules. But she knows the provisions in Articles 205 and 206 as this is essential in the day-to-day administration to escape from administrative hassles. She listed a number of major and contentious issues in the Panchayat administration, namely, joint signature system, convening of the Gram Sabha, insufficient fund allocation, increasing expenditure on electricity, very limited powers conferred upon the Panchayat etc. The President learnt all these only from experience.

She stated that if more opportunities and encouragement are given to women Panchayat Presidents by enhancing the percentage of reservation for women, they will perform well. If power is really bestowed upon the Panchayati Raj institutions, they will carry out successful experiments. She has suggested that the sectoral departments have to consult the Panchayats for effective implementation of their programmes. By doing so, effective delivery could be achieved. She explained that because of her rapport with various sectoral departments, she was able to bring benefits to the right beneficiaries.

On Development

Her perception of development is centred round agriculture and employment opportunities for youth and women. She observed that those who worked hard in agriculture are getting profit and those who migrate outside can earn a lot. She said that by getting more information through mass media, particularly TV and radio, quite a number of families are improving their economic status. Infrastructure facilities, training and financial assistance are the major factors of development, she said. Special and specific need based programmes pertaining to villages will be very useful at the grassroots.

With regard to the village economy she suggested that irrigation sources have to be improved and women SHGs should be guided properly. They are eagerly forming groups and initiating micro financial activities. She emphasised that agriculture and employment opportunities are the means of development. She felt that if a party is built up from below, it would be a successful one. She did not join any party first. But recently she has joined the DMK. The programmes evolved by the then DMK Government were very much people oriented. Service to the poor is considered the ideology of the DMK. On gender issues, Ms. Eswari has the opinion that the social status of womenfolk has improved. As an example she narrated that the politically active men encourage their family women to enter public life and politics. On social justice, she observed that the atrocities perpetrated on the Scheduled Caste people are now reduced. She recollected an incident of community conflict. A man belonging to the SC had an illegal affair with a woman belonging to the Backward Class (BC). The BC community people killed the man in an angry mood. A police case was registered and the culprit was punished. This type of violent behaviour has now decreased. She suggested that social justice to women and suppressed communities could be easily achieved through Self-Help Group (SHG) women by creating awareness among the women and the suppressed communities.

Socialization Process

As an educated lady, Ms. Eswari helped the other women in their activities. She guided them in getting Government schemes for women and the poor. She gradually understood the social issues and social transformation process as her father is a member in the Village Committee. After becoming the President, she improved her relationship with women and men. She enrolled herself as a member in the Lions Club. She constituted a Vigilance Committee to monitor the eradication of alcoholism. By visiting various offices, she cultivated the practice of interface with officials. Now she can deliver an address on the stage without any difficulty. Thus she has achieved socialization.

She has a two-wheeler and she drives on her own. She stated that the perception of society of the women who are in public life has not yet changed. But the society is trying to understand the women leaders when they achieve things in their career. By newspaper reading, viewing TV and reading books, Ms. Eswari is improving her understanding of the importance of the involvement of the people in development. On occasions, people contribute generously for public causes. But normally people are underestimated by the officials. When people are respected and informed properly they participate in every development activity.

Ms. Eswari associated herself with the PWD staff when the channel maintenance and desilting work was undertaken. Attending the consultative meeting of the TWAD, she was able to explain the inadequate water supply and succeeded in getting two more OHTs for her Panchayat. Due to her proper follow up and persistence, a check dam was allotted by the PWD by which 500 acres of land are getting adequate water for irrigation. She took seriously the villagers' requests and resolutions in the Gram Sabha meetings. She took up the issues with the concerned officials, higher political representatives and the district authority and succeeded in her attempts. During the period 2000-2001, construction of a TV room and a cement concrete road were undertaken. All the works were executed by her and the Vice-President who happens to be a member of the same community. She made all the accounts transparent and hence the Vice-President extended his wholehearted support.

Performance

In the beginning she faced many problems and after understanding the basics of the Panchayati Raj system her initiative to undertake activities was challenged and she faced struggles. But, after some time, by sheer hard work she achieved many things for her Panchayat.

During 1996-97 she tried her best to get a new transformer installed in her Panchayat by influencing the Electricity Board. Retaining wall construction and improvement of a few roads was successfully done. By influencing the Highways Department, she tried to provide BT roads in the villages. During 1997-98, attention was given to roads which had not been taken up earlier. Electricity was provided to a hamlet where so far no service connection had been given. She provided toilet facility to the primary school and extended water supply pipeline to the toilets.

When the innovative programme of Namakku Naame Thittam was announced, she encouraged the local community leaders to undertake desilting and maintenance work in two ponds. A volunteer came forward to undertake this assignment as a donation provided he was permitted to execute the contract. As the villagers agreed to this the desilting was done by the donor. She got notebooks and uniform dress for poor students from a few clubs.

Her regular meetings with the MLA helped her to get many of the schemes through the MLA's recommendation. She succeeded in getting an allocation for road-gravel work from the District Panchayat. Her relationship with the Union Chairperson is very good. The Chairperson is a woman belonging to her village constituency. Allocations for roads, noon meal centre, school building and small bridges were given to her Panchayat from the Union General Fund. She concentrated her efforts on achieving sanitation in her Panchayat. Under the CRSP (old scheme) 20 toilets were provided. All are in use. Under the new scheme (Rs. 500 estimate) 274 toilets were provided but the beneficiaries planned to modify them by spending additional money. So most of the toilets built under this scheme are being still utilized. She periodically meets the village health nurse. The nurse hands over the tablets and medicines to Ms. Eswari who gives the same to the right persons. With the help of the Makkal Nala Paniyalarkal, she maintains the library. She permits a few persons to take books home for reading also.

A Case of Traditional Panchayat *vs.* Formal Panchayat

When an allocation for the construction of a new ration shop was made, after long and continuous consultation with all, Ms. Eswari identified a place convenient to both Balamuthur and Kudikadu villages. But the Vice-President, who is the representative of the traditional Panchayat, proposed another site, which is very close to Balamuthur but not convenient to Kudikadu. Ms. Eswari explained that the Panchayat office is also located near the site she had selected. Due to this difference, the work was not carried out and it was cancelled. The traditional Panchayat leaders want to establish their supremacy over the formal and Constitutional Panchayat. Because of the strongly rooted belief system in the villages people are not able to challenge the leadership of the traditional Panchayats, according to Ms. Eswari. The Vice-President and other community leaders did not expect this cancellation. They thought that Ms. Eswari would abide by the suggestion of the village community.

The Panchayat administration is properly carried out by the President. She regularly verifies the records and bank transactions. She visits all hamlets daily by cycle and meets the villagers of each hamlet. Whenever work is carried out, she gives special attention to executing the work properly. This monitoring exercise is observed by the people.

Panchayat Resources

The house tax was revised in the year 1997-98 by which a sum of Rs. 8,023 was additionally collected. The major source of income is stamp duty. The income other than taxes are auction of 20 tamarind trees and 120 coconut trees. The coconut trees are around Kudikadu Mariamman temple and tank. Most of the coconut trees are getting old and so it is proposed to replace them by young ones. After she became the President, she talked with the local people who used to bid in the auction. She decided to enhance the auction amount. So about Rs. 5,000 was additionally collected over the previous year. But due to poor prices for coconut, the auction amount during 2000-2001 was reduced. With regard to income from ponds, Ms. Eswari stated that the concerned village community gets the tender and re-auctions the rights for more money. This practice is an age old one and so the Panchayat could not do anything about this. The amount they get by re-auctioning goes to the traditional Panchayat. There are about 10 acres of temple land under the control of the Village Committee. The other common properties are vested with the revenue officials.

Regarding encroachments on common properties, Ms. Eswari said that in one grazing yard the approach path belonging to the SC community was encroached upon by two individuals belonging to the BC. It is an old issue. She discussed it with the concerned encroachers but could not make them budge. Moreover, the revenue officials are not helping the Panchayat in removing the encroachment, she complained.

Issues in Execution of Work

With regard to the Panchayat fund and work under this fund, there is no issue except the joint signature of the Vice-President, whereas the scheme funds can be operated only with the permission of Union officials. Moreover, the Union engineer and his staff play a significant role. They have to prepare estimates, issue orders, check the measurements, maintain the 'M' book, and recommend payment. Advance is not permitted for the work execution. Through personal efforts, the materials are arranged by the President. Any undue delay in release of the bill amount will complicate the work as well as payment for the materials. Understanding this trap, the Union engineering section staff demand money. When Ms. Eswari executed a road work, she suffered a loss. When the officials expected bribes she explained her predicament and did not give any money.

She said that the officials expect bribe as the executors of work are getting the project. When 35 *katcha* houses were allotted to her village, she explained the practical problems involved in the execution of the scheme. So the beneficiaries themselves executed the work. The President helped them in getting needed materials like bricks, cement, tiles, and timber from a local trader. When the fund was received, the amount was paid to him. Unless the President takes this type of risk more items of work cannot be received by the Panchayat.

Village Setting

The village of Balamuthur is a multi-caste village, having three hamlets, namely Kudikadu, Talukkai and Pottalakudikadu. The Kallar caste is the majority community and the SCs, Vellalas, Ambalams and Chettiars are the other castes. Village craftsmen like carpenters and goldsmiths are also living in Balamuthur. Caste sangams are not formed. A Village Committee is functioning in which all castes have representation.

The village community generally has a traditional mindset. When the Vice-President, with the support of community leaders, compelled the President to select a site in Balamuthur for a building, the President refused to do so. Hence, the Vice-President refused to affix his signature on the cheques. The Village Committee expects that the President should act according to the suggestions given by the Committee. The enmity was settled by the initiative of the President of a nearby Village Panchayat who is related to both the President and the Vice-President. The village organizations like Village Committee wish to influence or control the Village Panchayat.

There is a registered milk society in which the Vice-President of the Village Panchayat is serving as President. When the payment due to the members of the society was delayed and there was a dispute over the fixation of payment rate for the milk according to its fat content, Ms. Eswari, in her capacity as Village Panchayat President, enquired of the staff upon receiving complaints. They replied that, as the members brought milk mixed with water, the rate was reduced. This was regarded as undue interference in his administration by the Vice-President.

She observed that if the new grassroots institutions like Panchayats, cooperatives and SHGs are captured by the conventional and self-interested leaders, the development process will be baulked.

SHGs are also functioning in the Panchayat. One group was formed and strengthened by an NGO and Ms. Eswari guides the other six groups. The SHG members are close to the President. They understand the Panchayat affairs and wholeheartedly extend their support to the President.

Youth do not organize themselves. But they have formed a Rajinikanth Fans Club. It undertakes no serious social activities. There are temples for deities like Ulagammal, Mariamman, Pillayar and Uthirapathy. The celebration is organized by the concerned Village Committee of each hamlet. The SC community members are permitted to worship. There is no untouchability, no two-tumbler system in this Panchayat area.

Major Social Issues

Arrack sale was one of the major issues in the village. The political parties functioning in the village are AIADMK, DMK, CPI (M), TMC, MDMK and BJP and these parties did not take any steps to prevent the sale. Ms. Eswari and the SHG women took steps to stop the sale. In the hamlet of Kudikadu, a man belonging to the BC raped a women belonging to the SC community. The issue became serious, as the SC community was not ready to accept the verdict of the local Panchayat. A police case was registered and the person was arrested and sentenced to imprisonment. The BC community ostracized the SC families of the particular street. They were not called upon to perform the customary rites during death ceremony and they were not engaged for drum beating during celebrations. More than one and half years have passed but there is no improvement in the social relationship. The BC community is getting help from the SC families residing in other streets. Ms. Eswari could not find any means to settle this issue.

There is another social institution, namely the community well. There are four community wells, two in Balamuthur and two in Kudikadu. The wells were dug under a Government scheme. About forty farmers of Balamuthur and 35 farmers of Kudikadu are the beneficiaries. Of these five and six are SC farmers of the respective villages. The community wells are fitted with electric pumps. The electricity is free of cost to farmers. The beneficiaries have constituted themselves into an association. They have fixed the charge for irrigation as 25 rupees per hour for members and 30 rupees for other farmers. The collected amount is kept for the maintenance of the motor pumps and for desilting the wells. The association employs an operator at a monthly salary of Rs. 600. The President of the Village Panchayat maintains good relationship with the office bearers of this association. They used to attend the Gram Sabha meetings.

Agriculture is the main occupation. About 300 families are engaged in farming. They are all small and middle level farmers. Apart from paddy, grams, groundnut, sugar cane, soya, gingelly are the crops produced in the village. The village lands also get irrigation from the Cauvery channel distribution system.

The President is in association with the Prohibition Enforcement Committee organized by the village community. A Youth Sports Committee is also constituted but the youth do not take any initiative. The traditional system of community leadership in temple celebration is still prevalent in Kalakadu Mariamman festival.

Accounting and Auditing

All the years' accounts have been audited and no major objections have been raised in the audit. The officials' instructions and guidance change when new officials take charge. Hence the President should be provided with clear rules and regulations with regard to various procedures in account maintenance. Panchayat meetings are properly conducted. There are two wards for which there are six members. Of them, four are male and two are female. There is no SC member. From 1996-97 to May 2001 the Panchayat Council has met 57 times. The Gram Sabha has met 9 times with a maximum attendance of 144 and a minimum of 13. Ms. Eswari said that the villagers are not showing interest in attending the Gram Sabha meetings. She takes necessary efforts, but in spite of that, only poor attendance is recorded. The accounts are read out at the meeting. The people expect wage compensation as on most days they are engaged in agriculture.

Only a few *Dalits* used to attend the Gram Sabha meetings. After the formation of the SHG, more women have started attending the Gram Sabha meetings. The Panchayat office is housed in a good building with electricity and toilet facilities. Needed furniture is available. Ms. Eswari is not regularly available in the Panchayat office. But everyday she visits the hamlets and the work spots and meets the members and villagers in their places. She is determined to do social service. She wishes to contest in the next Panchayat election also even if it is reserved for the general category. She wants to serve the society whether she is elected or not. She is ready to contest even in the general category.

CASE - 2

BODITHASANPATTI GRAM PANCHAYAT
ANDIPATTI BLOCK, THENI DISTRICT

Socio-Economic Background

Ms. Amalorpavam, 70 years old, has studied upto the 9th standard, worked as a teacher for more than 39 years and retired from service. She hails from the Parayar community. She is a Christian and she lives in a tiled house, with electricity facility and house tap connection but without toilet facility. Her husband was also a teacher, but he is no more. Her two sons and one daughter are living in other places. She is the only person living in the house now with a pension of Rs. 5,800. She has no land or vehicle.

Recruitment Process

When she was in service as a teacher she used to help the villagers in many ways. She helped the school going children by giving notebooks. She also wrote petitions to help women to get loans and benefits. Since she worked as a teacher in the same village, she was respected by all the caste groups. Many children studied under her guidance. She also moves with the villagers in a pleasant way. This helped her to succeed in the Panchayat elections. The village community has constituted a Committee in which the members belonging to the majority communities Gounders, Chervais, Parayars and Naidus are included. The Village Committee serves for the development of the village. It organizes the celebration of common festivals. The decisions of the Committee are accepted by all because if the villagers disobey them they will be ostracized from the community.

During the Panchayat election the President's position was reserved for SC women. The Committee decided to select the President and nine ward members unopposed. The Committee preferred Ms. Amalorpavam as she is from a respected family. Moreover, nearly all the Committee members had been her students. She was a simple person belonging to the Parayar community. The Committee selected her and nine ward members, of whom five were from the SC community, and 4 from BC communities. All the members accepted the decision of the Village Committee.

Village Set-up

There are 483 families in two villages. The population is 2760, 1225 males and 1535 females. The majority are from the Parayar community. The second largest community are the Gounders. The other communities are Naidus, Sakkiliyars, Asaris, Kuyavars and Pandarams. The Village Committee deals with all common matters like celebration of festivals, hearing disputes between families and other affairs.

There is an association named Dr. Ambedkar Association organized by the village youth. This association celebrates Dr. Ambedkar's birthday. Pongal Day celebration is also organized. Sports and cultural programmes are organized at the time of Pongal and prizes are given to the winners of the events. The youth attend the Gram Sabha meetings and request cooperation at the time of the festivals celebrated in the villages. There are a number of Cine Fans Association for Prasanth, Rajinikanth and Vijay. They celebrate their idols' birthday only. There are six SHGs in the Panchayat. The groups are organized in each community separately. They are in the network Sevanilayam and Arokiyaagam, two NGOs operating in the villages. Arockiyaagam (NGO) is running a community health centre. The health staff visit and administer medicines to the ailing persons. They organize special drives to identify skin diseases and leprosy and give medicines to the patients continuously. The NGO staff members spread awareness about skin diseases, female infanticide, female education, small savings and self-employment for women.

Village Temples

The Mariamman temple is a common temple but the SC community cannot enter it. They are permitted to worship from outside only. At the time of celebrating the temple festival only caste Hindus pay the fixed amount householdwise. SC, Christian, Parayars, Sakkiliyars, Kuyavars and Pandarams do not contribute. There are two churches, one CSI and the other RC, in the Panchayat. All caste members visit the church for prayer. There is no caste discrimination. There is no caste and religion rivalry in the Panchayat.

Village Economy

The economy of the villages is generally centred round agriculture and animal husbandry. Most of the land is rainfed. There is also well irrigation. In these lands crops like cotton, banana, groundnut and onion are cultivated. In dry lands cholam, kambu and pulses are cultivated. Some of the families migrated to Kerala State for agriculture and allied work. They return to their village only during festival times like Pongal. Nearly 50 to 100 villagers get employment in construction work and painting work and do some small businesses like mango, sweets etc. in Andipatti, which is a nearby town. Most of the women are saving their money through SHG groups.

Political Parties

In this Panchayat most of the political parties, namely, AIADMK, DMK, CPI, CPM, TMC, MDMK have a presence. The dominant party is the AIADMK. There is no office building for any party. The various political parties actively participate in political events, but there is no help from them to the Village Panchayat. Ms. Amalorpavam is a retired teacher. She does not have any family work. She regularly visits to the BDO office and the District Collector's office to get some scheme for the village people. She is not in any political party. She meets the District as well as the Union Councillors and the MLA to get some funds for the village. These frequent visits help her to get some funds from them. She got Gandhigram training in the Theni Collector's office. After the training she approached the MLA and the District Collector to get schemes. She said that Gandhigram training is very useful to approach the higher officials and the MLA to get some schemes and that if this training is given in the beginning it will be very useful to know about the schemes and go to the offices without any timidity and hesitation.

Common Property Resources

There are some common property resources in the Panchayat: forest area 0.3 hectare, drought area 0.3 hectare, not used area 0.2 hectare, poramboke land 0.2 hectare and tank area 0.05 hectare. In the Panchayat, poramboke area trees are planted on the bunds of the tank and in the village poramboke lands also trees are planted. There is no way to construct any shop for increasing the Panchayat's income.

Perception of Panchayati Raj

When the elections were announced this Panchayat was reserved for SC women. The Village Committee decided to select a good candidate for the Village Panchayat President's post. Ms. Amalorpavam was selected because she is working in as a teacher for nearly 40 years, and, as an educated women, she would be able to move with the officials easily.

Ms. Amalorpavam said that there is a lot of difference between the two Panchayats: in the earlier Panchayat there was a District Board which looked after primary education, particularly appointments etc. After 1981, primary education was taken over by the Government. In the same way agriculture and health have also been taken over by the Government. There was no reservation for SCs and women. The Panchayat President was always a male dominated.

In the new Panchayati Raj system there is a change: women can become Village Panchayat Presidents because there is a reservation for SCs and women. The Panchayat gets funds from the Government directly. The Panchayat people decide their basic needs. The Panchayat is accountable to the villagers.

Development/Democracy

Ms. Amalorpavam said that 40 items of work were carried out in the last 4½ years. Every year, she got some programme from the Government. The following are the items of work carried out by the President of this Panchayat. In the year 1996-97 under the DANVA scheme, she got loans for Rs. 3,25,000; in 1997-98 a ground level reservoir was constructed at a cost of Rs. 60,000, a hand pump was installed from Panchayat funds at a cost of Rs. 30,000, and from the Drought Relief Fund a 5 HP electric pumpset was purchased at a cost of Rs. 27,775; in the year 1998-99 a TV room for the SC colony was constructed at a cost of Rs.12,500, burial ground road maintenance work was carried out at a cost of Rs.7,800 a new water pipeline was laid from the 10th Finance Commission Fund at a cost of Rs.10,900, and, loans were obtained for SHG members (13 members, Rs.3,60,000); in the year 1999-2000, a threshing flower was constructed at a cost of Rs.59,800, burial ground maintenance work was done at a cost of Rs. 8,000, a cement road was laid from the 10th Finance Commission Fund at a cost of Rs. 21,000, a borewell was sunk at a cost of Rs.57,080, an OHT was constructed through the PWD at a cost of Rs. 3,00,000; in the year 2000-2001, concrete roads were laid in two places at a cost of Rs.60,000 from the District Councillor's Fund, Panchayat office maintenance was done at a cost of Rs. 15,000 from the Panchayat Union Fund, a hand pump was installed at a cost of Rs. 30,000, a youth playground was formed from the MLA Fund at a cost of Rs.25,000 and, from the District Collector's Drought Relief Fund Rs. 40,000 was provided to install a hand pump. Apart from all this she regularly obtains OAP for elderly persons and other assistance for widows and disabled people.

Panchayat President's Opinion about Work Carried Out in the Village

Ms. Amalorpavam is an active President. At the same time she knows how to move with the villagers, evict the encroaches etc. At the time of forming the concrete road in the village she had to evict some encroachers first. If any person obstructs her plans, she approaches the Village Committee to solve the problem.

Opinion about Village Development

To Ms. Amalorpavam village development means giving 100 per cent employment to the villagers, streetlights to all the Panchayat areas, full drinking water supply to the villagers, road facility and needed transport facilities and health facility.

She is a retired teacher and knows how to give attention to their education, strength, environmental neatness, school functioning and how to strengthen the parent-teachers association etc. She frequently visits the school and requests the teachers to increase the strength and the quality of the education. She visits the noon-meal centre and ensures that appropriate nutritious food is given to children and their mothers.

She meets the SHG group members and requests them to repay the bank loan properly first and then develop their standard of living.

Monthly Meetings

Information regarding monthly meetings is sent through the clerk. Three women members (SC-2, BC-1) participate in the meetings and demanded basic facilities for their wards. The President shows them the Panchayat income and expenditure statement and openly gives it to all the members. All the work is distributed among the ward members on a necessity basis. There is no rivalry or conflict in the Panchayat meetings.

Gram Sabha Meetings

Gram Sabha meetings are announced through bit notice and tom-tom. The President invites the Village Committee members, SHG members, school teachers and Department officials (agriculture, electricity). She personally request the ward members to participate in the Gram Sabha meetings. In the Gram Sabha meetings the people decide upon the work to be done. The SHG members demand loans for their members, basic facilities like drinking water, road, transport, and health.

The Village Committee members participate in the Gram Sabha meetings and demand certain basic facilities like extension of pipeline and street lights.

NGOs and the Village Panchayat President

There are two NGOs working in the Village Panchayat. The SHG formed by the Sevanilayam project staff members got a loan for Rs. 3,25,000 to purchase a tractor for the SHG. The staff members of the NGO take care of the repayment of the loan. Another NGO called Arockiaagam checked for skin diseases and gave medicines to the people. There is a medical centre run by the NGO. Medicine is given to the people free of cost. Ms. Amalorpavam stated that the people of the Panchayat use these facilities.

Audit and Accounts System

The present audit system is good, because every three months the accounts are closed, the deposit amounts are returned to the contractors, bills are obtained, and mistakes are corrected by the officials to prepare for the annual audit. This system helps to remember the transactions and give correct answers to the government officials regarding them. This system prevents corruption. Usually Ms. Amalorpavam meets the hospitality charges for the officials.

General Information about the Village

1.	Panchayat building	1
2.	Overhead tanks	3
3.	Public taps	39
4.	Household connections	73
5.	Handpumps	8
6.	Open wells	3
7.	ANM centre	1
8.	NGO clinic	1
9.	*Balwadis*	2
10.	Primary schools	2 (CSI-1, PUC-1)
11.	Noon-meal centres	2
12.	Library	1 (part-time)
13.	Ration Shop	1
14.	Sub-Post office	1
15.	Street lights	52
16.	Self-Help Groups	6
17.	Temples	2
18.	Churches	2

CASE - 3

EECHAMPOONDI GRAM PANCHAYAT KATTUMANNARKOIL BLOCK, CUDDALORE DISTRICT

Socio-Economic Background

Ms. Amutha Lakshmanan is the Panchayat President of Eechampoondi Village Panchayat in Kattumannarkoil Block. She has studied upto the 8th standard, is aged 39 and belongs to the SC community. She has four children, two sons and two daughters. At present one son is studying a one-year computer course and the others are school going children. Her husband is a government employee working as an extension assistant in Sankarapuram. She has one acre of dry land, but there is no regular income from that land. She has two cows and their milk brings regular income to the family. There is no individual tap connection to her house. She lives in a hut. It is electrified with a single light and there is no toilet facility.

Currently she has associated herself with the Women Panchayat Presidents Association of North Zone (Villupuram, Cuddalore, and Thiruvannamali Districts). She is the Secretary of the Association. Besides this she is also the President of the SC Women's Association at the district level.

As the Secretary of the Women Panchayat Presidents Association, Ms. Amutha has also focused on certain issues related to *Dalits* in the Association. She conducted a public meeting highlighting the murder of the Oorappackam Panchayat President. She is very active in the SC Women's Association activities and she has suggested the removal of clause 205 of the Tamil Nadu Panchayat Act, she had a resolution passed in the Women Panchayat Presidents Association at the district level to this effect. She has also suggested that the SC Women's Association President has to continue for another 5 years in the same post without any dislocation.

Ms. Amutha said that there is no political background for her entry into the Panchayat. She does not have any political affiliation. She is interested in mobilizing the people on a non-party basis for development activities. She is keen on creating awareness among the poor, particularly the women and *Dalits* for good governance.

Village Profile

This Panchayat has one hamlet, namely Balwaikandan. In Balwaikandan Village, people of SC and BC are living in equal ratio. In Eechampoondi Village, the SCs are the major community and the other communities have less than 10 households each. The total population is 1,223, of which males are 606 and females are 617. Among the SCs 456 are males and 473 are females. There are two wards in this Panchayat and there are six ward members. The total households are 402, of which 10 are *pucca* houses, 40 tiled ones and 275 huts. The rest are group houses and mixed houses.

Two OHTs are available in the Panchayat and their capacity is 60,000 and one lakh litres respectively. There are 16 public taps and no individual tap connection. There are 12 hand pumps and there are no open wells. With regard to health and sanitation, there are no specific facilities for draining of sewage water. No drainage system is constructed on the streets. Though 25 households have individual toilets, they are not using them properly, but going outside for toilet purposes. There is no health centre in the village, but one is functioning effectively in nearby Kattumannarkoil.

There is a *balwadi*, a noon-meal centre, and a primary school in this Panchayat. There is no higher secondary school in the Panchayat, but one is available in Rettiyoor, about 3 km from the Panchayat. Regular readers come to the Ayyan Library and they take books home after registration from this small library.

Facilities like market, butchery shed, bus shelter, community hall, cinema theatre and post office are not available in the Panchayat. There are two public distribution centres. The total number of ration cards is 350 and 52 more persons have already applied for ration cards. Initially this Panchayat had 35 streetlights. Later 12 streetlights were added.

There is no caste association or women's association in this Panchayat. But REAL, an NGO, is functioning and they have been concentrating on forming a Self-Help Group in this Panchayat. An Ambedkar Youth Association has been formed and they help the public during festival periods. By and large local work has been done by the Youth Association. There is no cooperative society, church or mosque in the Panchayat. There are four small temples.

Forty families are engaged in agricultural work because they are having lands. They are all caste Hindus. There is no land for the SC community and they are engaged in agricultural coolie work. The major crop is paddy and the water source is river irrigation.

Since 1935, there has been a common pond but it has been encroached upon by other Panchayats. Ms. Amutha has complained to the block officials and they are taking necessary steps to remove the encroachments. She pointed out that the encroachers were getting an income of Rs. 20,000 per year from that pond.

Ms. Amutha said that 200 families are engaged in rearing goats and 150 families are engaged in rearing milch animals. No family is involved in poultry farming but a few persons are engaged in poultry activities. No veterinary centre is available in the Panchayat.

Ms. Amutha pointed out that two political parties are functioning in the Panchayat: one is the PMK and other is the Viduthalai Siruthaigal Party. In Eechampoondi Village the majority of the people are in the Viduthalai Siruthaigal Party and in Balawaikandan Village the majority of the people are with the PMK. On the whole it is a caste based alignment.

Ms. Amutha suggested that the Small Savings Scheme is the best scheme in the Panchayat and that is conducive to development. Environmental protection awareness among the people is the need of the hour, she suggested. The people have advocated three facilities for effective environment protection, namely toilet facility, housing facility and drainage facility.

Recruitment Process

The villagers felt that Ms. Amutha had good character and has worked for the welfare of women by forming Mahalir

Sangams. She gained rich experience in activities relating to the development of women while she was living with her husband in Sankarapuram. It was because of this that she contested in the Panchayat election. Four candidates contested against her but they were not involved in women development activities previously. For this reason the villagers thought that she should be elected Village Panchayat President. She won by a margin of 23 votes. In electioneering, she followed the door-to-door canvassing technique, visiting every family twice. She assured the people that she would provide drinking water supply, streetlights and housing facilities. Village leaders, the youth and coolie women participated in the canvassing. She herself developed articulation skills and spoke to the public and developed self-confidence. Besides her husband, a large number of people supported her. She said that Rs.7,500 was spent for her election.

During the election, the opposing candidates developed hostility towards her. Even after the election, two of the opponents have not even spoken to her. But the villagers have a good opinion about her and she has stayed in the village and addressed the problems of the people. In this way she has developed self-confidence and started working with officials and the people for the development of the people in her Panchayat.

Perception

Ms. Amutha knows of only the 33 per cent reservation for women in the 73rd Constitutional Amendment Act, and has little awareness of the Tamil Nadu Panchayati Raj Act. With regard to development she suggested that certain facilities are essential for development and that they should be given special attention, namely, sanitation, environment, agriculture, water supply, pre-natal care, post-natal care, child development, women's development and creating employment opportunities. In addition she suggested that literacy plays a vital role in any development scenario. Besides literacy, strict discipline is needed at any level. The Government should allocate adequate funds for village development activities. She said that a large number of people have migrated to Kerala and Bangalore for employment. Agriculture and animal husbandry are the major component's of the village economy today. There is no cultivable land for certain groups of people. Hence they migrate from Tamil Nadu to other states.

A large number of alcoholics are found in this Panchayat and that is the main obstacle to human resource development. Another obstacle is dowry. Without dowry marriages cannot be arranged for women. Secret small savings is essential for every village woman (without informing the husband) for emergency expenses of the family. In this way the village women are empowered economically, according to Ms. Amutha. Before marriage, some amount has to be deposited by the parents in the name of their daughters. After marriage that amount will be helpful for the welfare of the daughter's family.

There are SHGs formed in this Panchayat. The majority of the SHG members are not literate. This is the major reason for inadequate individual development. Each group has savings; the minimum amount is Rs. 5,000 and maximum is Rs.10,000. Through loans provided by banks employment opportunity was created for the skilled women in the SHGs. With regard to common property resources, four lakes are available and the Panchayat is getting a regular income of Rs. 5,000 from the lakes and Rs. 2000 from the tamarind trees in the Panchayat. Ms. Amutha has understood the importance of social justice. She emphasised that it is essential for all marginalized groups. She has developed leadership qualities due to the support extended by her husband, the members of the SHGs and some of the officials.

Performance

Ms. Amutha pointed out that basic facilities such as constructing steps to ponds, TV room, retaining wall, school building, hand pumps, group houses and bridges were provided in the Panchayat. The major work was the construction of a bridge by the PWD at a cost Rs. 36,000. The work is nearing completion.

She listed the following important items of work carried out in her Panchayat:

Development Activities from 1996-2001

S. No.	*Name of the work*	*Village*	*Scheme under which*	*Amount in (Rs.)*
		1996-97		
1.	TV room	Balawaikandan Colony	JVVT	11,000.00
2.	Steps	Balawaikandan Colony	JVVT	11,000.00
3.	TV room	Balawaikandan Colony	JVVT	11,000.00
4.	Retaining wall	Balawaikandan Colony	JVVT	29,000.00
		1997-98		
1.	TV room	Eechampoondi Colony	JVVT	12,000.00
2.	Steps in canal	Balwaikandan	JVVT	16,000.00
3.	Retaining wall	Pudukulam	JVVT	16,000.00
4.	Retaining wall	Thiddal street	JVVT	17,000.00
5.	Group houses	Eechampoondi	IAY	5,80,000.00
6.	School building	Eechampoondi	EAS	2,72,000.00
		1998-99		
1.	Retaining wall	Balawaikandan	JVVT	20,000.00
2.	Retaining wall	Balawaikandan	JVVT	30,000.00
3.	Retaining wall	Eechampoondi	JVVT	21,500.00
4.	Hand pumps-2	Eechampoondi	SFC-grant	20,000.00
		1999-2000		
1.	Cement road	Eechampoondi Colony	JVVT	45,800.00
2.	Cement road	Eechampoondi Street	EAS	1,00,000.00
3.	Retaining wall	Eecham poondi Road	General Fund	1,50,000.00
		2000-2001		
1.	Cement road	Eechampoondi Colony	JGSY	45,800.00
2.	Vadavattri Bridge	Eechampoondi Colony	PWD Veeranam Plan	36,000.00
3.	Road maintenance	Eechampoondi	Medical Dept.	50,000.00

These are the items of work carried out in this Panchayat during 1996-2001. Ms. Amutha pointed out that more group houses are needed for the homeless persons. Employment generation is essential for educated women. In this Panchayat more than 200 educated women are available but they do not have any gainful employment. They have skilled women also.

Yet they cannot find employment for the women. The President is struggling hard to generate employment opportunities. She listed the following details of Government grants:

JVVT details for 1998-99

Income		*Expenditure*		
JVVT amount	71,764	Group houses	2,33,152	
Interest	980	Retailing wall	26,152	
Group houses	3,38,502	TV room		6,980
Initial balance	50,048	Steps		6,360
		Final balance	1,88,650	
	4,61,294			4,61,294

1999-2001

Income		**Expenditure**		
JVVT amount	26,046	Retaining wall	41,470	
JVVT amount	39,068	1998-99 work amount paid		29,970
Interest	3,718	Group houses		79,600
Initial balance	1,88,644	Cement		7,530
	2,57,476	Cement		7,570
			Total	1,66,090
Final balance	91,386			2,57,476

Earmark Fund 1998-99

Income		**Expenditure**		
Funeral assistant	8,400	Funeral expenditure		4,500
Interest	5	Bank interest	45	
Initial balance	996	Final balance	4,856	
	9,401			9,401

1999-2001

Income		**Expenditure**		
SFC-grant	8,544	Retaining wall	8,100	
Bank interest	41	Ayyan library material		3,020

(Contd.)

For Ayyan library	5,000	Final balance 7,321	
	13,585		18,441
Initial balance	4,856		
	18,441		

From JVVT funds the major work done was house construction and from earmarked funds, it was funeral assistance.

The followings are the income expenditure details of this Panchayat from 1996 to 2001.

1996-97

Income Sources		*Expenditure Sources*	
House tax	395.00	Travelling allowance	1,050.00
Library tax	38.50	Salary for OHT operator	3,900.00
Professional tax	1840.00	Pongal bonus	400.00
Vehicle tax	106.00	Other sources	340.00
Maintenance records	735.00	Street maintenance	490.00
Stamp duty	43,863.00	OHT maintenance	1,701.00
House tax matching grant	437.00	Hand pump maintenance	2,141.00
		Street light maintenance	4857.00
Funeral grant	1,800.00	For training purpose	90.00
Initial balance	14,049.00	Funeral assistance	1,200.00
		Advance amount	12,049.00
		Final balance	33,924.00
	62,869.00		62869.00

In this year, stamp duty was the highest source of income to the Panchayat. The Panchayat has received the house tax matching grant from the Government.

1997-98

Income		*Expenditure*	
House tax	4,286.00	Salary	8,581.00
Library tax	429.00	Travelling +setting	9,023.00
Professional tax	3,272.00	Written items	1,156.00
Other sources	148.00	St.light E.B.charge	1,845.00
Deposit	100.00	Power pump E.B. charge	4,031.00
Interest	123.00	Maintenance of well	1,755.00
Stamp duty	26,700.00	Maintenance of hand pump	11,537.00
Weaker pan. grant	3,540.00		
Union level source	33,924.00	Maintenance of OHT	3,212.00

(*Contd.*)

SFC grant	36,701.00	Maintenance of St. lights	11,622.00
Auction from trees	300.00	Maintenance of TV	11,667.00
Earmark fund		Maintenance sanitation	1,300.00
equality	1,700.00	Maintenance of roads	17,399.50
		For roads	
		For deposits	663.00
		New equipments	7,195.00
		Funeral assistance	1,700.00
		Other expenditure	1,722.00
		Final balance	16,824.50
	1,11,223.00		1,11,223.00

For 1996-97 the income/expenditure details are not available according to Ms. Amutha. In 1997-98, income has been received in the form of SFC grant, stamp duty and Union Fund. The Panchayat has incurred expenditure for maintenance of hand pumps and streetlights and also roads.

1998-99

Income		*Expenditure*	
House tax	5,190.00	Salary for Pan. Asst.	5,255.00
Library tax	508.00	Salary for OHT operator	14,162.00
Professional tax	3,760.00	Salary for TV operator	950.00
Auction from trees	318.00	T.A. for Pan. asst.	1,770.00
Auction from old		T.A. for Pan. president	3,600.00
things	570.00	Sitting fee Pan. president	750.00
Interest	1,384.00	Sitting for ward member	1,900.00
SFC-grant	80,552.00	Bonus	500.00
House tax match		Written items	737.00
grant	8,572.00	Record/other forms	1,042.00
Stamp duty	27,904.00	Sanitation	4,690.00
Initial balance	16,814.00	TV maintenance	700.00
		Newspaper	1,633.00
		Paid for PWD	545.00
		Other equipments	560.00
		E.B. Charges	1,953.00
		OHT maintenance	15,575.00
		Hand pump maintenance	3,287.00
		Mark-2 pump maintenance	1,116.00
		St.light maintenance	16,879.00
		Road maintenance	28,502.00
		Bridge maintenance	960.00

(*Contd.*)

		Thorns cutting	1,920.00
		Building maintenance	5,600.00
		Funeral assistance	1,000.00
		Retaining wall	2,000.00
		Final balance	26,658.00
	1,45,573.00		1,45,573.00

1999-2000

Income		*Expenditure*	
House tax	3,475.00	Salary for Pan. Asst.	4,640.00
Library tax	347.50	Salary for OHT ope.	9,800.00
Professional tax	3,128.00	Salary for TV ope.	750.00
Auction from trees	520.00	TA for Pan. asst.	1,650.00
Auction from wastage	280.00	Pongal bonus	750.00
SFC-grant	1,12,258.00	Sitting fee for Panchayat president	4,500.00
Weaker Panchayat grant	3,643.00	Sitting for ward members	2,700.00
Stamp duty	40,978.00	Written items	620.00
House tax match grant	10,330.00	Records	3,842.00
		EB charge	20,038.00
Birth death special grant	50,000.00	Newspaper	1,636.00
		TV Maintenance	640.00
Initial balance	900.00	Lease amount to PWD	1,206.00
Initial balance	26,658.00	Sanitation	4,320.00
		Festival expenditure	4,360.00
		Bank balance	20.00
		Funeral assistance	5,000.00
		Hand pump maintenance	4,072.00
		Mark-2 pump maintenance	2,510.00
		OHT maintenance	17,932.00
		St. light maintenance	25,189.00
		Road maintenance	1,920.00
		Thons cutting	2,995.00
		Bridge construction	11,480.00
		Retaining wall	36,800.00
		Cement	850.00
		Previous amount	3,000.00
		Final balance	77,413.00
	2,52,518.00		2,52,518.00

Two types of committees have been formed in this Panchayat. One is the Education Committee and the other is the Supervising Committee, *i.e.* for watching the Panchayat work. Ms. Amutha said that there was no problem in collecting tax. She raised the house tax from Rs. 5.25 to Rs.11.00 for huts and for tiled houses from Rs.11.00 to Rs. 22.00. The house tax depended upon the size of the house.

The traditional Panchayat leader gave 3 cents of land for construction of a public distribution shop in the local area. The cost of construction was Rs. 5,500 but the new building is not yet opened. Ms. Amutha pointed out that since there is a good relationship between the Block officials and the Panchayat there is no problem with regard to accounting and auditing.

In Panchayat meetings, very often ward members used to ask questions on the demands of the people in their own wards. Ward members regularly attended the Panchayat meetings. As for Gram Sabha meetings, these members are not interested in them and do not attend regularly, because they are interested only in demanding group houses and loan facility for their own wards. To ensure quorum in Gram Sabha meetings a separate circular is issued to the ward members and other important persons. The Gram Sabha meetings are also announced over the temple public address system for the benefit of the public. Ms. Amutha said that the Government grant has to be increased. The following are the major demands voiced in the Gram Sabha meetings :

1. Fulfilment of basic needs.
2. Decision-making power.
3. Present school should be upgraded up to 8th standard.
4. Laboratory facility is needed for teaching science subjects.
5. For each classroom awareness pictures/charts are needed.
6. Playground is needed.

Ms. Amutha has helped to improve the school. She has spent her own money for the Republic Day and Independence Day celebrations.

She commented on the poor health status of the women in the rural areas. They are not taking care of their health. They do not have awareness about health care. Further their health care depends on the resources available with the menfolk in their family. A VHN visits the villages periodically but the VHN does not have adequate medicines. Even in the health centres they do not have adequate medicines. The Village Panchayat office is in a dilapidated condition and requires immediate attention. The Panchayat President cannot sit in the Panchayat office due to heavy damage to the building. The office transactions are conducted under a big tamarind tree near the building. Even today ward members, villagers and the Panchayat President sit under that tamarind tree and discuss Panchayat matters. There are problems in mobilizing the community for development activities as their needs are not met through the schemes and programmes of the Government.

CASE - 4

ERAMANAICKANPATTI GRAM PANCHAYAT PALANI BLOCK, DINDIGUL DISTRICT

Socio-Economic Background

Ms. J. Malliga, the President of Eramanaickanpatti Panchayat, belongs to the SC community. She has 1.5 acres of wet land (tank irrigation) and cultivates the land. She has studied up to SSLC and has worked as a noon-meal centre teacher (earlier occupation). Now she is living in a nuclear family, *i.e.*, along with her husband and her three female children. She lives in tiled house with electricity facility, toilet facility and individual water tap connection. Two of her daughters are visually disabled (blind). Her husband is a retired cashier (pension Rs. 2,500 per month). Their sources of income are the pension and Rs. 5,000 from the land.

Recruitment Process

Her Panchayat was reserved for SC women. Earlier she was working as a noon-meal centre teacher. She resigned the post and contested in the Panchayat elections. Totally five persons contested in the elections. She won the election by a margin of 450 votes. She gave an assurance to the people regarding the work to be done in her period: (a) drinking water facility, (b) street lights, (c) road facility, (d) colony houses, and, (e) DOWCRA loan facilities. The people remembered that the candidate's father-in-law in earlier days, started a primary school which proved very useful to village school-going children. So they cast their votes in favour of his daughter-in-law. This was one of the reasons for her victory in the elections. The school students canvassed their family votes for their former teacher. She moves with the people closely and helps the pregnant ladies in many ways, like giving nutritious tablets, iron tonics etc. So, her association with women proved very useful at the time of the election.

Her family background also helped to get votes in the election. Her father-in-law was educated and started a school; her husband was a bank employee; and, her daughter has studied upto B.Sc. This was also another reason for her victory in the Panchayat elections. In the village she moves closely with caste Hindu people and helps them in education, and maternity finance and she maintains a close relationship with all the families. Community unity helped her to succeed in the Panchayat election.

Socio-Political Environment

In this Panchayat nearly nine caste groups, namely Gounders, Pallars, Sakkiliyars, Paraiyars, Naickers, Thevars, Vanniars, Barbers and Chettiars live together. All of them except her own caste people supported Ms. Malliga. The *Dalit* community was angered by the transfer of school management to others by the family of Ms. Malliga. Caste Hindus supported her because her family was educated and helped them to improve their children's education and provided women with education, particularly the Gounder community. Another important support was that of the students, because she was the teacher of the noon-meal centre.

The school students requested their parents to cast their votes for their teacher. She contested the election without any party support, and stood as an independent. She does not belong to any political party even now.

Perception: Concept of Panchayati Raj

She knows the 73rd Amendment but is not able to explain the importance of the amendment. But she can explain the New Panchayati Raj System in terms of reservation for women three-tier system, Gram Sabha and the duties of the Panchayat President. After the introduction of the new Panchayati Raj system in Tamil Nadu women leaders have emerged as good leaders because, as Panchayat Presidents, they move with block and district officials and get Government programmes implemented. At the time of street concrete road formation her opponent in the election and another person attempted to block the work. Then she got a court order and completed the road work.

She said that only India has reservation for women in local self-government and that the Gram Sabha represents the democratic system and the decentralization of power. The Tamil Nadu Panchayati Raj Act gives preference to reservation for women and SC/ST people. In addition every 5,000 people elected a Panchayat Union Ward Member and every 50,000 people elect a District Council Ward Member. The system of joint signature by the Vice-President creates many problems according to Ms. Malliga.

Development

In her vision if the basic needs of the people are fulfilled, it is called development :

- Create awareness regarding infant death in the villages.
- Create awareness about dowry problem in the society.
- Eradicate the illiteracy.
- Create awareness about child marriage and early marriage.
- Give women education.

Village Economy

Agriculture is the main occupation, particularly vegetables production: *makka cholam* (maize), tomato, beetroot, ladies finger, brinjal and cucumber. It provides employment and boosts the village economy. Other important occupations are building work, agricultural coolie work, sericulture and knitting of coconut thatch.

Many people of this village (nearly 25% to 30%) go to Palani and nearby villages for building work and 10 per cent of the people are engaged in mango and guava fruit business. The farmer families (*i.e.* those who own land) have milch animals and increase their family income. Regarding improving the village economy, Ms. Malliga said that the Government should sanction more welfare programmes in order to develop small business skills in the villages. Secondly, the Government should give training to the women in several small trades like making cooking powder, pickle making and knitting plastic baskets.

Political Parties

In this village parties such as AIADMK, DMK, BJP and TMC have a presence. Among the parties AIADMK stands first, followed by DMK, TMC, and BJP. Ms. Malliga is not involved in any party activities. She contested the election as an independent candidate. She clearly explained that she does not know about the parties and their ideology because she is not involved in any political activities. In fact the women of the village are not involved in any political/party activities. Women empowerment in politics is needed in this Panchayat.

Gender Issues

There is no discrimination between SCs and BCs in the Panchayat. All caste Hindus move freely with the SC people and are allowed to participate in all functions and they are allowed into the temple also. The women are free from male domination because they work hard in all spheres equally with men (agriculture, businesses and shops).

On Social Justice

Ms. Malliga had to face an incident once: after the Panchayat election she appointed a BC person as the Panchayat clerk. In January 1998 the BC clerk was taken off the job and an SC person was appointed Panchayat clerk. The people, at the time of the Gram Sabha meeting, which the ABDO attended, surrounded the ABDO and wanted to remove the SC Panchayat clerk. After this incident Ms. Malliga was directed to consult the people and the Panchayat Ward Members. In this village social justice is practiced only partly. The caste Hindus did not accept a Scheduled Caste Panchayat clerk. The two tumbler system prevails in the tea stalls. But free movement of SC people wearing chappals on the caste Hindu streets is allowed. At the time of festivals the caste Hindus allow the SC people inside the temple.

Common Property Resources

This Panchayat's water sources are Pattikulam, Vekkaiyankuttai, Senkuttai and Uranikuttai. Water sources for these tanks are limited. The Panchayat has a plan to plant *babul* trees in the tanks. Earlier too they planted babul trees with the help of the Social Forestry Programme and got some money for the Panchayat.

Committee Formation

Ms. Malliga received a communication to form seven committees in the Panchayat. She formed five committees, but they exist only on paper and are not functioning. She pointed out that it is very difficult to give power to the Committees and if the members are given duties, they expect money for the work.

Tax Collection

House tax and professional tax give financial strength to the Panchayat. After the first year, Ms. Malliga increased the house tax. The collection of taxes is very difficult because people do not realize the financial position of the Panchayat and the importance of remitting the tax in time. The Panchayat clerk had to go to every house more than five times and only then the people pay their house tax.

Resource Mobilization

The Panchayat has mobilized resources other than tax: coconut trees (60 Nos. for Rs. 9,000 for a 3 years on contract), fish tax for the last two years (32+8 = 40 thousand rupees), and, household individual tap connection deposit of Rs. 62,000. Ms. Malliga plans to construct some shops on Panchayat land and get perennial income for the Panchayat.

Accounting and Auditing

She doesn't know how records are maintained in the Panchayat since the accounts are maintained by the clerk only. The Panchayat has completed the auditing up to December 2000. The present system of account and audit is useful, because it is done every three months. If any mistake is discovered, the persons involved remember the incident and can rectify the mistakes. The officials of the BDO office and the district officials are cooperative. They correct the mistakes and show the way to maintain the records. The Panchayat President is dependent upon the Panchayat clerk for the accounts. She must know the accounts fully. If the Panchayat President does not know anything of the accounts it is easy for the clerk to trap the President. In general the authorities use their power to extract work in offices. Some officers use their power to force subordinates to do their personal work and some officials get money and work without giving any problems. This is happening everywhere. In the case of Panchayat accounts and auditing, the officials expect some money for the end of the year auditing (*i.e.* in the month of March). This practice prevails from the Panchayat clerk to higher officials at the block level. In this Panchayat though the accounts are maintained properly, the higher-ups do not appreciate what the subordinates do.

Corruption cannot be eradicated in India because, when a case is filed in court for corruption, it keeps going on. Corruption is not avoidable in the administrative sphere.

Conducting the Panchayat Meeting

Ms. Malliga conducts the Panchayat meeting every month. Nearly all the six ward members attend the meeting. At the meeting the *Dalit* members insist on providing basic facilities like drinking water, street lights, road facilities, individual loans etc. Ms. Malliga moves closely with the ward members and whatever programme arrives from the Government is given to the ward members and the Vice-President of the Panchayat. No untoward incidents occur during the Panchayat meetings.

In the Panchayat meetings the President, the Vice-President and the ward members discuss the total amount received from the Government and other sources like collection, MLA Fund, MP Fund and what items of work are to be carried out in the Panchayat in future besides what items of work have been carried out. These matters are discussed without reference to micro level planning and macro level planning. This is the first time that the people have entered the Panchayat activities and so they are not able to think of micro planning because this is a learning period.

Conducting of Gram Sabha Meeting

Gram Sabha meetings are conducted in front of the Panchayat office. The topics for discussion in the meeting are displayed on the information board. The agenda, place, date, special invitee's names etc. are printed on bit notices and distributed to all the households through the Panchayat clerk, the operator and the ward members. Tom-tom was employed in earlier days to inform of the Gram Sabha meetings to the people.

In the Gram Sabha meetings the people are given account of the work completed, the work going on and the work to be carried out. Gram Sabha members give their concurrence to the items of work and their suggestions about the items of work to be carried out. The President, the Vice-President and the ward members request the people to support the encroachment eviction in the villages. So far 135 resolutions have been passed in the Gram Sabha meetings, but only 25 to 50 resolutions have been carried out in the villages.

An incident occurred in the Gram Sabha meeting relating to replacing the BC Panchayat clerk by a SC Panchayat clerk. In January 1998 at the 26th Gram Sabha meeting, the people *gheraoed* the ABDO to reinstate the BC clerk. Women's participation in the earlier meetings was poor. Now-a-days women's SHG members participate in the Gram Sabha meetings and ask several questions relating to their basic needs, particularly the *Dalit* SHG members. Suggestions to improve the attendance at the Gram Sabha meetings are: the District Collector's "Manuneethi Day" should be conducted on the Gram Sabha meeting day; for beneficiary programmes, beneficiaries' selection should be done at the Gram Sabha meeting; and if anything is to be given free to the people, it must be decided at the Gram Sabha meeting.

Environment Activities

Ms. Malliga got the drainage system in the village cleaned with the help of the middle school students and applied bleaching powder. The surroundings of the Panchayat office are cleaned every month and bleaching powder is applied. She arranged for a medical camp for the school children, checked the diseases and supplied medicine to the students. At the time of village festivals the main streets are cleaned by the youth of the village. They also apply bleaching powder and give safe drinking water to the villagers and the guests of the village.

Social Activities

Earlier Ms. Malliga was a noon-meal centre teacher. So she now concentrates on children's education, health, schooling, sanitation, pregnant women's health, giving iron tablets and tonics to them. After occupying the village Panchayat President's post she continues the same work. She has provided a hand pump in the school premises.

Assigned Duties: Collection of Tax

The Panchayat collects house tax, professional tax, earmarked fund, interest, local tax, entertainment tax, stamp duty, tree tax, urimai tax, and receives house tax matching grant. All the taxes came to around Rs. 90,835 in the year 1995-96, Rs. 92,835 in the year 1996-97, Rs. 94,895 in the year 1997-98, Rs. 94,219 in the year 1998-99 and Rs.1,01,390 in 1999-2000.

The State Finance Commission's contribution was Rs. 2,90,538 for three years, *i.e.* 1997-98, 1998-99, 1999-2000. Income from the trees was Rs. 20,560. Building rent fetched Rs. 4,350. Individual house tap connection deposit fetched Rs.49,000.

Income from the 10th Finance Commission Fund was Rs. 24,688. Scheme fund for two years (1998-99, 1999-2000) under JVVT fetched Rs. 2,09,550. The Millennium Wells Scheme fetched Rs. 55,000. The Indra Memorial Housing Colony Scheme contributed Rs. 3,41,300.

These are the income sources for this Panchayat. Ms. Malliga pointed out that collection of house tax is a difficult task and funds like building fund are not received in time due to late release by the Government. She visited the BDO's office frequently to get the funds. She would approach the MLA and get some money from the MLA Fund and lay a blacktop road.

Maintenance of Public Assets

She takes care of the tank area. If anybody occupies the public land they are evicted. Ms. Malliga safeguards the Panchayat trees and earns income from the trees and maintains the roadside trees also. She maintains the Panchayat office, the TV room, the motor room and the noon-meal centres properly. Funds from the Government are regularly deposited. Ms. Malliga maintains these accounts. Every month she conduct the monthly meeting and discusses with the ward members regarding the items of work to be carried out, the accounts, the demands of the people (*i.e.*, basic needs) and the plans for the Gram Sabha meeting etc. Record maintenance, office cleaning, village cleaning etc., are overseen by Ms. Malliga. If any work is carried out in the

Panchayat area, she visits the area and supervises the work. She has to look after the Panchayat administration too.

Unassigned Responsibility

1. She looks after pregnant ladies with regard to supply of iron tablets, tonics, taking weight, inspecting after delivery for child care and mother care etc.
2. She look after streets and the drainage, keeping them clean all the time, with special care taken at the time of festivals.
3. She approaches the area MLA and gets some funds for welfare activities (blacktop road).

General

Ms. Malliga's father-in-law started a primary school in the village, her husband worked in a bank and retired, and she was a noon-meal centre teacher. So, all the family members have worked for the welfare of the community/village, particularly regarding education. This is the reason she became the President of this Village Panchayat. She has been working for the last two decades for women's development by providing education, ANC, PNC and child health care.

CASE – 5

GURUVAPPANPETTAI GRAM PANCHAYAT
KURINJIPADI BLOCK, CUDDALORE DISTRICT

Socio-Economic Background

Ms. M. Amirtham is an elderly illiterate woman of 50 years old holding the position of the President of Guruvappanpettai Gram Panchayat. She belongs to the Most Backward Community. She can only affix her signature on papers. She lives with her husband and two sons who are married and have six children.

Her husband is a retired Electricity Board employee who has gradually involved himself in public activities. She has two acres of dry land and no regular income from this land. She has her own tiled house and a tap connection to her house. Her husband has a two-wheeler and his pension is Rs. 4000 per month. She has developed a close link with SHGs after being elected President of the Gram Panchayat. Her two sons are involved in the activities of political parties. But she has not associated herself with any political party. She has developed association with school teachers, DANIDA-WS, and local traditional communities. She and her husband engage in social service activities, particularly participating in community activities and have earned a very good name for this.

Village Profile

The total population of this Panchayat is 752 of whom 373 are males, 379 are females. There are 2 wards and 6 ward members, of whom 4 are males and 2 are females. There is no hamlet in this Panchayat and there are no Scheduled Caste families. This Panchayat is peopled by one caste group, namely, Vanniars. The total number of houses are 177, of which are15 *pucca*, 24 tiled, and the rest mixed houses. With regard to drinking water, an OHT with a capacity of 60,000 litres is available in the Panchayat. There are 21 public taps and 2 hand pumps. The water supply is adequate to meet the demands of the people.

For health and sanitation, there is no public toilet facility, no health centre, and no compost yard. But a health centre is available in Kurinjipadi, two km from this Panchayat. A Village Health Nurse visits twice a week, checks the pregnant women and takes care of them. The VHN has to go to 3 villages. So she attends to the women's needs quickly. The Panchayat has only a 3 km road. A *balwadi*, a noon-meal centre and a primary school are available in the Panchayat. For higher education the children go to a school in Kurinjipadi. The Ayyan Library books are kept in the Panchayat office. They are being used by the public regularly. There is no separate room for the Ayyan library. There is no market, butchery shed, bus shelter, PDS, community hall or cinema theatre in this Panchayat. There is no caste organization in the Panchayat. In general the youth attend the Gram Sabha meetings and any other meeting organized in the village, particularly meetings organized by the DANIDA team.

The people celebrate temple festivals in the Panchayat periodically. If there is no money for temple celebrations, people get money from private finance companies or borrow from others at the local level. The majority of the people are farmers and they cultivate paddy, sugarcane, groundnut and other cash crops. The major source of irrigation is lake and borewell. Fifty-five families are engaged in milk trade and rear milch animals. The milk produced is collected by vendors at the rate of Rs. 8 to 10 per litre. There is no cooperative milk society in the Panchayat. The farmers also engage in poultry farming and goat rearing. There is no veterinary centre in the Panchayat. With regard to political parties, the Pattali Makkal Katchi has got the most number of members and other political parties such as the DMK and the AIADMK have only a few members.

Village Setting

There is a popular Ayyanar Koil in this Panchayat. Outsiders also come to this temple periodically. Ten *Poojari* families are living in the Panchayat. Their work is to maintain the Ayyanar temple and the other local temples. One community hall is available, which belongs to the Ayyanar temple.

Guruvappanpettai is one of the project villages of the DANIDA assisted Water Supply and Sanitation Project in Cuddalore District. This is a water starved village in Kurinjipadi Block. So it appealed to the DANIDA for water supply facilities. Problem analysis and needs assessment were made with people's participation by DANIDA staff members. The villagers had to contribute 1/9 of the total cost of the water supply system. Since it is a mono-caste community, they paid upto Rs. 30,000 from the village common fund. Besides, the project staff said that they would have to remove all the pit type house tap connections, which are illegal. The community members started feeling the pinch only when the project staff asked all the households to close the pit type taps in front of every house. First of all, the pit type tap connections were removed from the President's and the

Vice-President's houses and then the others started to remove their pit type taps. Incidentally, both the President and Vice-President are women and submissive and obliging by nature. When they removed their taps, the others followed suit.

The villagers keep the livestock near the village school and the residential area. This disturbs the environment and the smooth functioning of the school. The cattle owners do not listen to the advice given by elders and school teachers.

Recruitment Process

After the retirement of Ms. Amirtham's husband from the Electricity Board, both have gradually involved themselves in public activities, giving donations for festivals and other public activities. They actively associated themselves with the youth club members and school students. So the local youth requested her to contest the Panchayat elections. Ms. Amirtham and her husband also thought that it was an opportunity to serve better through an institution. Her character and her relations with the public, particularly with the youth and school children, attracted the attention of the community. Her husband's active participation in community activities shaped the opinion of the public in favour of her. In addition, the village people also felt that Ms. Amirtham was the best candidate for Panchayat President compared to the other three candidates. The other candidates contesting against Ms. Amirtham did not possess adequate experience in the field of social work. So Ms. Amirtham won by a margin of 31 votes.

During the canvassing period, every week, Ms. Amirtham visited the village and assured the public that basic facilities would be provided. The village youth were her major supporters. She spent Rs. 10,000 for the election, particularly for providing tea, snacks and other eatables to her supporters who accompanied her during the campaign. There is no rivalry in the village after the election.

Ms. Amirtham stated that, before she was elected to the position of Panchayat President, there were no infrastructure facilities in the village and now she has developed the infrastructure facilities through the Panchayat system. Water facility, electricity connection for street lights, and roads have been provided. Officials frequently visit the village. Besides, the DANIDA team members also play a vital role in providing protected water supply to the people through the Panchayat.

Perception on Development

Ms. Amirtham has adequate perception of Village Panchayat development thanks to DANIDA. She was not aware of the 73rd Constitutional Amendment Act and the Tamil Nadu Panchayat Act. After she involved herself in the DANIDA programme, she acquired information about the 73rd Constitutional Amendment, the Tamil Nadu Panchayat Act and people's participation in development activities. She said that the scope of the new Panchayati Raj system is wide and its success depends on the cooperation of the officials.

Development

To Ms. Amirtham development means activities akin to fulfilling the basic needs of the people with the active participation of the people in the development programmes and schemes provided by the government. Any activity that exploits nature beyond a certain level will ultimately affect the natural balance which will work against development. The government officials have to visit the Panchayat and discuss with the President periodically to assess the development programmes carried out in the Panchayat. Sometimes Ms. Amirtham is not involved in the development activities because she is illiterate. She felt that the development process should be based on the management of the common property resources of the Village Panchayat. She admitted that the government has now built up a number of infrastructure facilities in the Panchayat, such as health centre, marriage hall, school building and veterinary centre.

Ms. Amirtham said that the village economy depends upon the utilization of land resources. A number of people are landless and they migrate to other places. The improvement of the village economy is based on the employment opportunities available to the youth and effective training is needed for SHG and other women to generate more economic activities.

With regard to politics, Ms. Amirtham emphasised that politics is not necessary for the rural areas, because, in India, politics means conflict among the members and groups of different political parties. If there is a political party at the village level, the members tend to develop themselves and not to help the village people.

Regarding gender issues, Ms. Amirtham stated that guidance, counselling and awareness is necessary for the women's groups. Once a month she herself conducts a regular meeting, sharing the women's problems. Problematic issues are discussed and sorted out. There is a Kala Jatha programme related to the water supply and sanitation programme sponsored by DANIDA and this creates awareness among the people. In this way women have to be empowered.

Ms. Amirtham again stressed that regular/periodical training is essential for members of SHGs to develop their skills in order to develop the economy through gainful employment opportunities. She pointed out that the women groups were normally weak in the training aspect and that they must be involved in the development process. She felt that training provides more information, empowerment and knowledge.

With regard to social justice, since this Panchayat is fully dominated by a single caste, there is no question of discrimination. But discrimination on the basis of gender prevails. Basically, at the village level there is no cooperation among families. But it is essential for development. Today there is a limited employment opportunity for the youth. It is for this reason that she stressed that training is needed to generate employment opportunities. Ms. Amirtham has developed healthy practices such as periodical consultation with local traditional community leaders, discussions with block officials as well as local women's groups, contacting the DANIDA office whenever necessary, periodical consultation with ward members both formally and informally, listening to all kinds of complaints patiently and exploring all possibilities of solving the problem. When she is not able to solve a problem she immediately contacts the concerned person and informs her/him of her inability and gives the reason.

Besides, her self-confidence is being developed by the DANIDA staff members' guidance and encouragement.

Performance

She conducts the Panchayat meetings periodically. She sees to it that all the six members are present in all the meetings. She has ensured 100 per cent attendance in the Panchayat Council. They continuously discuss the problems of the people and Panchayat administration. The ward members demand programmes and schemes for employment generation. As for Gram Sabha meetings, Ms. Amirtham admitted that it is not possible to conduct the Gram Sabha meetings effectively due to poor participation of the people. The youth always disturb the Gram Sabha meetings by raising irrelevant questions outside the purview of the agenda. Since demands discussed in the earlier meetings are not always fulfilled, the youth disturb the meetings.

In 1996-97, a retaining wall was constructed at a cost of Rs. 12,600 under the JVVT Scheme. Besides a BT road was laid for one km to Melapudupettai at a cost of Rs. 3 lakhs from the Xth Finance Commission Fund. The village people were satisfied at the completion of the BT road work. In 1997-98 the road leading to the school was subjected to maintenance from the Panchayat fund at a cost of Rs. 8,970. The work of maintenance of streets was also completed at a cost of Rs. 3,120. A T.V. room was constructed with JVVT fund and the work of maintenance of graveyard road was also completed during the same year.

In 1998-99, Ms. Amirtham gave importance to the maintenance of streets and the OHT and to the construction of small bridges on East Street. In 1999-2000, 4 important items of work were executed under the JGSY Scheme, namely,

(i)	Six group houses	Rs.	1,33,284
(ii)	Maintenance of Panchayat Office	Rs.	3,213
(iii)	Maintenance of Nutrition Centre	Rs.	4,244
(iv)	Bathing Ghat in Koil Lake	Rs.	18,705

The above items of work were discussed in the Gram Sabha meeting.

In 2000-2001, the following items of work were carried out from the Panchayat fund, the earmarked fund and the JGSY Scheme fund. Thorns and bushes were removed from the premises of the school at a cost of Rs. 4,680. Three sodium vapour lamps were installed at a cost of Rs. 11,070. The work of maintenance of the graveyard road was undertaken and completed.

These are the items of work which have been completed in Guruvappenpettai Panchayat from 1996 to 2001. Apart from these, Ms. Amirtham has taken much effort for providing drinking water facilities with the assistance of DANIDA and street light facilities and to maintain streets and roads in good condition during this period.

Seven Committees have been formed but only on paper. They are not functioning effectively. House tax collection is a difficult job. She revised the house tax, increasing it marginally. For huts the tax revision was from Rs. 5 to Rs. 11 and for tiled houses it was from Rs. 10 to Rs. 22. The other source of income is the lake, but the lake is not maintained properly. If the lake is maintained properly the Panchayat will get more income.

According to Ms. Amirtham the government gives more funds for SC and ST development and hence villages which have more number of SC and ST families get more funds. If the Panchayat has no SC and ST family, it does not get sufficient funds for development work. The economic conditions of the other castes are not considered for grants. In her Panchayat, in the past four years, there has been no objection in the auditing.

In the Panchayat meetings, very often the ward members ask about the street light facilities and the installation of pipelines for water supply. These problems have gradually disappeared. The Gram Sabha meetings are not so effective as they do not attract the members. She is taking earnest efforts and even then there is no response. Even for a small piece of work she has to consult the Gram Sabha members in the meeting. For strengthening the Gram Sabha meeting she suggests the following :

(i) One day's wage to be paid to the wage earners.

(ii) Any distribution of material should be made through Gram Sabha.

(iii) The people's demands are to be met.

Assumed Duties

Neem saplings were planted around the school building. Environmental awareness was created among the people through the Gram Sabha meetings. For achieving 100 per cent student enrolment, Ms. Amirtham has taken continuous efforts. She met the parents and held discussions about the importance of education. Besides, for school development, she has done the following: maintenance work of the school building, including toilet construction and whitewashing, installation of flag post for Independence Day and Republic Day celebrations, providing notebooks, pencils and pens, and, felicitating teachers. This expenditure is met from her own pocket.

During rainy seasons, steps are taken to fill up all the five tanks. She found a good deal of encroachment of public properties by poor people for their own use, such as bathrooms, toilets, cattle sheds and so on. It was very difficult to remove such encroachment. But she gradually took steps to remove the encroachments despite the difficulty of facing opposition from her own supporters.

Maintenance of Panchayat Office

The Panchayat office is situated very near the school building and the surroundings are not maintained and hence are filled with weeds and thorns. Inside the Panchayat office sports materials are kept along with the public TV. Chair and tables are also kept in the same room which has a small door. Through this small door, public have to watch the TV programmes. In the other room are kept the Ayyan Library books and also rice and other foodgrains belonging to the nutrition centre.

Details of Income/Expenditure of Guruvappanpettai Gram Panchayat, Kurinjipadi Block

1997-98

Income		*Expenditure*	
House tax	565.00	Salary	6,280.00
Library tax	55.00	TA	4,000.00
Professional	3,648.00	Written items	129.00
Opening A/c	100.00	OHT maintenance	4,771.00
SFC – grant	7,157.00	Road maintenance	13,070.00
Stamp duty	51,901.00	Other, expenditure	600.00
Bank interest	21.00		
	63,453.00		29,600.00
Initial balance	13,357.00	Final balance	47,410.00
	77,010.00		77,010.00

1998-1999

Income		*Expenditure*	
House tax	1,468.00	Salary	10,515.00
Library tax	147.00	TA	5,744.00
Professional	2,850.00	Written items	400.00
SFC-grant	10,742.00	EB Charge	21,835.00
Stamp duty	18,702.00	St. light maintenance	6,864.00
Bank interest	829.00	Water maintenance	1,020.00
		St.light maintenance	300.00
		St.improvement	19,500.00
		Bank deduction	45.00
	34,738.00		66,213.00
Initial balance	47,410.00	Final balance	15,935.00
	82,148.00		82,148.00

For 1996-97, the income/expenditure details are not available with the Panchayat. In 1997-98 stamp duty and SFC-grant were high income sources. In 1997-98 road maintenance cost was high and also OHT maintenance. In 1998-99 E.B. charges were high and also maintenance of streets.

1999-2000

Income		*Expenditure*	
House tax	1,700.00	Salary	14,655.00
Library tax	170.00	TA &Sitting fee	11,545.00
Professional tax	1,050.00	Written items	1,095.00

(*Contd.*)

SFC grant	19,964.00	Handpump maintenance	3,485.00
Stamp duty	20,434.00	St.light maintenance	5,289.00
Ho.tax.matc.gr	2,889.00	Lib. tax paid	264.00
Bank interest	538.00	St.light improvement	1,680.00
		Other expenditure	427.00
	63,453.00		29,600.00
Initial balance	15,935.00	Final balance	24,137.00
	62,677.00		62,677.00

In the year 2000-2001, house tax matching grant of Rs. 2,889 was received. The SFC grant was high compared to the previous year. The stamp duty amount also increased when compared to previous year. With regard to expenditure maintenance of hand pumps and street lights cost much.

2000-2001

Income		Expenditure	
House tax	4,438.00	Salary	10,845.00
Library tax	444.00	TA	8,830.00
Professional tax	3,990.00	Written items	955.00
SFC grant	24,364.00	EB Charges	6,000.00
Stamp duty	21,246.00	OHT maintenance	1,324.00
Auction of old things	59.00	Hand pump maintenance	685.00
Bank interest	843.00	Expenses for GS	500.00
Deposit changes	7,444.00	Assigned grants received	7,281.00
Registration fees	100.00		
		Street maintenance	4,140.00
		Sodium vapour lamp	2,730.00
		St.light improvement	8,972.00
		Sanitation maintenance	4,680.00
		Playground maintenance	2,650.00
Initial balance	24,137.00	Final balance	27,269.00
	86,961.00		86,961.00

In 2000-2001 from the SFC-grant, stamp duty and house tax, the income has increased. At the same time electricity charges, street maintenance, street light maintenance have cost more. Ms. Amirtham suggested that the government has to increase allocation of funds to small Panchayats and weak Panchayats.

All the pit type taps were removed in this Panchayat. Over 87 pit type taps in about 70 households were removed. As a result they are getting safe drinking water with the help of the DANIDA-WS project. The bold decision taken by Ms. Amirtham and the Vice-President (also a woman) paved the way for development to take root in Guruvappenpettai.

Change in Guruvappanpettai Village Panchayat was made possible through the efforts of the woman President who is firm, assertive and takes decisions for the common good of the community. The story of illegal pit type taps and disconnection by the people themselves upon the counsel of the DANIDA-WS Project at Guruvappanpettai Village should be a lesson for other villages in the neighbourhood to follow. Finally, Ms. Amirtham has decided not to contest again in the Panchayat elections due to her age.

CASE – 6

KALAIYUR GRAM PANCHAYAT PARAMAKUDI BLOCK, RAMANATHAPURAM DISTRICT

Socio-Economic Background

Mr. U. Subraminan is the President of Kalaiyur Village Panchayat. His age is 31 and he is married. He discontinued his college study in the second year of his B.Sc. programme in the year 1990. With the idea of getting training as a teacher he discontinued the course. But, due to financial crunch, he could not get a seat in the training school. For some time, he served as a bus conductor in a private transport company in Madurai. With the idea of self-employment, he resigned the job and he got trained in an ITI in two wheeler mechanism. When the Arivoli Iyakkam (education to all) was implemented, he joined it as an animator. In the year 1992, he became an LIC agent. He belongs to the SC community.

Village Profile

Kalaiyur is one of Village Panchayats in Paramakudi Union, Ramanathapuram District. K. Puthanenthal, N. Puthanenthal, N. P. Singarayapuram, Narivila, Kandukondan Manickam and Thouzhukudiyieruppu are the hamlets of the Panchayat. The predominant caste is the SC and more than 300 families belong to the SC community. The next dominant caste are Thevars and the Yadhava caste follows in the third place. Other communities like Chettiars, Asaris, Servais, Udaiyars (Christian), Naickers and Cobblers also reside in Kalaiyur, but they are numerically insignificant.

Places of Worship

1. Karumalaiyan temple is a famous temple where the *Poojari* is from the Yadhava caste. Offering of goat to Karumalaiyan is an important celebration. Exorcism is also conducted here. All communities attend the temple festival, which is celebrated oncc in two years.
2. Muniappasamy temple and Vinayaga temple are found in every hamlet. All the communities worship in them.
3. Ayyanar temple, Karuppusamy temple and Amman temple are also found in Kalaiyur.
4. There is a church in the name of Royappar-Chinnappar at Singarayapuram where the Udaiyar Christians are living.

It is reported that there is no untouchability during the celebration of festivals. There was a custom that the tree earmarked for the carving of Karumalayan Swami should be lifted by caste Hindus. But in the past two or three years the SC youth voluntarily came and lifted the tree and came into the temple. The caste Hindus did not block this. It is significant that the caste barrier was broken through a temple festival. This is contrary to the existing practice in other parts of the State.

Caste Associations

Caste associations are not functioning in Kalaiyur. Even though disputes and riots took place in and around other villages of

Paramakudi Taluk, Kalaiyur is an exception. The respective caste leaders do not encourage the people to form caste associations. Moreover they will not openly come out to receive and honour the leaders of the respective castes.

But the youth from the Scheduled Caste openly started mobilising themselves. They decided to fix a photo of Thiru. Emanuvel and Dr. Ambedkar in a public place and to form an association called the Emanuvel Peravai. Subramanian advised them to desist from such activities as he regarded them as potential causes of unnecessary disputes. The youth agreed out of respect for the opinion of the Subramanian. They removed all name boards. In N. Pethanenthal, the local SCs have formed a Village Committee and convene a meeting of all the SCs once a week. They have their own building constructed from their common fund. The committee never encourages caste disputes or disorderly behaviour of the youth in public.

As Pethanenthal hamlet does not possess protected drinking water, the Panchayat extended a pipeline from the main village Kalaiyur. The majority of the residents in Pethanenthal are SC families. But the SCs of Kalaiyur objected to the supply of water to Pethanenthal, though the other caste of Kalaiyur agreed to provide water to that hamlet. Subramanian, with the support of officials, extended the pipeline to that hamlet, for which he earned the wrath of his own community. When the officials sanctioned a new borewell, the SCs of Kalaiyur did not permit him to execute the work in the hamlet of Pethanenthal. The dominant community is interfering in the Panchayat activities and preventing the good work of providing water supply which is a humiliation

There are seven SHGs functioning under the women's development programme. The SHGs are facilitated by an NGO. The SHG members participate in Gram Sabha meetings and present their demands in writing. The women have expressed their opinion that the Panchayat could implement any number of programmes but the President should present the accounts in Gram Sabha meetings.

Common Property Resources

There are two water tanks, each 3.25 km long. Out of the two, one is under the PWD with an extent of 160 hectares. Trees are grown in the tank regarding which a dispute is going on between the PWD and the Forest Department. The villagers used to cut the trees after auctioning them. When the President took efforts to make the tender proper, the villagers did not allow it, and hence it was stopped. The villagers told the Panchayat to get funds from the government for carrying out repair work on the banks of the tank. Since the earmarked fund of the Village Committee has to be spent for other purposes, they refused to give money for maintenance activities to the Panchayat. In the Panchayat common land (porambokke), 20 tamarind trees were left unprotected earlier and hence the public cut down the branches. Subramanian said that, after he became the President, he prevented the same. Now the trees have grown fully. The Panchayat earns Rs. 1,000 from these trees. Every year the fruits of the trees are auctioned.

There are three tanks in Kalaiyur and one tank each in the four hamlets accounting for a total of seven tanks in the Panchayat. Each tank is looked after and maintained by the village community itself. The social forestry coverage is auctioned once in three years. Recently Rs. 68,000 was earned by the Panchayat from this auction. About 15 acres of common (porambokke) land is available in the Panchayat. All 15 acres are encroached upon by seven individuals who belong to both Scheduled Caste and Backward Class. The revenue officials did not lend support when the Panchayat took efforts to remove the encroachment. Subramanian said that so far the people did not know that these are common properties. Now the people know how many common properties are in the Panchayat and who have encroached upon them. Now the people are asking questions about the lands. Soon people themselves will pass resolutions and make the encroachers leave.

Political Parties

After the police atrocities in Kodiyankulam Village, there was a general feeling among the people belonging to the SC that the

AIADMK is pro-Thevar. The SC leaders screened a video film on the Kodiyankulam incident and advised the SC youth of all villages to consolidate their strength to prevent any further atrocities on the SCs. Subramanian was a supporter of the DMK during the elections but, afterwards, he switched his loyalty to the AIADMK. Subramanian felt that from 1996-99 onwards, when he was with the DMK, the MLA and the Chairman of the Panchayat Union did not extend proper support to him.

The ex-President, a caste Hindu, tried to control all Subramanian's activities in return for his support during the election campaign. He belongs to the DMK. He advised Subramanian to join the DMK and so Subramanian became a member of the DMK Party. But the ex-President did not allow Subramanian to meet the government officials. The ex-President wanted Subramanian to walk behind him. Moreover, the MLA also gave undue recognition to the ex-President by by-passing the Panchayat President Subramanian.

Due to this humiliation, Subramanian joined the AIADMK. Now, within a short period of 1.5 years, he has been given the position of Union level presidentship of the Selvi. Jayalalitha Peravai, a wing of the AIADMK Party. Subramanian's relative is an MP in the Rajya Sabha. He helped him in getting programmes for Kalaiyur Panchayat.

Subramanian said that the officials give respect and recognition to the ruling party supporters or cadres. Any political affiliation with the ruling party helps to establish rapport with officials and thereby many activities could be carried out in the villages, particularly for development. Subramanian maintains that the political affiliation of a person belonging to the SC helps him to mingle with caste Hindus by which the discriminatory attitude of the caste Hindus could be reduced. According to Subramanian, the DMK Party gives more importance to farmers whereas the AIADMK Party gives priority to basic amenities. All the major political parties are having units in this Panchayats.

Village Economy

The majority of the people in the village are farmers. About 500 families own land, out of whom only 20 families have borewell irrigation. Most of the SC families do not have land for cultivation. The young members of these families are educated and try to migrate to towns and cities to seek employment. The poor SC families get loans from private moneylenders by mortgaging their available vessels and jewels to meet even their basic needs. After the advice of the educated youth, they are now mortgaging their properties with banks. The farmers cultivate cotton, chilly, gingili, coriander and brinjal in their lands. Earlier ragi and sorghum were grown. Now, due to drought, these crops are not cultivated in their lands.

Landless labourers used to get employment in chamber brick kilns. At present the proprietor of this kiln prefers workers from other villages outside this Panchayat and they are asked to stay at the site itself and completely engage themselves in all activities without limit. Moreover, the use of machine like tractor and JCB has replaced the manual labour work even for preparing the brick. Preparation of charcoal is the commonly available avocation to all poor people. Rearing of milch animals is resorted to by those who can afford it. The Yadhava community is generally involved in goat rearing and rearing milch animals. Employment opportunities can be created through Employment Assurance Scheme if the desilting of all big tanks and small tanks are regularly carried out and the Social Forestry Scheme is promptly carried out according to Subramanian. The new programme known as Watershed Development is very useful to the villages but, as the work is undertaken by the Union, the Village Panchayat does not have the authority to undertake it, Subramanian complained. Politics among the members of the Watershed Committee disturbs the development activities, he felt. In the case of the Union tanks, the control of the Revenue Department on tenders has been removed. The Village Panchayat can get more funds out of the auction of trees, by enhancing the tender amount without any malpractice. From this income the Panchayat can further develop and protect the trees planted under the Social Forestry Scheme, according to Subramanian.

Recruitment

Subramanian started his social service activities by helping the poor to avail themselves of government schemes. With the advice of the former President, he used to visit various offices in connection with village problems. These activities helped him to earn a good name among all the community members in Kalaiyur. When the Panchayat election was announced and the Presidentship was reserved for the SC, most of the people advised him to contest. The ex-President too encouraged him to contest. His friends and community leaders tried to select him unopposed by initiating discussion with all those concerned. Five other SC men had filed their nominations. Before the election date, four of them withdrew their nominations but one refused to do so and so a contest could not be avoided. The opponent was an elderly person and a big farmer also.

The canvassing was serious. Three visits were made to each hamlet. As the hamlets are situated at long distances, a tractor was engaged to take the supporters for the canvassing. Relatives, friends and family members accompanied Subramanian. The candidate who opposed him received support from a caste Hindu landlord who even spent money for him. About 20 days were spent for campaigning and more than Rs.25,000 were spent for the election as a whole. Villagers agreed to cast their vote in a mass but demanded a small amount of money for the Village Committee. In the competition Subramanian won by a margin of 137 votes. His educational qualification, free movement with all caste groups, commitment to social service and his promise of taking initiatives to bring government schemes brought victory to him, accord to the Subramanian.

Panchayat Administration

Subramanianan said that there are nine Ward Members out of whom five are males and three are females. Most of the Ward Members belong to the SC community. Only one Ward Member is a caste Hindu. One seat was reserved for general women but, as no one filed her nomination from the caste Hindus, one SC woman who filed her nomination and she was declared elected. Twice a month the Panchayat Council meeting is convened tentatively on the 6th and the 30th. The members attend the meetings. In the Council meeting, the availability of funds and the execution of items of work are discussed. Subramanian said that the income and expenditure of each month is read out during the meeting. The ward members feel that, as the details of the work are known to all, there is no necessity to read out the accounts. They insist on deciding on other items of work according to the availability of funds and they are not ready to spare time for discussing accounts and bills. This is due to the faith the members have in Subramanian.

As the Ward Members know the procedure for government grants and the various grants like JVVT, SFC and the earmarked ones, they do not compel Subramanian to do any work immediately. They know that their turn is inevitable, but the women members do insist on giving priority to their demands which could be met. Their demand is mostly for either street light or pipeline extension.

Gram Sabha

Sufficient attention is given to create awareness among the people about the importance of the Gram Sabha. Yet attendance at Gram Sabha meetings is always thin and to get the quorum Subramanian has to struggle a lot. Around 100 persons attend the Gram Sabha meetings regularly. Earlier mostly men attended the meetings. Now the women members of SHGs are attending and the women participate seriously in the Gram Sabha meetings. Construction of a community hall is a long pending demand of the people. They demand metal roads between the hamlets. Due to limited funds, the Panchayat is not able to take up this work. The MLA and the Union Chairman earlier promised to allocate funds for the construction of a community hall. But, later, they failed to keep their promise due to their indifferent attitude towards this Panchayat.

Activities

During the year 1997-98, under the JVVT scheme, Panchayat building repair work, desilting of four wells and gravelling of the approach road to the graveyard belonging to the SC were taken up together for Rs. 50,000. Under the Employment Assurance Scheme (EAS), the Union sanctioned Rs. 40,000 for the construction of a culvert and Rs. 7,500 under Flood Relief Work to repair the approach road. From the 10th Finance Commission award, pipeline extension work was carried out at a cost of Rs. 12,000. Gravelling work on approach roads got priority in the year 1998-99 under the JVVT and Rs. 69,000 was spent for that work. Construction of a ration shop and blacktopping of one km of road were done from the Union allocation under EAS during the year 1998-99. A Rajya Sabha M.P. related to Subramanian has sanctioned Rs. 6.00 lakhs for metalling of roads.

During 1999-2000 the JVVT grant was increased. A number of items of work were carried out in this year: culvert, colony street approach road, the graveyard road belonging to the SC, concrete road and provision of steps in the oorani (small tank) earmarked for drinking water. As the allotment for the concrete road was insufficient to complete the street, from the Panchayat funds Rs. 76,000 was additionally spent. As per the government norms, 22.5 per cent of the JVVT grant was spent for the creation of infrastructure for the SC community.

Rs. 24,000 was allotted under earmarked funds. According to the felt need of the colony people a pipeline was extended as the water available at the colony is too saline to be drunk. To meet the expenses on the pipeline extension, Rs. 11,000 was additionally spent from the Panchayat fund.

This year the Union did not release any grant. But from the M.P. Area Development Fund, Rs. 2.00 lakh was spent for oorani maintenance, construction of a bathing ghat and Rs. 2.50 lakh for the metalling of the roads. Subramanian said that the MLA and the M.P. funds were spent only on basic facilities as decided by the villagers in the Gram Sabha meeting.

In the year 2000-2001, CRSP was provided to 15 individuals, of whom seven spent an extra amount and built toilets according to their design. Rs. 35,000 was allotted for 15 group houses for SC families. In consultation with the SC community leaders, the beneficiaries were selected and the work was successfully completed. A bathing ghat was provided in a oorani (tank) and a retaining wall was provided to another oorani where frequent breaches occurred during the floods. To regulate the flow of water during floods, a small culvert was also provided under the JVVT Scheme. About Rs. 1.20 lakh was spent for the above-mentioned activities. From the Union fund, a new school building at a cost of Rs. 2.60 lakh was constructed in Puthanenthal hamlet.

Subramanian said that NABARD aided kanmoi (tank) maintenance was carried out by the PWD at a cost of Rs. 9.60 lakhs. Road improvement for two km. by laying two layers of BT at a cost of 28 lakh and cement layer for two km. at a cost of Rs.10 lakh were also carried out with NABARD assistance. Under the District Primary Education Programme, at a cost of Rs. 5.50 lakh, a school building was constructed and toilet facilities were provided from the Union fund in the school. For the middle school toilets water supply was given from a neighbour who avails of water from the Jeevandara well. The farmer agreed to provide water regularly to the school toilets. *Balwadi* repair work was done from the Union fund. The staff quarters of the VHN was in a damaged condition. The hand pump in the quarters was also in a state of disrepair. As there is no permission to undertake repair work by the Village Panchayat Subramanian could not help. However, through the contribution of the public, these were attended to.

Five new streetlights have been provided and lighting facility at one graveyard has also been provided. Under the Watershed Programme, one hamlet, namely Puthanenthal was covered. Desilting of the oorani at Puthanenthal, inlet channel maintenance and kanmoi maintenance work were carried out under this programme at a cost of Rs.1.67 lakh. Chemical fertilizer is provided at subsidized rates to individual farmers who are covered under the Watershed Programme.

Subramanian said that the quality of the watershed activities is good compared to the Union funded work. The farmers are made stakeholders in the Watershed Committee and hence they monitor the quality of the work and bring to the notice of higher officials any mistake committed in the process of implementation.

Perception of the President

Subramanian said that he came to know through the press that many programmes are available for rural development activities through the New Panchayati Raj system. When the election was declared he did not know anything about New Panchayati Raj System. He was not aware of the 73rd Amendment and its importance. Now he has come to know the salient features of the new system. Subramanian commented that the Union Councillors are functioning as independent representatives without any coordination with the Gram Panchayat. On the issue of development in rural areas, he suggested that the government should give top priority to improving the cultivation of dry land through various innovations. Science and technology must be properly utilized in dry land improvement. Drip irrigation and other modern water management systems have to be explained to small farmers, and thereby agriculture can be improved and employment opportunities created.

Subramanian suggested that training for the rural youth in various trades has to be given. The educated youth do not have adequate skills and hence they are engaged only in the construction industry. They need and expect new avenues. The government must plan to build the capacity of the educated youth to equip themselves in new trades like engineering and computer technology. The uneducated youth engage themselves in the construction industry and in agriculture. There are youth groups engaged in preparing illegal alcohol. The SHG women are now engaged in rearing milch animals. They also get training in village and cottage industries. Subramanian perception of polity is very clear. He said that the poor and the marginalised communities must affiliate themselves with political parties to ventilate their felt needs. Political mobilization process is the only way the problems of the poor can be addressed.

Regarding the gender issue, Subramanian said that the rural people understand the significance of education and so send their children to school. But, for higher studies, people need more money, and hence they stop giving education to their children beyond the middle school/high school level. He further said that women in general are now awakened. Earlier they just felt sorry for the condition of persons addicted to alcohol. But now-a-days they rail against them, complain to the police, even meet the District Collector en masse and insist on taking action against the arrack distillers in Kalaiyur Village. The SHG women of Kalaiyur even prevent the sale of toddy and gambling in the village. Now they demand public toilet for women with water facility. These point to the empowerment of rural women. Some women used to openly threaten that complaints will be registered against those who demand more dowry after the marriage. Earlier they would not come out to talk like this in a public forum.

He felt that if periodical meetings with women SHG members are convened by key departments like Revenue, Police, Social Welfare, Health and Education, the general awareness among villagers will improve and people's participation in local bodies will also improve.

Regarding the scope of the New Panchayati Raj system, Subramanian feels that the basic needs of the villagers could be fulfilled by the Panchayat. The Panchayat is now functioning with minimum interference from officials. In future the system will further strengthen.

Subramanian said that if the people come to know the names of the schemes and fund allocation procedure their involvement will improve and that even after the change of government in the State, the work is carried out without interference from the ruling political party. But he expressed his fear that if the election is delayed after the completion of the tenure, the officials will spend the money on unnecessary activities. He is of the opinion that people will agitate if elections are postponed.

Panchayat Finance

Taxes are properly paid by the villagers and to avail of the matching grant for house tax collection, the left out amount is paid from Subramanian's pocket. In 1999-2000 the house tax rose as here under :

Type of house	*From*	*To*
Huts	Rs. 6	Rs. 11
Tiled houses	Rs. 11	Rs. 16.50
Pucca houses	Rs. 6	Rs. 22

The revision was not made in accordance with the plinth area and the value of the house. Only a little enhancement was made as otherwise the people would not come forward to pay the house tax, according to Subramanian.

Audits have been done till 2000. No major objections have been made in the auditor's report. Once, without knowing the obligation to deduct the income tax from the contractor's fee, the cheque was given to him for the execution of the pipeline work. The auditor discovered this violation of the rule and ordered that the money be paid by the President.

Corruption

Subramanian said that to avail of the Employment Assurance Scheme (EAS) from the Union, some amount has to be given as bribe to the Union representatives. He said that he did not pay on percentage basis but just paid *ad hoc* amount.

Subramanian said that if the Government officials are strict in their supervision, the work is executed properly, irrespective of the commission paid.

His Idea for the Future

Subramanian has decided not to contest again in the Village Panchayat election. But he plans to contest for the Panchayat Union Council. He has decided to actively engage in the AIADMK Party and influence the MLA and the MP to allot more funds for water supply and road improvement work in his village.

He feels that a few youth of the SC community behave rudely with the public and spoil the name of the entire SC community. The village elders cannot able to control them. By degrees the social control over the hooligans is loosened. Even in the Village Committees corrupt elements are getting entry easily. Against this backdrop, Subramanian feels that, in future, the administration of Panchayats will not be smooth. Only a strong personality who can respond to the challenge from these elements can administer the Panchayat. The Village Committees are not coming forward to extend their support for augmenting the income of the Panchayat. But they always expect government money.

Subramanian suggests that the common property resources management should be completely vested with the Panchayat rather than permitting the Forest and Revenue Departments to hold them. The Social Forestry work could be done by the Panchayat provided the earmarked grant is allotted to the Panchayat. He plans to build up his career through politics.

CASE – 7

VITTANERI GRAM PANCHAYAT KALAYARKOIL BLOCK, SIVAGANGAI DISTRICT

Socio-Economic Background

Smt. J. Manimegalai, the President of Vittaneri Village Panchayat, from an agricultural family, is aged 38, has studied upto the 10th standard, is a Hindu and belongs to the Most Backward Community of Maravars. Her husband is a functionary in the Muventhar Munnetra Kazhagam, a caste based organization as well as one of the members in the traditional Village Committee. In addition to the income from their two acres of wet land, her husband, as a painter, earns a handsome amount from his work. Living in a tiled house of moderate size with her four sons, Ms. Manimegalai is seems to be content with what she has. Two of her sons are working in private establishments and one of them married and he lives independently.

Her parents were once settled in Burma. But, during the Indian Independence period, they returned to the motherland and settled in Madras. Her father worked in the Madras port. After his return to the home country, they used to visit their native village, *i.e.* Udavayal, a hamlet of Vittaneri Panchayat. She was married to a local relative and started her carreer as a volunteer and then animator in the Total Literacy Mission. Her husband encouraged her public activities. They are not rigid and are very accessible to all castes, including those belonging to the SC community in their village, and the surrounding villages. They both used to extend their services to the poor families, particularly in getting the welfare benefits of government schemes and programmes and slowly they earned a good name.

When Manimegalai was an animator in the Total Literacy Mission, she took interest in understanding the nuances of politics. When her father was in Burma he associated himself with the Tamil Sangam activities. He used to influence her in matters connected with the development of Tamils. Hence she evaluated the Government of Tamil Nadu from the perspective of its performance *i.e.* activities carried out in her village during the period of the DMK since 1974. Providing road for access to the oorani (tank) which is the only source for drinking water, providing streetlights and a community well to the village were in her memory. These activities were carried out by the DMK Party when it was in power which attracted her and her husband towards it. They became the sympathizers of the DMK.

Her involvement in the Total Literacy Mission activities from 1982 to 1996 helped her to shape her attitude and personality as a good social worker. Her husband's smooth and positive approach strengthened their reputation.

Recruitment Process

Vittaneri is one of the 16 Village Panchayats reserved for women in Kalayarkoil Union. There are four hamlets, namely Vittaneri, Udavayal, Kurukkuthi and Sathani in this Gram Panchayat. It is a multi-caste Panchayat peopled by Servais, Thevars, SCs, Asaris, Maravars, Valayars, Pandarams, Vellalars and Nadars. But the dominant castes are Maravars, Thevars and Servais, all belonging to one clan, namely the Mukkalothors.

When the position of President of Vittaneri Village Panchayat was reserved for general women, Manimegalai decided to contest. Her husband encouraged her to contest. The ex-President of the Village Panchayat belonged to her hamlet and the villagers advised her to contest in the election confidently. Moreover, the families belonging to the marginalized sector openly expressed their support to her. The other caste people knew her family background, their positive approach to public issues like temple celebration and other social activities and wished for the success of Manimegalai.

Two other candidates contested in the election, one from Vittaneri and another from Sathani. They did not have public orientation. Hence Manimegalai won the election.

The Other Reasons for Her Success

1. Her husband is not involved in any political party activities.
2. Women volunteers of her hamlet joined her for canvassing.
3. A full day campaign was conducted by all the families of her hamlet. They visited all the villages and sought votes for her.
4. The staff of the Total Literacy Mission joined her for canvassing.
5. The local unit of the DMK, even though she was not a member, worked for her success considering the family background as her father and her father-in-law were DMK supporters.

She did not project any issue during the canvassing. But people's expectation was very high that too for facilities like road and drinking water. A bit notice representing her symbol was printed requesting the voters to cast their votes in favour of her. There were further expenses. Friends and supporters regularly accompanied her. They used to have their meals at her house during the canvassing period. Her sister-in-law stayed for a week in her house to help her in the activities. Hence she could devote her time fully to canvassing. The total expenditure was below Rs.10,000. The canvassing was a smooth affair and no untoward incident occurred during the canvassing.

Socio-Political Environment

Though the village is a multi-caste one, social harmony prevails there. The religious activities provide an opportunity to understand one another in the village. In all hamlets, except Kurukkathi, there are Amman and Ayyan temples and the marginalized sector has free access to all these temples. There is no two tumbler system in any tea stall in the hamlets. The villagers of each hamlet used to visit the nearby villages where a tea stall is available. In one tea stall the untouchability was practised. It was stopped since whole the community protested against it.

Even though nobody is permitted to fetch water from the tank for other than drinking purposes, the youth from the SC community question the decision of the Panchayat and since the tank is near their settlement they want to take water for all purposes. But this has not taken a serious turn since in this Village Panchayat the traditional committees are functioning. On all social and cultural matters the traditional Panchayat takes decisions. People accept the decisions of the Panchayat. But there is no conflict between the traditional Panchayat and formal Panchayat. The traditional Panchayat maintains its own accounts. They maintain inner democracy by reconstituting the committee every two years. Practically they decide on all community matters. Whenever they need the support of the formal Panchayat they ask the Panchayat and *vice versa*. All activities are determined only in committees and later all are reviewed by the members in the general body.

The traditional Panchayat maintains a corpus fund and from the corpus fund the committee gives money for needs at a low interest. This traditional Panchayat understands the role of the formal Village Panchayat and makes use of the Village Panchayat for getting necessary welfare schemes. It gives money to the Panchayat to get schemes from the government. The committee members used to meet the President and the President shares the Panchayat affairs with them. This positive relationship between these two institutions helps each other. Manimegalai's husband is one of the committee members of the traditional Panchayat. Now he is the organiser of Valarkalvi Mayam, the post-literacy activities. Hence, Mrs. Manimegalai is able to get along well with the Village Committee.

Manimegalai said that she frequently met responsible persons of the Village Committee in other hamlets also and gained their confidence. This positive relationship between the two helped her in administering the Panchayat activities and in the selection of beneficiaries for government programmes and schemes.

Other village organisations which play a contributing role in the Panchayat affairs are SHGs sponsored by the NGO. Even before the implementation of the SGSY Scheme by the government machinery, the NGO, TRUS was working in Vittaneri village and formed SHGs. There are seven SHGs with 125 women member representing all sections of the community. They are all registered and maintain a bank account with savings of Rs. 8000. They practise micro-finance, charging 3 per cent interest for their internal lending. They meet every Tuesday at the President's house in the case of Udavayal and in the case of the other SHGs at the respective organiser's house. So far the maximum individual loan given is Rs. 1000 with five instalments of repayment. Adult literacy, health, child welfare are discussed in the meeting of the SHGs. The sectoral department officials from Agriculture, Animal Husbandry, Health and Social Welfare visit and discuss their department programmes with the SHG members and the Panchayat. The SHG members attend the Gram Sabha meetings regularly. Manimegalai has served as organiser of the SHG in Udavayal. There is no cinema fans association or any other youth association in the village. The Muventher Munnetra Kazhagam of Mukkalathors, Veera Saivar Peravai of Pandarams, Mutharaiyar of Valayars, Yadavar Peravai of Konars are the major caste organisations working in the villages. Apart from the Muventhar Munnetra Kazhagam no other association is functioning well.

The AIADMK, the DMK and the TMC are the major parties functioning in this village. Only at the time of elections the parties organise meetings and other programmes. But in the villages there are no serious party activities. It is said that in general the ruling party people work actively as villagers seek their support to deal with issues related to various departments. The political party functionaries, when they meet the President, enquire about the Panchayat work. While attending the Gram Sabha meetings, they express their opinions on the Panchayat administration. Manimegalai said that she never showed any undue favouritism to her party men. She claimed that the IRDP loan beneficiaries are selected from the list given by the Gram Sabha and they are really poor families irrespective of party background.

Manimegalai said that the village institutions are not considered rivals to the Panchayat. They never act against the Panchayat's activities. This may be due to her fair administration.

Her Perception of the Concept of Panchayati Raj

Manimegalai learnt about Panchayati Raj through her Total Literacy Mission training programme. In the training programme they explained the salient features like Gram Sabha, reservation for women and power to the Panchayats and people. She was able to compare the functioning of the local bodies in Kerala and that of those in Tamil Nadu. She recollected the efforts taken by Rajiv Gandhi in establishing the New Panchayati Raj System.

She admitted that she did not have the Tamil Nadu Panchayat Act, but she used to read the newspapers such as *Dinamalar* and *Thinathanthi* for Panchayat news. She used to purchase the women's magazine *Mangayar Malar*.

She appreciated the steps taken by the DMK Government to conduct the Panchayat elections. She believes that the three-tier system is essential and that the Chairpersons of local bodies should be given a honorarium as it is done in Kerala State.

With regard to issues in the New Panchayati Raj System, she said that there are a volley of questions to be sorted out to enable the Panchayats to function effectively as institutions of self-government. The entire administrative system at the grassroots is highly complicated and a variety of players are in the system without clear-cut roles assigned to them. Officials control the entire system. The Panchayat leaders are at the mercy of the officials.

The scope of New Panchayati Raj will be changed according to the mood and temperament of the ruling party. If the state government encourages and supports the local bodies, they will be empowered. Otherwise their functioning will be crippled. She narrated the latest development after the assembly elections. The government grant due to the Panchayat is not available.

The local ruling party MLA and the local AIADMK party functionaries met the block officials and influenced them to delay the activities. This unnecessary interference will disturb the spirit of the local bodies. As Panchayati Raj becomes a regular and permanent institution basic amenities and infrastructure facilities for the people will improve.

Perception of Development

As for her perception of development, Ms. Manimegalai quoted Gandhiji's notion of development, *i.e.*, meeting the basic needs and living with nature peacefully. Economic development is essential for villages as the agricultural operations are limited. She commented that due to the serious efforts taken by the government the yield of the agricultural sector has increased many times. The government has to play a vital role in improving the rural economy in the following ways :

- Ensuring irrigation resources,
- Encouraging women's participation,
- Encouraging agriculture related activities,
- Providing training to the youth in various rural activities, and
- Providing training to the youth in various small scale industrial activities.

Perception of Village Economy

In the agriculture sector, employment is limited as lands are getting shrunk. One cannot earn much profit in agriculture. Due to the vagaries of the monsoon, agricultural operations are a challenge. Most of the youngsters belonging to agricultural families have left the villages, and are trying for employment in cities and abroad. Animal husbandry is slowly sliding down. The introduction of the tractor and other modern equipment has replaced animals in agriculture. As a result bullocks have been sold. There is no village or cottage industry in the vicinity of this Panchayat. The young men have migrated to cities. The educated youth have got driving licence and left India. Most of the migrated youth engage in vending, catering, rickshaw driving, and automobile driving in towns and cities. The SHG is the new approach to improve the village economy. The benefits from the government are enjoyed again and again by the same families, unless the Panchayat intervenes.

Manimegalai listed the following as the major obstacles to the process of development :

- People do not have any aspiration to develop themselves.
- Confusion prevails in implementing hundreds of programmes of the government in the rural areas.
- The below poverty line list is not genuine. Many genuine cases are left out and ineligible persons are included.
- The present day younger generation belonging to rural areas are not serious about their life. They do not have the initiative and drive to develop themselves.

SHGs have to be strengthened and oriented towards socio-economic activities. Illicit distillation and sale of arrack is widely by prevalent in villages. Women's equality is not yet acceptable to all men. To bring about development in the villages, all Government Departments and their schemes have to be channelised properly through the Panchayat. The latest initiatives of SHGs do not have relevance to the Village Panchayats. There is no coordinated effort from the sectoral departments. All sectors, Government, NGOs, local bodies SHGs and individual woman have to joint hands to bring about development. The Panchayat must be positioned well in these joint efforts.

Perception of Gender Issues

Women are now treated with respect in villages. But wage discrimination still exists. The menace of alcoholism is increasing and the sufferers are women. Due to lack of proper education they become prey to exploiters. As examples Manimegalai cited certain incidents which happened in her village. A married man was involved in an extra marital relationship with an unmarried woman and induced her to come away from her home. The same man, while staying in Chennai, developed an illicit relationship with another unmarried woman and brought her to the village with her jewels and money. As a woman Panchayat President, Ms. Manimegalai spoke on this issue to women police officials. According to their advice, the local Panchayat met and discussed the problem. The man was found guilty and they imposed a fine of Rs. 2001. The unmarried girls were advised to discontinue their relationship with him. Ultimately justice was not done to the unmarried girls. Justice was done only to his wife. This kind of atrocity is going on in the villages. Menfolk are not sensitive to these issues. Manimegalai is gradually creating awareness among the SHG members to fight against such atrocities.

Manimegalai said that if the husband and the family members understand the problems of women, society will also understand them. Her own husband respects her; he even cooks food when she is away in connection with Panchayat work. He has faith in her and allows her to attend training programmes, meetings and other programmes without any hesitation. Development will come about only if women are economically empowered. Education and employment skill orientation are two main necessities for women's empowerment. The political empowerment of women is a stupendous task. Women are interested in playing a role in society but the family duties and responsibilities do not allow them to take up such responsibilities. Moreover they have to depend on their husbands for their protection from societal problems. The reservation for women in local bodies provides an opportunity to women. But only if the women develop the right spirit and self-motivation, such opportunities will empower women politically. To keep up the spirit of the women leaders, orientation programmes are essential.

Perception of Social Justice

For the past fifty years, efforts have been made through social movements to establish social justice. As a result the marginalised sectors and the most backward communities have gained power and status through education and employment opportunities. Discrimination and untouchability are now absent in Manimegalai's village. Political parties are the main culprits in bringing about differences among the social groups. The ruling party leaders and the Ministers unnecessarily encourage the communal forces to mobilize the people for their political gain. If every community is given equal opportunity they will all disown these leaders.

Perception of Common Property Resources

The common properties like oorani, kanmoi, threshing floor, grazing land, trees and paths are now misused by dominant groups. But in quite a number of cases, the village community has established its control over these properties. For example, the protection of karuvelan trees is properly done by her village community. Due to the failure of the monsoon, the oorani and the kanmoi are not properly maintained; otherwise the village people themselves maintain them as they have to do so to get irrigation water. All the families possess a little or more dry land and they use it for grazing or fuel-wood cutting. Hence the village commons are not disturbed by anybody in her village.

Socialization Process

Initially Manimegalai's involvement in the Total Literacy Mission activities helped her to understand the problems of people belonging to different sections. She cultivated the habit of savings and hard work which won the heart of her husband. He encouraged her patience, faith and interest to serve the people which he considered appropriate to a model organizer.

Her father encouraged her to do service to society when she lived in Chennai. By reading books in the Valarkalvi Mayyam she understand many things. Her positive approach to issues and her respect for individuals are her outstanding qualities in the estimate of the marginalized sector. Her political orientation is very useful to her in establishing good relationship with officials and village leaders. She plans to involve herself seriously in SHG activities as well as the DMK women's wing activities continuously in future.

Performance in the Village Panchayat

Upon assuming power, Manimegalai, during 1996-97 undertook maintenance work in two hamlets from the Village Panchayat funds. When the State Finance Commission grant was released, oorani maramathu work at a cost of Rs. 12,000 was undertaken. By influencing the District Councillor, she got sanction for a BT road at a cost of Rs. 35,000. Under the JVVT Scheme street maintenance was carried out at Udavayal, a kitchen shed was provided to the *balwadi* and a retaining wall was constructed at Udavayal during 1997-98. Maintenance work in the irrigation tank was carried out in Vittaneri hamlet. The Jeevandhara Millennium Well dug at a cost of Rs. 1,81,000 benefiting the poor was also her achievement.

During the period 1999-2000, when the people demanded improvement of the graveyard road in Udavayal and Sathani hamlets, these were at a cost of Rs. 30,000 under the JVVT Scheme. Repair work on the drinking water supply line and extension of the line were also carried out.

During 2000-2001, maintenance of the graveyard roads at Kurukkuthi and Udavayal was carried out, a bathing ghat was constructed at Vittaneri at a cost of Rs. 20,000 and the irrigation tank was repaired at a cost of Rs. 10,000 under the JGSY Scheme. From the SFC grant road maintenance was carried out in three hamlets and five group houses were provided for Sathani Village people. Maintenance work was carried out for streetlights, handpumps, drinking water public taps and motor pumps at a cost of nearly Rs. 1,00,000 in the past five years.

Execution of Work

The manner of making use of the Panchayat fund, State Finance Commission grant, and JVVT grant was decided in the Panchayat meetings. During the Gram Sabha meetings people's demands were discussed and consolidated. According to the availability of funds and the urgency of the need of the people, items of work were selected and carried out. Selection of sites was done in consultation with the concerned hamlet elders and responsible people's opinion.

Manimegalai cited an example of how problems emerge in the field while executing Panchayat works. It was decided to construct a bathing ghat at the Vittaneri. While the measurement was being done for the construction, the local people complained that the proposed space for the bathing ghat was too little and so they refused to permit the construction. Manimegalai explained the funds availability and the Panchayat's financial position, but the people refused to listen to her. Hence she met the village elders and explained the situation to them. Later the village elders came and pacified the villagers and then the work was completed.

As undue delay in releasing grant to Panchayats continues, the execution of various items of work within the stipulated time is a serious problem to the Panchayat President. Ms. Manimegalai said that she patiently waited in the Union office to meet the higher officials during their visits and frequently submitted the people's demand to the Minister and the District Collector. Only her continuous efforts yielded dividends. Her cordial relationship with the District Councillor, even though she belongs to another party, helped her to avail of the District Council's assistance.

Ms. Manimegalai regretted that the people used to criticize her in spite of her efforts. But she took it positively as frustration from too much of expectation from the Village Panchayat. If the villagers understand the details of the limited power the Panchayat enjoys and the meagre resources of the Panchayat, they will not trouble the Panchayat.

At Kurukkuthi hamlet, when a TV room was constructed, a few persons came and suggested a different site for installing the TV. Due to the difference of opinion, the work was delayed. At last, with the help of the village elders and the VAO, a suitable site was identified and then the construction was completed. By her political influence she was able to get funds for a 3 km BT road for her Panchayat.

As she is seriously involved in Panchayat affairs, she is not able to look after her family and its agriculture. Moreover the meagre travelling allowance given is not sufficient to meet the expenses. Only financially sound persons can bear these losses. Her husband and family members have to adjust with her frequent absences from her house. Otherwise no woman

President can come out daily, visit various offices, patiently wait for officials to meet and share the village problems with them. To convince the officials, she has to explain the conditions in detail. All these are possible for Manimegalai because of the support extended by her husband.

All the works in her Panchayat are carried out by the Panchayat only. She does not follow the practice of allotting work to Ward Members. Due to this quality is ensured and, at the same time, a small savings is also effected. One of the Ward Members, out of envy, complained to the block officials about the quality of the work. The officials came and verified all the details. They could not find any fault and they spoke to the Ward Member who had complained and advised him not to disturb the work.

Manimegalai felt that when the work really benefited the people, the villagers will not cause any trouble. But if they suspect that the President has made any personal profit, they will certainly start murmuring. The President has to be flexible. Ms. Manimegalai cited an example. When the people of Vittaneri hamlet asked to be permitted to clear the thorny bushes along the roadside, she permitted them to do so. Since there is no provision to use Panchayat funds, she herself donated the money for employing workers to clear the thorny bushes. Caste differences and political competition are the major obstacles in public life. To overcome all these obstacles, in Manimegalai's opinion, the Village Panchayat Presidents should be fair to all and never involve in caste and political activities.

Committee Formation

A Vigilance Committee was formed earlier to monitor the functioning of the ration shop, to prevent illicit liquor sale and to supervise the provision of basic amenities. For two years the Committee met periodically but the members, three men and four women, including three SC members, did not show any interest in attending the meetings since they did not get any sitting allowance. When a complaint arose regarding non-issue of the correct quantity of rice earmarked for ration card holders, Manimegalai met the staff of the ration shop. They explained that they did not get 100 per cent stocks and so there was less for distribution to the latecomers. But the President asked them to divide the issued quantity equally among all the ration card holders. Thus the problem was solved. She did not receive any government orders regarding the formation of various committees.

Tax Collection

Collection of house tax is not a problem. The village people used to pay the house tax but one has to visit each house two to three times to collect the tax. Immediately after she assumed power, the Panchayats were asked to enhance the house tax. But it was not done, as the people would not cooperate. Only during 1999 a revision was carried out. For new houses they collected Rs. 2,000. Due to the absence of any business and industrial establishment the Panchayats could not get more income. By auctioning the fishing rights in five ponds Rs. 4,000 was carned and by auctioning the karuvelan trees in three *kanmois* (tanks) Rs. 44,000 was earned. The Village Committee got the auction, employed a watchman to safeguard the trees and earned a good deal of income from the trees. As the government does not permit the Panchayat to employ watchmen, auctioning to the Village Committee is a good option.

The Vittaneri Kanmoi (tank) is under the administration of the PWD. The fuel trees in this kanmoi were auctioned by the PWD. The Panchayat's share is not yet handed over to the Panchayat. An earlier share of Rs. 44,000 was given at a time of financial crisis. That amount was spent for the payment of dues to the Electricity Board. As the area is very dry, no further improvement can be made in the village commons. There are seven ooranis (small tanks) and eight *kanmois* (big tanks) in the village with an *ayakattu* (cultivable lands) of 600 acres. Everywhere only thorny bushes and trees are growing. The details of other poromboke lands (commons) are not known to the Village Panchayat. According to Manimegalai there must be a separate budget allocation during the initial period to manage the commons and improve the same.

Government Grant

This Panchayat received grants from the government based on the State Finance Commission recommendations. The details are given below:

1997-98	*1998-99*	*1999-2000*	*2000-2001*
Rs. 12,000	Rs. 9,000	Rs. 52,820	Rs. 6,300

Payment is made in a belated manner and there is no regularity in payments.

Auditing

For all the years except 2000-2001 the audit was completed. No serious objections were made by the auditing officials. Money is given to the auditors but Ms. Manimegalai said that it was just for incidental expenses like food and fuel for the vehicles of the team. The existing system of inspection and auditing is a good arrangement. The officials explained the procedures to the clerk and the President. The officials asked the clerk to bring all the records to their office. They do not send for the President during auditing. Manimegalai said that only those Panchayat Presidents are present during the auditing whose clerk does not keep proper accounts.

She has knowledge of accounts, but does not know the systematic and procedural maintenance of all records and account books. She verifies the bank pass book entries, cheque book entries, cash book entries and the bills. The accounts are maintained by the clerk. Her husband also used to supervise the accounts with her. The clerk used to convey to her the findings and the observations or any other comments made by the auditing officials. She narrated an incident. During the celebration of Independence Day last year, she purchased some articles for Rs. 60 whereas the permitted amount is only Rs. 40. The officials made a note that the extra amount spent on this item has to be recovered from the President. But the auditing official asked her to give in writing that in future the mistake will not occur. In this way the officials gave guidance and helped in finalizing the accounts.

Moreover once in six months a Union officials used to visit and inspect all the records and comment on the accounts. This periodical inspection came into practice after malpractices were detected at the end of the financial year in a few Panchayats.

Corruption

Corruption is widely prevalent, particularly in the Union engineering section. The Union engineering officials are authorised to measure the constructions, make entries in the 'M' book and prepare for inspection. They have also to prepare a work progress report based on which the bills would be settled. Any delay will create complications as the work is carried out without receiving any advance. For a speedy transaction the contractor or the President used to give money to the Union engineering department. The Union Engineer is more powerful than the District Collector in this regard.

Moreover, as technicians, the Union Engineer and his officials know that the estimated amount is more than sufficient to complete the work in accordance with the quality specified. When the contractor or the President fails to maintain the quality, the Union Engineer and his officials demand money. When the work is done properly the officials resort to delayed payment and so even the non-corrupt Presidents have to give some money to the Union Engineer and his officials.

The Block Development officials do not demand money. But they accept whatever is given. The problem arises due to the following reasons: delay in releasing grants; visiting the spot to take measurements, and delay in making entries in the 'M' book. Even after the completion of the work months pass before the visit of the Union Engineer. By the time the work might change appearance. Fearing this and the consequence of this, the contractor and the Presidents bribe the Engineering Department officials illegally. Though there is a rule permitting the employment of private technician for verification and reporting, the signature of the Union Engineer is essential. Hence the Union Engineer is a key person in the system of corruption.

Manimegalai maintains that corruption cannot be completely eliminated. Moreover the contractor who earns a profit will give money to the officials despite the vigilance maintained. However it is not a large amount. In the case of group houses inspection and measurement a considerable amount is given to the Union Engineer. But in the case of joint inspection by block officials and the Engineering Department officials and the People's Committee, the inspection is quick and prompt.

Panchayat Meeting

One Panchayat meeting is conducted every month which all the members attend regularly. The lone *Dalit* member does not talk seriously, but conveys the expectations of his people. There are six Ward Members, four men and two women, with one SC man. The women Members demand road and water supply facilities to their wards. Earlier they not known the financial position and the system governing the government's grants. Later they understood them and so limited their demands. The Panchayat meeting is conducted smoothly. There are no untoward incidents in the Panchayat meetings.

Gram Sabha Meeting

The Gram Sabha meeting is held on the stipulated days. Only one meeting was held at Udavayal hamlet. There are 1,413 voters but the average attendance was reported as less than 10 per cent and only once the attendance was 10 per cent. Manimegalai said that she took all steps to mobilize the people for the Gram Sabha meetings. A public address system was used to announce the details of the programme in all the hamlets. The clerk met the members and the village community leaders and informed them of the Gram Sabha meeting and its agenda. The attendance will improve if decisions taken in the Gram Sabha are implemented.

Demands pertaining to road, drinking water, *balwadi*, black-topping of roads, construction of ration shop, maintenance of road to graveyard and streetlights are discussed in the Gram Sabha meetings. Some of the demands of the people have been met under the schemes of the government. But when they attend the meeting, they raise a volley of questions. Moreover some individuals expect individual benefits. The SHG members attend the Gram Sabha meetings and submit some demands. The details of income and expenditure are read out, but no one seriously listens to them and verifies the records. The SC members' attendance is very limited.

Manimegalai observed that a huge amount of money has been spent on schemes like Samathuvapuram. Such schemes can be avoided as a large amount of money is utilized by a few families, that too party cadres. More poor families must be covered by government programmes and the selection of beneficiaries should be done in the Gram Sabha. If this is done more poor people will attend the Gram Sabha meetings.

Environment Activities

Significantly environmental activities are being carried out only by the traditional Panchayats. They make rules and regulations for utilising the common pastures. They impose conditions on the procedure for rearing goats as they spoil the saplings in the common lands and in the forest land.

Social Activities

For enrolment of students in school, Manimegalai used the members of the SHGs.

There is no sweeper in the Panchayat and hence special steps are being taken by Manimegalai in this regard. The VHN used to meet each pregnant woman in the Panchayat and the ward members used to help her in mobilizing children for immunization. A health sub-centre is located at Vittaneri and the VHN is staying in the sub-centre.

For the school, a handpump and additional school building are needed. Toilets are not available in all the three primary schools. Manimegalai met the District Collector in this regard. Steps are to be taken in future for providing toilet facilities at the schools. Girl children used to study upto the eighth standard in this village. After that they used to go for employment in factories. Manimegalai regrets that girl children are not continuing their study further. But she has not taken any step to address this issue in the Gram Sabha meetings as the parents are indifferent to it.

Innovation

An innovation has been made in Manimegalai's Panchayat. Instead of paying money to the Electricity Board (EB) for the fittings of new streetlights, she herself purchased components needed for the new streetlights and assembled them, since the EB charged 4500 rupees whereas the real cost is only Rs. 1,200 to Rs. 1,500. Five new tubelights fitted on the posts are already available. When it was explained that it was subject to audit objection or legal action by the EB, Manimegalai said that, if it meant violation of rule, she was ready to face the consequences.

She cited another innovation: when a new road was formed, there were three electricity posts which stood in the way and so had to be repositioned. The EB demanded Rs. 20,000 for repositioning the three posts. Manimegalai did not accede to their demand but took the issue up with the local Minister. Upon his advice, she met the highest district official of the EB and explained the problem. The district officer agreed to help. After that the local EB officials revisited and re-assessed the proposed expenses and fixed Rs. 8,000 as the cost.

Problems in Maintaining the Public Assets within the Guidance of Government

The earmarked fund meant for drinking water system maintenance is not sufficient. The motor pumps and pipeline are subject to damage and expenses cannot be limited. In the case of non-functioning tubelights, in about 50 per cent of the lights, the chokes have been replaced more than twice, whereas the government permits change of chokes only twice. For buildings, maintenance there is no grant. Hence maintenance of public assets is really a problem due to financial crunch in the Panchayat.

The Panchayat office is an old building and the wiring was done after the new Panchayat administration was introduced. Necessary furniture were purchased. But the doors and the windows are not in good condition. The toilet is not in good condition. Manimegalai cannot take any step to reshape the premises. The records are kept at the President's house for the sake of safety. She does not have the habit of visiting the office regularly. As the office is at Vittaneri, only once or twice a week she goes to the office. But she used to meet the people by visiting their areas periodically.

Accountability

During the Gram Sabha meeting the accounts are kept open for public scrutiny. Moreover the income and expenditure statement is exhibited in three public places where many people gather everyday. But people do not take this seriously as they know what is done in their area. They know that Manimegalai shows interest in public work but they do not take the concept of accountability seriously. Manimegalai complained that the Vice-President, who cooperated so far, now expects money for affixing her joint signature. Even though the Vice-President is a good woman, the husband of the Vice-President unduly influences her in her activities.

She maintains good relationship with officials, frequently visits the Panchayat Union office and sectoral departments like Social Welfare, Agriculture and Health and the offices of TWAD, EB, and DRDA. As most of the other women Presidents rely on their husbands when visiting offices, the officials encourage Ms. Manimegalai in her independent functioning. Moreover, in general, the officials of the Police Department, and the Revenue Department recognize the Presidents' role and respect them. Manimegalai narrated her efforts in stopping the sale of illicit arrack in her village. Along with a few women members of the SHG she met the Police officials. The Police officer respected them and immediately took action. Her continuous efforts resulted in success. Manimegalai observed that, as there is no functional linkage between the Union Council and the Village Panchayat, she could not have good relationship with the Councillor. Social issues like alcoholism and discrimination against women are not seriously taken up by the Councillor.

Her Future Plan

She wishes to contest again. Then only the remaining work could be completed. At the same time she plans to strengthen the SHG activities so that economic activities could be taken up. Two of her sons are employed, one in Chennai and the other in Coimbatore. The son settled in Chennai is married and he is independent and the other is unmarried. The remaining two sons are with her. She has no female children. Hence Manimegalai plans to continue to involve herself in public activities, transferring the family responsibility to her would be daughter-in-law. Her husband is already in public life and so he encourages her public spirit. Their independent earning from two acres of wet land is a good support for their livelihood. Hence they are working to sustain the name earned after she became the President by involving themselves more in public activities. The reservation for women in Panchayat institutions provides enormous opportunities to channelise their energy into nation building and community development activities.

CASE – 8

KANDRATHEERTHAM GRAM PANCHAYAT THIRUMANUR BLOCK, ARIYALUR DISTRICT

Socio-Economic Background

Mrs. Selvi is the President of the Kandratheertham Village Panchayat. She belongs to the SC community and is a Hindu. She is literate and has completed her primary education. She is married and her husband is working as a mason. Their family is nuclear. Their economic status is very low as they do not own any land or other property. Selvi herself is working as an agricultural labourer. They live in their own house, a *pucca* house, but a small one. They have two daughters. One is in school studying in the second standard and the other is a baby.

Her Recruitment Process

Selvi's husband is an educated young man and known to the former President. The former President suggested to him to field her Selvi the Panchayat election and accordingly he consulted her. Her husband is a calm type but maintains social relationship with all communities. He does not have any bad habits and so he is treated as a cultured SC young man. Moreover, as a mason by profession, his hard work and honesty is known to many. Based on this merit, it was suggested that Selvi's candidature was welcome.

There were three candidates in the fray and all were poor. In Kandratheertham, the main village, all the communities supported only Selvi. In the other hamlets the votes were divided. Though the former President belongs to the Vanniar community, he evinced keen interest in her victory. For about one week they conducted intensive campaigning in which village youth, men and women, accompanied her. In one hamlet, the public demanded her assurance to provide drainage facilities and group houses to the Backward Classes also. In the tough competition she won by a margin of 285 votes.

Village Set-up

Kandratheertham Panchayat has two hamlets, namely, Mettutheru and Packianathapuram. The Vanniars are the dominant caste. Other caste Hindu communities are Moopanars, Muthurajas and Udayars. There are Muslims and Christians also in the village. In the hamlet of Packianathapuram, almost all the families are Christians of SC, Servai and Muthuraja communities. There is no close social relationship among the communities. Each community considers itself superior to the others.

Agriculture is the main source of income. The major landholding is in the hands of the BCs and among the SCs only

10 to 15 families hold lands. Onion, paddy, sugarcane and groundnut are the major crops.

Marketing of agricultural products is not a problem. Most of the crops are profitable ones, except onion. Hence the landed gentry in the village is powerful.

Social Issues

Alcoholism is the main social issue, which affects a large number of families among the peasant community as well as the landless labour class. The village is situated on the banks of the Cauvery river and so the groundwater potential is rich. More than 200 borewells are available for irrigation and, due to availability of adequate water, intensive agricultural operations are undertaken in Kandratheertham Village. But the wages are very poor compared to landless labourers' wages in Thanjavur. As more number of poor landless labourers are available, the landholders fix the wages at Rs. 25 for women and Rs. 45 for men.

The SC landless families used to get money as advance for their labour from the farmers. If they fail to report when demanded, the farmers used to come over to the habitation of SC family and abuse the defaulter. Because of this a feeling of ill-will has developed between the BC and the SC community. This mostly happens to alcohol addicted SC labour families. The bootleggers sell arrack in the Panchayat area. As the public demanded the intervention of the Panchayat in this regard, with the help of the Ward Members, a signature campaign was organized to take action against the culprits. After this, the Police acted and the sales were stopped.

Political Parties

The AIADMK and the DMK are the dominant political parties in this Panchayat. Other parties like the PMK, the TMC and the Congress are also functioning. But there are no serious activities carried out by the political parties. They are active only during the elections. The party leaders do not give much importance to the Panchayat but the party of the local MLA influences it because he allocates schemes to the Village Panchayat.

Youth Association

Among the youth, one youth association affiliated to the NYK is in operation. They do not engage in any constructive activities. A few of them attend the Gram Sabha meetings and demand some facilities from the Panchayat. The SC youth do not have any association.

Other Social Institutions

There is one common association in Kandratheertham Village in the name of Makkal Mandram. It helps the Panchayat by taking the main issues to the knowledge of the district administration. When the number of trips by the public transport bus to the village was curtailed, the Makkal Mandram intervened. The Makkal Mandram committee members went to meet the District Collector and, with the help of the district administration, the earlier number of bus trips was restored. Once the representatives of the Makkal Mandram complained regarding the poor quality of the BT road work executed by a contractor by using the funds of the Union Council and the work was stopped. Later the defect was rectified. Most of the village leaders take active part in the Makkal Mandram.

Construction Workers Union

The labouers like masons and helpers who are engaged in construction activities have their own association. The leaders of this association come over to the Panchayat office and demand welfare activities for the village. Selvi feels that, in general, the representatives of social institutions have the habit of questioning and demanding from the Panchayat rather than understanding and associating with the Panchayat.

Women's Groups

Under the guidance of an NGO, there are six women's groups functioning in the Panchayat. They meet once a month in their respective streets. They could not get government loan though they started their activities two years back. But the NGO, which supports the group, extended loans to them. After the formation of SHGs, there was awareness on small savings, children's education and public issues among women, but, due to alcoholism, the development achieved by the women is getting wasted. The members of SHGs attend the Gram Sabha meetings and demand work on their streets.

Religious Institution

Village daities like Mariamman, Karuppanasamy, Chellai-amman, Semban and Kaliamman are worshipped in this village. The *Poojaris* of these temples are from Pandaram, Moopanar and SC communities. There is a church in Packianathapuram. Harmony prevails between the Hindu and the Christian communities. Untouchability or denial of temple entry to the SC does not prevail in the Panchayat.

Perception of Panchayati Raj

Selvi said that she did not know anything about Panchayats when she contested in the election. Without the guidance and encouragement of officials, she could not handle the administration. When the Vice-President failed to cooperate with the Panchayat she explained the problems to the Ward Members and then met the AD (Panchayat) and the District Collector. After a struggle she was able to replace the Vice-President. After this incident she realised that any issue could be handled if she involves herself directly. She learned bicycle-riding in order to go to the Union office whenever necessary. To administer the Village Panchayat a good deal of knowledge and courage is needed for the President, according to her. When the Vice-President out of self-interest, demanded to change a name from a list of beneficiaries of a group housing scheme, she did not know how to manage the issue, since those who were selected were really eligible poor people. To seek guidance, her husband visited the Union office. But the official there said that the President had to come personally and learn the rules and procedures. When she arrived, the officials encouraged her and properly guided her in Panchayat work. Women Presidents have to be equipped in many ways to effectively administer the Village Panchayat.

On Village Economy

As the wages for agricultural activities are very limited, it is advisable to give new skills training for new employment opportunities at least to young men and women. Landowners are living independently and they know how to develop themselves, whereas the poor and landless need support and guidance to improve their life. Economic activities have to be implemented for the poor.

Gender Issue

Selvi believes that, in villages, it is not easy to change the mindset of the public on gender justice. But women are gradually getting importance due to their education, employment and representation in Panchayati Raj institutions.

Performance

When the investigator visited the village for interviewing her, Selvi was working on a farm as a labourer. She said that she could not remember the exact details of work executed in her Panchayat. She said that the Panchayat work is carried out through the Ward Members. Twenty group houses, 15 for SCs and 5 for BCs were constructed. The selection of beneficiaries was done fairly as there was a demand from many.

The other items of work like construction of culverts, two TV rooms, two kitchen sheds, laying of cement concrete road and metal road, installation of 13 new streetlights and providing night light connections to huts were carried out.

From the Panchayat funds mainly road improvement activities were undertaken. In the year 1998-99, roads were improved in all the three hamlets at a cost of Rs. 18,000 in two hamlets each and of Rs. 15,000 in the other hamlet. In the year 1999-2000 and 2000-2001 again road work and improvement of graveyard roads were undertaken at a total cost of Rs. 46,000 and Rs. 77,000 respectively in the main village of Kandratheertham. From the earmarked fund a small culvert at a cost of Rs. 10,000 and a cement concrete road at a cost of Rs. 64,000 were executed.

The other major items of work were undertaken with the help of JVVT grants. In the year 1996-97 Rs. 61,000 was spent for constructing a culvert and two kitchen sheds for primary schools. In the year 1997-98 six culverts of Rs. 15,000 each were constructed. Many streets which are isolated during the rainy season have now been provided with culverts and two small bridges were constructed at a total cost of Rs. 40,000 in the year 1998-99. In the year 1999-2000 one small bridge, one retaining wall and one bus shelter at a total cost of Rs.1.20 lakh were completed. The approach road to the AD colony was upgraded with metal at a cost of Rs. 85,000 along with a culvert at a cost of Rs. 24,000.

Sources of Income

The major sources of income are :

1. Auction of fishing rights,
2. Stamp duty,
3. SFC grant, and
4. Entertainment tax.

There are 11 tanks in the Panchayat and through auctioning of fishing rights in these tanks the Panchayat gets a considerably good income. In the year 1997-98, Rs. 11,525, in the year 1998-99, Rs. 53,690, in the year 1999-2000, Rs. 20,110, and during the year 2000-2001, Rs. 7,500 were collected and deposited in the Panchayat's account. A total of Rs. 92,825 was earned, as per the statement of accounts in the Panchayat office. From 15 tamarind trees the Panchayat earned an income of Rs. 18,500. As there is a cinema theatre within the jurisdiction of the village, entertainment tax share is received by the Panchayat since 1998-99. So far a total sum of Rs. 73,691 has been earned as share of entertainment tax.

The major expenses are under the heads of payment of electricity bills (annual average Rs. 60,000) maintenance of streetlights (average Rs. 40,000) and maintenance of roads, bridges, and culverts (average Rs. 59,000). Installation of new streetlights and new drinking water taps and improvement of roads have also been done. Forty-five individual water tap connections have been provided along with 70 public taps. Since 205 tubelights, 23 sodium vapour lamps and five television sets are functioning the electricity bill is always on the higher side.

Conducting Panchayat Meetings

There are nine Ward Members, of whom six are men and three are women. The meetings are properly convened and all the Ward Members attend regularly. When the problem created by the Vice-President was reported, all the members extended cooperation to replace him for the smooth running of the administration. When the items of work were allocated to wards, the concerned Ward Members opted to carry out the work and the Council decided accordingly. The members used to pay attention to the quality since the people often pointed to the poor quality of the work carried out in the Panchayat. As the problem of water supply has been solved, people now expect cement concrete roads.

Gram Sabha Meeting

The Gram Sabha meeting is organised in the school premises. An average of one hundred people attend it. Many participants are from the SHGs. The members of SHGs present their demands in written from after reading them out loudly. In spite of the President explaining the financial position of the Panchayat, the people press their demands. To mobilize more participants for the Gram Sabha meetings the Panchayat gives special invitation to SHG members.

Social Development Activities

Drinking water supply and toilet are provided in two primary schools and in one high school. Repair work was undertaken in two *balwadis* along with the replacement of damaged door with the Union funds. During the time of weighing of children and immunization Selvi used to visit the *balwadis*. ANC and PNC are given to those who need them. She maintains a good relationship with the nurse and the nurse is living in the village itself in a rented house as there is no building for the health sub-centre. During the PNC, along with the nurse, Selvi too visits the families and requests them to take measures for birth control. Verification of the sex of the embryo through scanning is in practice among the pregnant women of the middle and the lower middle classes also but there is no report of female infanticide.

At last funds have been sanctioned for the construction of a health sub-centre. A site has been located for the same but it is under encroachment by many families who dump their wastes in that area. The non-availability of sites in other areas to the required extent was explained to all and, with the help of the public, the encroachments were removed. Rs. 2,000 has been, received as a loan from the Makkal Mandram to initiate the work.

Public Office Administration

The Panchayat clerk is a very hard working young man. He helps the Panchayat President in all activities. Accounts are properly kept and audited. The officials extend cooperation by properly guiding her whenever she faces difficulties.

The OHT operators are helping in tax collection by accompanying the clerk. In the year 1997 the house tax was revised. The house tax is collected at the rate of Re. 1 per Rs. 100 value of the house. Before revising the total house tax was Rs. 8,270 and after revising the total house tax was Rs. 16,540. The officials do not demand any money as they know that all the Panchayat work is not carried out by Selvi. They used to collect money from the concerned Ward Members who carried out the particular work.

Her Future Plan

Selvi said that she would contest again. Her honesty, simplicity and easy accessibility to all are listed as her strengths. Once she decided to resign her position due to unbearable discomfort created by the Vice-President and his supporters. But during, that time, she received necessary guidance and encouragement from officials and Ward Members and the problem was handled successfully. In the meantime she learned to administer the Panchayat. The training she received at RETC, Pattukottai, was helpful to her.

As basic problems like drinking water and streetlights are solved, she proposes that her next priority will be road improvement. There is still 8 km of mud road in the main village and the two hamlets which have to be replaced by BT roads. She has decided to seek re-election on this platform.

CASE – 9

KONDACHERI GRAM PANCHAYAT
KADAMBATHUR BLOCK, THIRUVALLUR DISTRICT

Socio-Economic Background

Mrs. Senthamil Selvi, the President of Kondacheri Village Panchayat, is 45 years old. She is an SC woman, educated upto SSLC. Her husband is a government employee. They have a son, 17 years old. She worked in the Social Welfare Board for a period of 4 years. So she has got awareness about social issues and is able to concentrate on social activities. As a member and the leader of an SHG she has mobilized maximum assets for the members of the group and gained name and fame. It is important to mention that even before becoming the President of the Panchayat she mobilized the village people and made a successful attempt to solve the drinking water problem. As she devotes much of her time and energy to social causes, her husband stands behind her. Since he is a government servant, the economy of family has never been troubled. Her only son also does not trouble her. The income of her family is Rs. 50,000 and she lives in a well built house with all basic facilities. For transportation the family possesses a two wheeler.

Village Setting

Kondacheri Panchayat is 9 km from the Kadampattur Block Office. With 5 hamlets under its jurisdiction, the population of the Village Panchayat is 1648, out of which the SC males and females are 223 and 228 respectively. The village is self-sufficient in drinking water supply with 4 OHTs, 40 common taps, 8 handpumps, 2 open wells and 100 individual tap connections. About 70 per cent of the households have toilet facilities. The major caste groups in the village are Chettiyars, Naidus, Mudaliyars and SCs. The entire Village Panchayat is illuminated with 58 tubelights and 30 mercury vapour lights. A middle school and a primary school meet the educational needs of the children in the Panchayat along with a creche and two noon-meal centres.

The majority of the population are Hindus and a few Christians are also found. There are a church and three temples is the Panchayat area. There are 7 women SHGs and men SHGs along with Cine Fans Associations and Youth Clubs. The major source of irrigation is tank and the crops produced are paddy, tomato, groundnut, and black gram. The range of annual income of the families is from Rs. 10,000 to Rs. 20,000.

The Perception

Kondacheri Panchayat is a General Women Panchayat. In the Panchayat election Senthamil Selvi was opposed by three SC and one BC women. Spending a sum of Rs. 20,000 at the time of the election, she won by a margin of 22 votes. Not having much orientation in administration, but well aware of the problems of the rural folk, she mustered confidence and started to move with the stream. As the Panchayat has traditionally and hereditarily been dominated by non-SCs, it was very difficult for her to manage the activities of the Panchayat. However, being oriented towards a Dravidian party, she gathered confidence and political awareness. The violence prevalent, particularly against women, has made her think that democracy is meant for a few alone. Apart from this she does not have any idea about democracy, development and socialization. She is particular that the problems related to basic facilities should be rectified urgently with the assistance of State and Centrally sponsored schemes. She wants the schemes to be large in numbers so that she can generate many activities to meet the needs of the people.

The Panchayat

The Kondacheri Panchayat has 5 hamlets and two wards, with six Ward Members out of whom 50 per cent are from the SC – two SC men and one SC woman, two BC men and one BC woman. The Vice-President belongs to a non-SC community. The Panchayat meetings were hard and rough in the initial stages and later they became quite smooth. The Panchayat maintains close association with officers at the higher level and so it could achieve quite much.

Performance

Senthamil Selvi was forced to face stiff opposition from her the election rivals. They joined together and troubled her by making derogatory remarks against her. The Vice-President was also not cooperative in the initial six months. However, when the President developed cordial relations with the officials, the Vice-President changed his attitude and started cooperating with her.

The achievements of Senthamil Selvi are renovating school building, supplying 100 per cent drinking water, and providing 70 per cent sanitation facilities. The selection of work is done on a priority basis with 50 per cent of facilities for the SC area and 50 per cent for the non-SC area. This pattern of execution of work throughout the Panchayat was maintained, and on that count, she was able to win the confidence of the people. The major source of funds for the Panchayat is JGSY Scheme as the income of the Panchayat is poor. Being an SC woman it is not easy for her to carry out the activities but she tries to the maximum extent possible to fulfil the needs of the people. As drinking water problem was acute, out of the SFC funds, a drinking water scheme was launched and it is now under operation. The total expenditure for the maintenance of the various facilities comes to around

Rs. 4.58 lakh and it increases every year as facilities are getting added.

The Gram Sabha meetings are not much of a problem as the benefits are distributed every now and then equally to all the segments of the society. A fixed agenda is followed and the quorum is maintained. The major work done in the Panchayat is discussed.

Table : Activities carried out

Sl. No.	*Year*	*No. of Items of Works*	*Major Source*	*Amount*
1.	1996-97	3	JGSY	46,500
2.	1997-98	6	SHC, JGSY	1,17,500
3.	1998-99	6	JGSY	8,07,300
4.	1999-2000	8	JGSY	1,27,750

Though there is a wide range of activities, Senthamil Selvi is not able to cover all the areas, because the Panchayat area is big with 5 hamlets and the income is small. A substantial amount of taxes and the matching grants are pending and so she is not able to generate more activities. She does not have a clear idea about governance and development. She is very particular to get the benefits for the people in terms of creating the basic minimum facilities and making some arrangements for employment for earning their daily bread. She said that if there is proper orientation, training and support, the women Presidents can function effectively.

CASE – 10

KOTTUR GRAM PANCHAYAT
THENI BLOCK, THENI DISTRICT

Socio-Economic Background

Smt. Indira Gandhi, President of Kottur Village Panchayat, belongs to the SC community. She has studied up to the 10th standard. Her family is a nuclear family, and her husband has studied upto SSLC. They have two acres of land, a well and an electric pumpset for irrigating the farm. They have one daughter and three sons and all are studying. Her eldest son has completed college education. Her house is *pucca* with facilities like electricity and toilet. They have two two-wheelers, namely, a TVS Suzuki and a Hero Honda.

Her father and father-in-law belonged to the Congress Party since Independence. Her father served as an MLA from 1952 to 1957 and, after his death, a memorial was built at the entrance to the village. Her husband is a DMK Party cadre and their family is known for their political involvement. Her husband is doing contract work for Panchayats in somebody else's name. Their family rears milch animals and supplies milk to the local milk society. She was the secretary of a Mathar Sangam organised by an NGO even before her election to the Panchayat. Their family's average income is Rs. 20,000 per year.

Village Setting

The village is situated 15 km from Theni, the District headquarters. The total population of the village is 5,681. Out of them 2,791 are males and 2,890 females. There is no hamlet in this Panchayat. There are five wards, and nine Ward Members. Among the nine Members five are males and three are females. There are 300 *pucca* houses, 400 tiled houses, 320 huts and 90 mixed houses in the village. There are several communities living in the village. The Parayars (SC) are the majority in this Panchayat. Other communities such as Pallars, Valluvars, Sakkiliars, Puthirvannans, Christians, Muslims, Asaris, Barbers, Chettiyars and Nadars are also living in the village.

The Deventhira Kula Vellalars, Muslims Vellalars, Arunthathiyars and Puthirvannans have their own caste associations. The caste associations, with traditional leaders, meet the Panchayat President and inform her of the problems in their areas. Youth have Cine Fans Associations for Rajini and Prasanth. They also help the Panchayat when encroachments are removed. There is an association for farmers. It is not a registered one. The leading farmers attend the Gram Sabha meetings. There are 21 SHG groups organised and supported by two NGOs, namely CENTEC and Sevasangam. The SHG members attend the Gram Sabha meetings regularly and they demand drinking water, streetlights and loan facilities.

Village Economy

The majority of the agriculturists are from the SC community. The land gets water from the Periyar Dam and some of the lands are dependent on well irrigation. Paddy, banana, vegetables, coconut, black gram and green gram are the agricultural products. In the dry lands sorghum and millet are grown. There are more than 500 families engaged in agriculture. Theni is a nearby town about 100 men and women go over to Theni for employment in the construction industry as masons and helpers and painters. A few families are engaged in production of coir rope and selling it in the weekly market at Theni.

Common Property Resources

There are three tanks in the village. To avoid soil erosion trees are already planted on the tank bunds and the Panchayat is rearing the same. A roadside poramboke is available from which a portion is allotted for construction of a shop under the new scheme called Poomalai and the construction is going on. There are 77 tamarind trees along the roadsides from which an income of Rs.1,000 per year is earned. There are 18 trees in the common land, but in the possession of individuals who pay Rs. 2 per tree to the Panchayat. Efforts are being taken for planting trees in the beds of the tanks.

Village Temples

All religious groups are living in Kottur Village. There are two churches, one mosque and thirteen Hindu temples in the Village Panchayat area. Religious harmony prevails in the villages as there is no dispute among the different religious communities. Under the AMT road improvement schemes, work was carried out in the area of one church, one mosque and four Hindu temples. Out of 13 Hindu temples two temples are maintained by the Vellalar community. All castes are permitted to come in and worship in the temple. A Mariamman temple is owned by the Parayars and another one by the Pallars and in both temples all groups are permitted to worship. During the festivals, donations are received from persons belonging to other communities also. There is no caste discrimination in the Panchayat. Though the President belongs to the Parayar community, she gives donations to all the communities. The message regarding meetings of the Gram Sabha is announced through church, mosque and temple as there are public address system facilities in these places of worship.

Political Parties

In this village many political parties such as the DMK, the AIADMK, the Puthiya Tamilagam, the PMK, and the Congress are functioning. There is no separate building for the parties. They are active only during the election time. After that there are no serious activities. Parties are not vibrant or effective as the caste associations are dominant in social activities.

Recruitment

When the Panchayat elections were announced and the President's post was reserved for SC women, a few elders from the Vellalar community met Indira Gandhi's father-in-law and suggested her name for the post of President. The villagers used to show much respect to her family as well as her in laws' family as all of them were Congress Party members. All the caste groups openly came forward to support Indira Gandhi. The opponent was a close relative of hers.

Indira Gandhi did not give any promises as she did not know the details of the Panchayati Raj System. But she assured the people that she would serve the villagers to the best of her ability. Door to door contact and distribution of notice were the main canvassing techniques. A few prominent leaders of the different communities used to accompany her during the campaign. No microphone was used. Indira Gandhi won by a margin of 1,700 votes. Her family background and the support of the majority of all the caste groups were the main reasons for her success. The election was smooth with no friction and even after the election there has been no ill-feelings.

Indira Gandhi projected herself as an independent candidate, even though her husband is a DMK Party man. But, after the election, she also joined the DMK Party, as people exerted pressure on her to do so since the DMK is the ruling party. They expected that the Panchayat would get many benefits from the government if she did so.

Perception of Panchayati Raj

Reservation for women and *Dalits* is very useful for the development of both these sectors through the Panchayat. For wider contact and for understanding the feelings of the people the Gram Sabha is a very good mechanism. The SHG groups can be equipped well through the Panchayat and arrangements can be made for loan facilities to them. The fund allocations under the MLA and the MP schemes should be based on the priorities proposed by the Village Panchayats.

Development/Democracy

Indira Gandhi carried out many items of work every year. In the year 1996-97, under the JVVT scheme, 30 colony houses were constructed, 100 metres of road to the graveyard was laid, six TV rooms were built and a school building was constructed at a cost of Rs. 13.31 lakh. In the year 1997-98 under the JVVT scheme, 10 small bridges worth about Rs. 30,000 were constructed.

Two roads of one km stretch were blacktopped from the District Councillor's Fund. From the 10th Finance Commission Fund, Rs. 2 lakh was spent for construction of a school building (Government Higher Secondary School). Under the JVVT Scheme, 40 colony houses were constructed at a cost of Rs. 1.16 lakh. Four toilet complexes were constructed at a cost of Rs. 4 lakh from the MLA Fund. Twenty household latrines under the

Central Government's health scheme were constructed at a cost of Rs. 60,000.

During the year 1997-98, the AMT scheme was implemented in this village. People raised a volley of questions on schemes and demanded more facilities in all Gram Sabha meetings. But it was very difficult to find out resources to meet the demands. Under the AMT scheme the following works were carried out in her Panchayat :

Sl. No.	*Work*	*Cost*
1.	Two ration shops	Rs. 2.30 lakh
2.	One km link road	Rs. 1.36 lakh
3.	Two small culverts	Rs. 0.60 lakh
4.	Two canals (2 km)	Rs. 3.00 lakh
5.	One additional school building	Rs. 2.27 lakh
6.	Five ground level reservoirs	Rs. 4.03 lakh
7.	One km blacktopping of road	Rs. 2.76 lakh
8.	Extension of drinking water pipeline	Rs. 0.65 lakh

In the year 1998-99 the Panchayat has got Rs.3.03 lakh under the JVVT scheme and Rs. 3.66 lakh under the Indira Awas Yojna. Indira Gandhi explained the importance of household latrines in the Gram Sabha meeting, SHG members meetings, and, whenever she met groups on the streets she explained the implications of open-air defecation. She convinced 33 individuals to construct household latrines in their houses under the CRSP scheme at a cost of Rs. 1.05 lakh. From the Union Fund metal spreading work was done on different streets for 2 km at a cost of Rs. 0.31 lakh.

In the year 1999-2000, under the JGSY Scheme, eight cement roads covering a distance of two kms at a cost of Rs. 6.10 lakh were laid. Three individuals constructed household latrines at a cost of Rs. 0.07 lakh under the CRSP Scheme. Four sodium vapour lamps were installed in the streets at a cost of Rs. 0.20 lakh from the earmarked fund. The Ayyan Thiruvalluvar Library was constructed at a cost of Rs. 0.05 lakh in the village.

During 2000-2001, under the SGSY Scheme, the Panchayat got Rs. 4.8 lakh and from the Union Fund Rs. 0.38 lakh. The Panchayat laid roads in six places covering 2.25 km at a cost of

Rs. 4.81 lakh. Two small culverts were constructed at a cost of Rs. 0.30 lakh.

Village Development

To Indira Gandhi a developed village is one which should provide all basic facilities to lead a decent human living and it should enable all the adults, both men and women, to get gainful employment to manage their livelihood. But, in reality, though villages have facilities, they could not be used to meet the demands of the people, because their activities are always supply driven and not demand driven.

After the implementation of the AMT programme nearly one-fourth of the demands have been fulfilled. Indira Gandhi went to the schools and requested the teachers to increase the strength, maintain attendance and the quality of the education. In the year 1996-97 the Panchayat constructed an additional school building for the Government Higher Secondary School. Pregnant women and children get nutritious food and tablets regularly and this is being monitored personally by Indira Gandhi. Whenever she meets the SHG members, she speaks to them of age at marriage of women, the importance of women's education and employment opportunities for women. In the year 1999-2000 she constructed a building for a milk society. This will help 75 to 100 women to improve their living conditions through the milk society.

Human Rights

Wherever women meet with injustice in the village Indira Gandhi questions it. There are instances where women were ill-treated in public places and when the Panchayat President questioned such activities at the village level it provided scope for the women's groups to assert themselves in public.

Socialisation Process

Originally her family was in the Congress Party. At the time of the elections she contested as an independent candidate. After the election shc joined the DMK Party because her husband was a DMK Party man and the DMK was the ruling party. There are two issues involved in this. First she was compelled to join the DMK Party by her husband since he is a DMK man. Secondly, she joined the DMK Party as it was the ruling party and her applications for schemes and programmes would be considered positively by the officials. This is now normal in Tamil Nadu. She has achieved many things by this approach. She got the AMT scheme for this Panchayat in the year 1997-1998. After implementation of the scheme the participation of the people in Gram Sabha meetings has increased.

NGO Link

Sevasangam is an NGO engaged in forming women's groups and it provides guidelines on small savings, maintaining health and generating employment opportunities. Nearly 15 groups have been formed and small savings have gone up in the groups. The groups got a revolving fund of Rs. 25,000 from the bank and the amount has been utilized by the group members for small trade. Indira Gandhi arranged the venue and meeting facilities for the SHGs for group meetings at night. NGO staff members spread awareness among women regarding ANC, PNC and age at marriage.

Committee Formation

Indira Gandhi formed a Peace Committee, a Parent-Teachers Association, and a Health Committee. All the caste groups are given due representation in the Committees and Ward Members are nominated Committee Presidents and as members in the committees. At the time of formation of committees there was no problem, but, after the formation, all kinds of problems occurred. Indira Gandhi gave importance to the Parent-Teachers Association. She has strengthened the school by constructing an additional school building. She used to discuss with school teachers to increase the student strength and to improve the quality of education.

CASE – 11

KUNTHALAPATTI GRAM PANCHAYAT VIRUDHUNAGAR BLOCK, VIRUDHUNAGAR DISTRICT

Socio-Economic Background

Mrs. L. Pauvanammal (35) is the Village Panchayat President of Kunthalapatti. Her husband is a farmer in Kunthalapatti. The village has only one hamlet, namely, Narayanapuram. The majority community is that of Naickers while Chettiars and Nadars are very few in number. Seven families belonging to the ST are engaged in scavenging work. Pauvanammal is an ordinary woman engaged in farm activities during the agricultural season and during the off season she used to work in a fireworks factory. She got married at the age of 16. Now she has three sons, and all are studying in school. She has determined to educate her children as she studied only upto the 7th standard.

When the election was declared for the Village Panchayat in the year 1996, the village community of Kunthalapatti decided to select Pauvanammal unanimously. The logic behind her selection was quite conventional. Her father-in-law's elder brother had served as President for two terms and another brother for one term. Her position within the family, her literacy, and her social closeness to other villagers were considered conducive to public activities.

When the village community of Kunthalapatti proposed her name, the villagers of Narayanapuram hamlet bargained for the candidature. As no compromise was arrived at competition became inevitable. Both sides took the competition very seriously. The village elders of Kunthalapatti joined together and canvassed for Pauvanammal. Door to door campaign, notice and poster campaign were the strategies adopted by Pauvanammal. Every evening, along with more than fifty men, she visited each house with a promise of providing necessary facilities to the village. After calculating the number of votes in Kunthalapatti, they decided not to visit Narayanapuram for canvassing. Pauvanammal won by a margin of 170 votes, as the majority of the families of Kunthalapatti cast their votes for her.

Village Setting

The village community is tradition bound. Within the Naicker community itself there are clans/vagayarakkal known as Vadakkuveedu, Therkkuveedu, and Kizhakkuveedu. Representatives from these families, along with the representatives of the two other castes, namely the Chettiars and the Nadars, constitute a Village Committee. The Committee is responsible for the celebration of temple festivals, conducting Nyaya Panchayat and other village activities. The committee has a common fund which is handled by the committee members.

The Committee selected the Panchayat Ward Members unanimously. If anybody wished to contest, the selection would be by lot. The Panchayat and the Village Committee have maintained a cordial relationship since the introduction of Panchayati Raj in the year 1958.

The other social institution is the Youth Association. Earlier the office bearers of the Youth Association misused the common fund and so the Association did not function effectively. Pauvanammal encouraged the present day youth and due to the political mobilization of other village youth, the youth of Kunthalapatti rejuvenated their Youth Association recently. About 20 young people joined together, organized Pongal festival, planting of trees and helped in organising the Gram Sabha meetings. As most of the youth have migrated to cities, the remaining youth carry on the Association activities.

There are a number of temples in Kunthalapatti. They are the temples of Kaliamman, Vinayagar, Krishnan, Muthalamman and Ayyanar temples where the festivals are celebrated. As there are no SC families in the village, there is no caste discrimination. But recently the SC community of a nearby Panchayat claimed that they have a right in the Ayyanar temple which is situated in Kunthalapatti. To prove their right, they referred to the fact that all the *poojaris* of the Ayyanar temple are from the SC community. Hence the caste Hindus could not have any claim over the Ayyanar temple. At this the caste Hindus decided to have their own Ayyanar temple separately. The SCs also declared that the wastelands adjoining the temple also belonged to them and so did not permit to construct a community hall there.

The revenue village is Senkunrapuram and the VAO certified that the Ayyanar temple and the adjoining wasteland belong to Senkunrapuram. The Kunthalapatti community was not ready to confront the SC community. The district authorities too advised them not to do so as the SC are the majority in the area.

Women SHGs have recently emerged as a social institution. With the help of ASSEFA, an NGO, and the efforts of the Union staff, eight SHGs have been formed. Pauvanammal involves herself seriously in the activities of SHG. She herself guides 3 SHG in Kunthalapatti. Every month, on the 10th day, the SHGs meet at the *balwadi*. Each member saves Rs. 30 per month and the total amount is rotated among the group members.

ASSEFA provides a number of oppotunities to the local community. Training is imparted to build the capacity of the artisans in certain skills. A night school is organised for school-going children and drop-outs. A tour was arranged to visit Kodaikanal and Vaigai Dam. In all these activities Pauvanammal extended her guidance and advice whenever necessary. She met the Project Officer of ASSEFA and availed of their scheme pertaining to girl children and hostel facilities for girl children. Various political parties, namely the DMK, the AIADMK, the MDMK and the TMC are functioning in the village. But the differences are never serious. The local leaders of all parties attend the Gram Sabha meetings. The MP of the constituency is the leader and founder of the MDMK. The President maintains a close relationship with the local MP as both belong to the same community. Moreover the maternal uncle of Pauvanammal is a close friend of the local MLA. This proximity helps her in the Panchayat administration. The village organisations in Kunthalapatti maintain good relationship with the Village Panchayat and extend cooperation. They understand the financial condition of the Panchayat.

To cite an example of political impact on the Panchayat, the local MLA sanctioned a cement concrete road to Kunthalapatti as per the recommendation of the local MP. This promise was withdrawn as the political alignment between the party of the MLA and the party of the MP changed. The ultimate loser was the Village Panchayat. It is said that Pauvanammal's husband is a local unit member of the AIADMK Party. But he is not an active party man. He never interferes in any of the activities of the Panchayat. But he helps in the execution of the Panchayat work by his wife.

Perception of the President

Pauvanammal does not know the salient features of the Panchayati Raj except the reservation for women in the New Panchayati Raj System. But, after becoming the President, she functions independently. She is aware of the importance of the three-tiers, the Gram Sabha, powers of the President and regular financial allotment to the Panchayats are of significance in the new system.

Earlier she could not comprehend anything regarding administration and accounts in the Panchayati Raj. She could not reply to the queries raised by the District Collector during his village visit. But the capacity building training given by the Tamil Nadu Social Welfare Board was an eye opener to her. She recollected the advice and guidance given by the Gandhigram Rural Institute team during the training by which she was transformed. Fear and reluctance are gone. She now meets all officials, explains the village problems, claims the right of the people and gets popularity as a successful woman President. She has been selected for various training programmes held at RETC, SIRD and TANWA. She has attended programmes organised by NGOs. She was the only woman President selected to go to Delhi by an NGO recently. The major issues according to her are the limited resources of the Panchayat and the prodigious popular expectations which not match. But she is confident that, in course of time, the Panchayat will be able to deliver a good deal of services to the people. Further she is confident that women will be recognised by the community.

The village economy will be improved only by agriculture related activities. By providing opportunities for employment in rural industries, the income of poor families will be improved. Animal husbandry is a profitable sector, according to her. Regarding polity she pointed out that the ruling party plays a role in deciding the allocation of resources. She does not belong to any party but she meets all higher level representatives and tries to get their help.

Regarding gender issues, she decried the wage discrimination against women. After the advent of the SHG, women are getting awareness, have stopped their useless gossip and are motivated to engage themselves in useful activities. Reservation is a new opportunity for women to enter public life. But it can be fruitful only if the husband encourages the wife. Women have to face ill-treatment by alcoholic men. Illiteracy among the village women is also a serious problem. The illiterate women do not make independent efforts to acquire literacy. Regarding ways and means to improve women through the SHGs, Pauvanammal suggested that adult literacy, self-employment training and continuous guidance in economic activities to women members should be the activities of SHGs. Regarding common property resources, Pauvanammal said that revenue officials must help the Panchayats to locate poromboke land and help them to protect the same. As for social justice, the mighty group is taking the upper hand now-a-days. Violence and threats are considered the right means to attain social justice. In her village there are a few families belonging to the STs and they are involved in scavenging work. They can come and buy eatables from the tea stalls but they are not permitted to sit in the stall. But if the SC and the ST are the majority, the practice of untouchability will be removed.

Socialisation

Until she became the President, she did not possess any experience of public life. Training programmes, the encouragement of her husband, thc cooperation of the officials and the support of the village people helped her to understand the Panchayati Raj. Her constant study of books, newspapers, and her listening to news helped her to understand the process of development. She plans to contest again. If defeated, she plans to organise women SHGs for economic activities. Moreover she has acquired new skills in carrying out civil work. Hence she plans to take up contract work by which she can provide good quality of work to the public and also earn a little.

Performance

Immediately after she assumed the office of the Panchayat President, Pauvanammal carried out maintenance work on the approach road to the graveyard under the JVVT scheme. Further, as per the wishes of the Ward Members and the village elders, maintenance work at the primary school was carried out. These two items of work were considered essential by the people. During the year 1997-98, under the JVVT scheme, a toilet was provided to the school and also a bus shelter. During 1998-99, as per the request of parents, wiring was done in the school from the Panchayat funds in addition to drainage work in the village. Next attention was given to provide drainage facilities. Due to the very unhygienic conditions in the streets, the villagers demanded drainage. The street environment became ugly and muddy due to unregulated flow of drain water. This has now improved a lot.

In the meantime, thanks to her rapport with the District Councillor, she could get a concrete cement road to her village. As the local MLA is a close friend of her maternal uncle, she got money for an OHT and, with the help of the Union Councillor, she got a borewell and a tap. As the local MP belongs to her community, she has established a good relationship with him. He sanctioned funds for the construction of a community hall. When the site was identified the SC community of Senkunrapuram disputed the right of ownership over the site. As per the advice of the villagers, a new site was selected and the construction was completed. But, unexpectedly, the whole construction collapsed. Pauvanammal met the MP and succeeded in re-doing the whole construction with a new estimate.

By frequently visiting the Union office and meeting the Chairman, she got three group houses for her village. As the ST families do not possess house site patta, the beneficiaries of the group houses scheme were selected from the poor caste Hindu families. Pauvanammal complained that most of the men Presidents do not give due recognition to the Union Chairman and so they cannot get Union Funds, whereas the women Presidents do not entertain any ego and, by sharing the village problems, they can avail of funds from the Union. Continuous efforts and follow up are the two important qualities that the President should possess according to Pauvanammal. Further, the President should not depend on the Panchayat clerk. Even though she has studied upto seventh standard only she is able to identify the registers, understand the entries in the pass book and know the defects, if any.

Kunthalapatti is a very poor Panchayat having around Rs. 1 lakh only as income by way means of house tax, stamp duty and professional tax. Due to paucity of funds, she could not purchase necessary furniture for the Panchayat office. Only after two years chairs and tables were bought. Even now there is no electricity connection. She tried to get public contribution as the Village Committee is having funds. She carried out all the JVVT work herself without giving these to contractors. The Union officials encouraged and guided her in the execution of the work. Her husband helped in transporting of materials; her sons helped in odd activities like watering the cement work etc. Due to this, the work was carried out to the fullest satisfaction of the people as well as the officials. At the same time there was a small profit for her.

People expect that the President must help. Once the villagers charged that the ration shop staff did not distribute the commodities properly. As the total number of ration cards is only 185, the Kunthalapatti villagers have to go to a nearby village, Senkunrapuram. The natives of Senkunrapuram used to get the commodities before the arrival of the Kunthalapatti villagers. Moreover they get good quality stuff. The issue was taken to the District Collector. The Collector directed to arrange for distribution of ration commodities at Kunthalaptti itself through SHG women. Pauvanammal told an SHG of this. As the activity was new to them, the SHG members wanted to get an orientation. Pauvanammal decided to take them to a nearby village unit where an SHG was handling the ration shop activities. In the meantime she succeeded in making an arrangement by which the distribution of goods should first go to the one village and in the next month the people of the other village would receive the goods first and further she tried to get a separate shop for her village itself.

So far she could not form any committee. But, after attending a programme which aimed at preventing selective sex abortion, she decided to form a Health Committee involving SHG women and young women from the Youth Association.

Tax Collection

She has ensured one hundred per cent house tax collection. She has enhanced the house tax for the tiled and *pucca* houses from Rs. 5.80 and Rs. 11.00 to Rs. 16.50 and Rs. 30.00 respectively. During 1996-97 the house tax collection was only Rs. 1,400 but now it has increased to Rs. 4,600. From the auction of 106 tamarind trees standing along the highways more than three thousand rupees was collected. Now the Senkunrapuram villagers also stake their claim to the standing trees. If they pursue it, the Panchayat will loose the income from the auction amount. Auditing is not a problem for Pauvanammal. She accompanies the clerk during the audit time. She sites in the Union office and offers her explanations to the enquiries of the officers. The audit has been completed up to 1999-2000. No major objections have been raised by the auditors. Regarding the practice of bribe in getting clearance, the officials do not demand any huge amount from her. When the President does good work and ensures good quality, the officials do not press for much money.

She conducts the Village Panchayat meetings smoothly. There are two women members in the Council. One regularly attends the Council meetings. The other woman member skips the meetings frequently and her father-in-law voices the people's demands during the meetings. The Gram Sabha meetings are periodically held. After the construction of the community hall, the Gram Sabha has been held in the hall. About 150 persons, mostly women and elderly persons, attend, whereas the youth do not take them seriously. But, after the revival of the Youth

Association, a few of them attend the Gram Sabha meetings. So far the Gram Sabha has met 12 times. Everytime the villagers expect the execution of the resolutions passed in the earlier Gram Sabha meetings. As the village is a small with only one hamlet, the Gram Sabha meeting details are announced to the people by door to door intimation.

There is a register for the maintenance of the CPR details. There are 9 kanmois (very big tanks), one pond (small tank), 16 odai porambokes (common land) and 3 porambokes and 9 road side porambokes. There are no encroachments except two tea stalls in the roadside pormaboke. There are five big neem trees in the village and the youth planted 10 saplings recently. Pauvanammal encouraged them in these activities.

Social Development Activities

The practice of consuming alcohol could not be contained. Most of the male adults are addicted to alcohol. As the sales is carried on in the nearby village, Pauvanammal cannot stop it. The men and women employed in the construction industry earn regularly. The women understand the small family norm and voluntarily undergo family planning surgery. Girls study upto the tenth standard and then go for employment in match factories. Some learn certain skills to get gainful employment. To augment the Panchayat's income, the community hall is rented out for celebrations and other functions. Seven marriages, three family functions, one political party meeting and one training programme were conducted in the hall. A rent of Rs. 350 per day is collected. Child labour has now been reduced. Pauvanammal strongly advocates education for girl children. But the parents do not permit their girl children to continue their education. Due to poverty, after completing the 10th standard, most of the girls go for employment. To maintain sanitation, drainages are provided at necessary places. The nurse visits the village regularly. The nurse attends to the ANC and PNC needs of the women. Pauvanammal regularly meets the nurse and helps in immunization and polio eradication programmes. To improve the school facilities, the NGO ASSEFA provided furniture to the school. The Panchayat provided toilets and carried out maintenance work in the campus. The Panchayat office is housed in an owned building.

Pauvanammal visits the Panchayat office regularly and meets the clerk and the people. Once in three days she visits the hamlet. As the Panchayat is situated on an important road, Pauvanammal always keeps the records ready expecting visits by higher officials at anytime.

Pauvanammal rose to the position of Village Panchayat President from that of an ordinary farm worker. Earlier she did not go anywhere except to her native village. After she became the President, she independently visits various places to attend training programmes, interact fearlessly with men, argues for her Panchayat with justifications and brings a lot of good things to her small village.

Reservation for women brings about a sea change in her life. The villagers earlier thought that, by electing her, they could run the Panchayat themselves. But contrary to their assumption, Pauvanammal administers the Panchayat independently and, to the satisfaction of many. Her involvement in NGO activities helps in getting a number of welfare schemes for the villagers. Now she is confident and ready to contest in the next Panchayat election. She will not imprison herself in the kitchen but is determined to engage in women's welfare activities through SHGs. As the village setting is conducive to her public carreer, she will shine further in her public career.

CASE – 12

KUPPAMPALAYAM GRAM PANCHAYAT KUDIMANGALAM BLOCK, COIMBATORE DISTRICT

Socio-Economic Background

Mr. M. Thangavel, the President of Kuppampalayam Panchayat, is 33 years old. He has studied upto SSLC. He is an agricultural labourer. He does not belong to any political party. He hails from a poor family of agricultural labourers and, in the dry area, he has developed an ideal to do service to the community. His wife is 22 years old and has studied upto the third standard. She is also an agricultural coolie. They live in a tiled house with electrification, but without the other minimum requirements. Both husband and wife earn their daily bread by going for agriculture work. They have no property of their own and no other source of income but also no debts. Thangavel belongs to the SC community. So he has little opportunity to engage in any enterprise. The practice of small family norm has made him happy. It is interesting to note that Thangavel does not possess any political identity other than his honest image in the Panchayat area.

Village Setting

Kuppampalayam is a small Village Panchayat in Kudimangalam Block of Coimbatore District. The village is very close to Poolavadi and it is in the Dharapuram Legislative Assembly constituency. There are only two hamlets, namely Kuppampalayam and Vellachettipalayam in the Panchayat. The population is 2,179, comprising 1,113 males and 1,000 females. One half of the population is SC and the Panchayat is reserved for SC men. The major caste groups in the Panchayat are Naickers, Gounders and SCs. There are 623 households. The total length of the Panchayat road is 8.8 km. There are two primary schools and two noon-meal centres. The Panchayat is poor one. There are 64 street lights and 68 water taps providing water supply. There are no sanitation services and a nurse belonging to PHC of Poolavadi visits the village regularly. The Panchayat is self-sufficient in drinking water supply and approaching sufficiency in electrification and roads.

Perception

Thangavel, hailing from a poor SC family, does not have any political orientation or identity. His interest and inclination towards service and his clean image from his childhood have made him venture into the local political process and to reach this position. He has no idea about politics and political processes. Just because of his interest in social service and being acquainted with all the local masses he was motivated to move into this post. Moreover he has been pushed into the post unanimously by the community. To Thangavel, democracy means people's participation in the process of development. He says that people have never realised their strength and that they expect too much from the government but are not ready to contribute. He has now acquired some knowledge about local governance and politics. As a regular reader of newspapers, he could acquaint himself with latest political events.

Performance

The Kuppampalayam Panchayat has nine Ward Members, six male and three female, including one SC male and one SC female. The conduct of Gram Sabha meeting is not at all a problem but the expectations of the people are very high because they have all been oriented to receive benefits from the government. The details of the Gram Sabha meetings conducted have been given below:

Sl. No.	*Years*	*No. of Meetings*	*% of Attendance*
1.	1998-99	2	8
2.	1999-2000	4	9.3
3.	2000-2001	4	10

It was said that the quorum was maintained sometimes by getting signatures after the meeting was over. It takes hardly one hour for one Gram Sabha meeting and the fixed agenda issued by the government is adopted in the form of resolutions. Not much official intervention is experienced at the Gram Sabha meetings.

The Village Panchayat Council meetings are conducted regularly with seven days' notice and an average of 95 per cent of attendance in all the meetings. There is absolute cooperation among the Ward Members, the Vice-President, the President, the Union members and the Block officials. The details of the Panchayat Council meetings are given below:

Sl. No.	*Year*	*Ordinary*	*Emergency*	*Special*	*Total*
1.	1996-97	4	—	2	6
2.	1997-98	8	3	1	12
3.	1998-99	8	1	1	10
4.	1999-2000	8	1	3	12
5.	2000-2001	6	4	1	11

The Panchayat has achieved 100 per cent self-sufficiency in drinking water supply but electrification and road work are yet to be completed. As the majority of the population are agricultural labourers they cannot contribute much but Thangavel could manage 100 per cent house tax collection. Since the population is small the Panchayat cannot receive much by way of grants. Though SFC grants are received the entire amount is spent towards payment of electricity bills.

There is absolute cooperation from the officials so that the President is able to draw their attention and receive certain schemes and programmes.

The items of work carried out by Thangavel over the years and the amounts utilised are as hereunder:

Sl. No.	*Year*	*No. of Works*	*Amount (in lakhs)*
1.	1996-97	4	8.20
2.	1997-98	7	2.41
3.	1998-99	5	4.68
4.	1999-2000	3	0.50
5.	2000-2001	2	0.79

Most of the funds have been spent on the creation of infrastructure facilities. But they still need to be increased.

Thangavel admitted that he is not aware of audits and accounts and that he depends on the Panchayat clerk and the Block officials. The audit has been done for four years and only the last year's is pending. There are no social against women and child labour problem is totally absent.

The four and a half years of experience have made him realise many things. He is ready to contest in the next election and he needs training because he has to enhance his capacity first so that he can perform more effectively. As a coolie he cannot give away his daily wages regularly and this position consumes most of his time. He needs a salary or financial assistance so that his family is not affected. Moreover the Panchayats must be assisted financially based on the needs and also the intensity of the problems experienced by the people. Priority should be given to making the basic amenities mandatory. Some change can be brought about in the social context rural life. As President of the Panchayat he has not realised his full power. So training will help to make him realise his powers and functions, roles and responsibilities. This is not relevant for him alone, but to all such Presidents.

CASE – 13

KUPPINAICKENPATTI GRAM PANCHAYAT THENI BLOCK, THENI DISTRICT

Socio-Economic Background

Mr. Pandi, the President of Kuppinaickenpatti Panchayat, is 35. He has studied upto the 5th standard and he belongs to a joint family. His mother, wife and three children and a disabled brother are living with him. All the children are studying in school. He is landless, but manages by engaging in cattle trade. It is a good source of income and his wife is rearing a buffalo. From selling the milk he is able to get around Rs. 1,000. Pandi goes to several places in connection with his cattle trade. Usually he gets Rs.100 per head of cattle transacted in the trade. Occasionally he works as agriculture labourer also.

Recruitment

The village community has constituted a village committee in which the members belonging all to the majority communities, namely Naidus, SCs and Thevars are included. The sitting MLA, hailng from this village, is also a member of the Village Committee. The Village Committee serves for the development of the village. It organises celebration of amman festivals and also delivers judgement on disputes. The decisions of the Village Committee are accepted by all because if the villagers disobey they will be ostracised from the community.

During the Panchayati Raj elections the President's position was reserved for the SC. The Committee decided to select the President and the six Ward Members unanimously. The Committee selected Pandi as he is a very simple person belonging to Cobbler community even though there is SC Parayar community in the village. It was felt that if a person belonging to the SC Parayar community were selected he would not be submissive to the Committee. The Committee selected six Ward Members, of whom three are from the Naidu community, one female from the Thevar community and one male and one female from the Parayar community. The position of Vice-President has been given to a Naidu male. No one opposed the decision of the Village Committee.

Village Setting

Kuppinaickenpatti is a single village Panchayat. There are 460 families. The population numbers 1,514. The majority are from the Naicker community, the second largest community being that of the Parayars. The other communities are Sakkiliayars, Nadars, Asaris. Families belonging to Chettiar and the Thevar communities are very few. Besides these communities there are families of Barber and *Dhobi* communities in the village. But their number is very nominal.

There is an association for the Naicker community in the name of Thirumalianaicker Naidu Maka Jana Sangam which facilitaties marriages and other celebrations. There is also a Village Welfare Committee consisting of representatives of the four main communities, namely Naickers, Parayars, Thevars and Chettiars. A Naicker is the head of the Committee. The Village Committee deals with all common matters like celebration of festivals, hcaring disputes between families and other common affairs in the village.

There is a Forest Committee organised by the Forest Department. The village is situated at the foothills of a forest range. The Forest Department officials prevent the entry of people into the forest as a number of tree sapplings have been planted by the Department. So the local people found no way to rear their cattle, particularly their goats. But the Forest Department came up with an alternative. A Joint Forest Management Committee (JFMC) was formed. A batch of twenty families who had goats were asked to dispose of their goats and they received a sum of Rs. 5,000 to engage in some alternate employment. There was a proposal to engage poor landless, labourer families in tree planting. A committee was formed to implement the activities in which the Village Panchayat President is the chairperson.

The youth of the Parayar community organized a Dr. Ambedkar Youth Association. Pongal Day celebration was organised by these youth. Sports and cultural programmes were arranged on the day of Pongal. These affairs were exclusively attended by the Parayar community. The youth attend the Gram Sabha meetings and demand streetlight maintenance, extension of pipeline to their colony etc. There are a number of Cine Fans Associations, and, of them, the Vijayakanth Fans Club and the Prasanth Fans Club are popular among the youth. The youth of the Naicker community back the Vijayakanth Club. The youth of the SC community run the Prasanth Fans Club. They celebrate their matinee idols' birthday only.

There are five SHGs in the village, each organized in a separate community. They are in the Kalanjiyam network sponsored by the DHAN Foundation, an NGO. Another NGO, namely Seva Nilayam, is implementing a community health scheme in this village. The health staff regularly visit and administer medicines to the ailing persons. They organise special drives to identify skin diseases and leprosy symptoms among the people. It is reported that there is no connection between the Panchayat and the NGO activities.

Village Temples

The Kaliamman temple is a common temple but the SC community cannot enter the temple. They are permitted to worship from outside only. During celebrations contributions are collected from each family except SC and minority families.

The temple celebration expenses are shared among Naickers, Chettiars and Thevars. The Cobbler community's temple is the Madurai Veeran temple. The Parayar community has two temples, namely Subramaniam temple and Nagammal temple.

The caste Hindus completely control the village. There is a careful marginalisation of one section of the SC Parayar caste. When the President's seat was reserved for the SC, the caste Hindus were determined to prevent the empowerment of the SC Parayars. As the majority of the population is on the side of the caste Hindus, the Parayar community have to be dependent upon them. The caste Hindus, instead of encouraging the Parayar community preferred to select a candidate from the very small Sakkiliyar community, which has only three families, while but the Parayar community has a strength of around 80 families. The President was elected unanimously since he is the son of an ex-sweeper of the Kuppinaickenpatti Panchayat. By electing the President unanimously the caste Hindus indirectly usurped the power of the President.

Village Economy

The economy of the village is generally centred round agriculture and animal husbandry. Most of the land is rainfed. About 150 families are small farmers and the majority of them are from the Naidu community. With the help of well irrigation crops like paddy, cholam, cotton, tomato and pulses are cultivated. There are coconut grovers also. Animal husbandry is the main subsidiary source of income, but, after the implementation of the afforestation programme by the Forest Department, goat rearing has been prohibited. But the villagers rear milch animals. The Forest Department authorities grant permission to graze the cattle inside the forest where the planted sapplings are more than five years old. The members of the poor families get employment in the construction industry in Theni, the nearby town, as well as the headquarters of the district, where the scope for the construction industry is large. Thcy have a regular income but most of the men spend the money earned in consuming liquor.

Political Parties

Almost all the political parties are functioning in the village. The dominant parties are the AIADMK and the DMK. There is no office building for any party. The leaders of the various political parties do not extend any help to the Panchayat. As a cattle trade broker, Pandi has to visit the weekly shandies at various places. The Vice-President, who is acting as the real President, finds no time to meet the MLA and the MP in connection with development programmes. When the Panchayat fails in its responsibility of establishing linkages with other elected representatives, at least the local political leaders might have taken efforts in this regard. But, in the case of Kuppinaickenpatti Panchayat, both the Panchayat and the political parties have failed to take the initiative to avail of schemes and programmes.

Performance: Monthly Meetings

The monthly meetings of the Panchayat Council are regularly organised. All the members attend the meeting. The woman SC member voices the most number of demands. It is felt that the President is the proxy of the Vice-President who is a Naicker. The meeting is handled by the Vice-President and in reality, though Pandi is the President, he merely participates as one of the Members and, merely gets Rs. 50 as sitting allowance. It is said that the fixed monthly TA of the President is utilised by the Vice-President.

Gram Sabha Meeting

Gram Sabha meetings are generally conducted in front of the Panchayat office. In these meetings also the President is present only for name's sake and all the transactions are handled by the Vice-President. About 150 persons attend the Gram Sabha meetings. About 15 per cent of them are women. Provision of streetlights and extension of drinking water through Panchayat taps are the two important issues referred to in the Gram Sabha meetings. The participation of *Dalits* is very limited.

Panchayat Finance

The total income for the year 1996-97 from various sources was Rs. 39,069. The major source was stamp duty accounting for Rs. 30,369. The house tax was collected 100 per cent and the house tax matching grant of Rs. 8,700 was received. Maintenance of power pumps and sanitation are the major expenditures.

In the year 1997-98 Rs. 50,455 was received as house tax and professional tax. The SFC grant was Rs. 49,755 and, under JVVT, Rs. 40,473 was received. In the same year the expenses were mainly payment of electricity bills, maintenance of pumps, streetlights, TV, public sanitation, construction of retaining wall, and, bus shelter constructed under the JVVT programme.

In the year 98-99 the JVVT allocation was Rs. 11,544 and the 10th Finance Commission grant was Rs. 8,425 only. Building licence income was around Rs. 10,000. The SFC grant was Rs. 49,755. The EB payment increased to Rs. 14,587. The cost of maintenance of hand pump, motorpump and streetlights also increased to around Rs. 24,000. Sanitation maintenance cost was Rs. 9,495. A road and a small culvert were provided at a cost of Rs. 10,000. A retaining wall and a bus shelter were constructed under the JVVT programme at a cost of Rs. 22,000.

In the year 1999-2000 the JVVT fund was Rs. 58,599. The SFC gave Rs. 74,595. The stamp duty collected was Rs.17,257 and, as the house tax was increased, an additional income of Rs. 10,000 was realised. The major expenses were the payment of EB bill to the tune of Rs. 1,450 and the maintenance of handpump, TV, motorpump, streetlights, and sanitation, accounting for Rs. 53,000. For pipeline extension, Rs. 14,500 was spent. For road maintenance Rs. 8,700 was spent. On TV room construction and formation of road Rs. 52,000 was spent.

Sixty indidvidual tap connections were given by the previous administration, but the deposit amount was not properly collected. So every year, through a drive, collection is made from the beneficiaries. There is an outstanding due of Rs. 7,960.

There is scope for fish cultivation and tree planting in the tanks. Five tree saplings have been planted in the Panchayat office campus and have been properly protected for the past ten years.

Observations

During the data collection the investigator have came across a wall poster related to a marriage celebration. In that poster, against the post of Panchayat President, the Vice-President's name was printed instead of Pandi's. As per the norms of the Joint Forest Management Committee (JFMC), the President of the Village Panchayat is supposed to be the President of the Committee. But, in this village, the Vice-President is the President of the Joint Forest Management Committee. When the investigator enquired after Pandi, a petty shop owner very casually referred to the Vice-President as President and asked a villager to fetch the Vice-President to the Panchayat office. Pandi openly admits that he is a proxy and that he does not have any independence in any matter as he was selected unanimously just for the sake of the caste Hindus. From newspapers it is learnt that he has again been selected unanimously by the Village Committee to serve as President.

CASE – 14

MAAMANDUR GRAM PANCHAYAT KAVERIPAKKAM BLOCK, VELLORE DISTRICT

Socio-Economic Background

Mrs. Shahilabanu, the President of Maamandur Village Panchayat, is thirty-six years old. She has studied up to the ninth standard. She is an SC woman – a Sakkiliyar. She lives in a joint family with her three daughters, one son and her mother-in-law. She is engaged in agriculture as the major occupation. Her family owns 10 acres of land, of which 1 acre is garden land with well irrigation and the remaining nine acres wet land with tank irrigation. The family has a *pucca* house. The house does not have an individual tap connection. For 20 years her husband looked after the agricultural activities. After his demise, she has been looking after the garden land and agricultural activities alone. The remaining nine acres of wet land have been given on lease to her relatives.

Recruitment Process

The village has seven caste groups and among them Mudaliars are dominant economically and politically. Since this Panchayat was reserved for SC women, the other caste people like Mudaliars, Yadhavas and Naickers asked Shahilabanu to contest in the Panchayat election because her husband had worked for the welfare of the villagers for 15 to 20 years with the support of the DMK Party. She is also from an educated family. All these factors prompted the people to select her as President. There are two main reasons for her selection: (i) Her husband belonged to the DMK Party and worked for the welfare of the people for 15 to 20 years; and (ii) Shahilabanu is quiet, obliging and educated.

Perception about Panchayats

In the present system, funds are received directly from the government, and this helps to meet the basic needs of the village. There is reservation for women in the present system. By this reservation women can be empowered, and they will be made to participate in the political activities, and administer Panchayats. In the earlier system, the BDO and other officials administered the Panchayat. The President and the Members were doing only the work of agents. But now the President can work on the basis of people's needs.

Village Economy

Sugarcane and paddy are the major crops cultivated as the lands have well irrigation. Under tank irrigation people cultivate paddy and cereals. In the dry land people cultivate maize (*cholam*) as the major crop.

The landless people go to nearby towns like Vellore and Bangalore for daily and monthly wages and are employed in construction work and small business because there they get high wages and large profits.

Political Parties

The major political parties of this village are the DMK, the AIADMK, the TMC, the Communist Party of India (CPI), and the PMK. The DMK is the dominant party. Since the village has a large number of votes in the Panchayat election, the Panchayat President is able to get more funds for development activities.

Social Justice

There is no evidence of discrimination on the basis of caste. In public places like tea stall, ration shop, public tap and *shandy* (market) there is no discrimination. But the people belonging to the SC are not allowed into the caste Hindu temples.

Socialisation Process

Shahilabanu's husband was a DMK Party man. He worked for the welfare of the villagers for 20 years. For this work the villagers appreciated him and respected his family. The other communities supported her in the Panchayat election due to her husband's dedicated service to the people. After the election her husband joined hands with her in the Panchayat activities.

At the time of conducting the monthly Panchayat meetings and the Gram Sabha meetings, Shahilabanu listens to the Ward Members and allots responsibilities to all the Members at their request. She motivates the beneficiary family members to take part by giving labour as well as by supervising so that the quality of the work will be ensured and also the expenditure controlled. She learnt a lot about Panchayat activities and work from her husband.

Panchayat Income

The Panchayat is poor. It does not have many sources of income except the house tax and funds given by the government. The house tax collection has increased to cent-per-cent. After the house tax was increased the people remitted the house tax without any murmur. They were interested in getting the matching grant for the collected house tax.

Panchayat Council Meetings

The monthly meetings of the Panchayat are attended by all the Members regularly. In such monthly meetings the two women Ward Members have participated regularly and asked for facilities for their wards. Since the President is a woman and that too an SC women, the women Ward Members felt at home in all the meetings. So, the women Ward Members, without any hesitation, participated in the discussions. The decisions taken in the Council meetings are discussed in the Gram Sabha meetings.

Committees

As per the government order the Panchayat has formed seven committees. Shahilabanu admitted that she did not know the details of the committees and their functions and uses.

Gram Sabha Meetings

Shahilabanu feels that the Gram Sabha meetings are useful to inform the people about the various items of work that are being carried out as per the demands of the people and to review the progress of such work. Resolutions are passed and plans are made based on the demands of the people. In the Gram Sabha meetings nearly 20 per cent of the participants are females. They demand road facilities, drinking water facilities, extension of pipeline to new areas, cement concrete roads to streets etc. Totally 30 per cent of the male and female participants are *Dalits*. They also demand basic facilities like drinking water to their area, streetlights, drainage, and employment opportunities for women. Shahilabanu laments that only 30 per cent of these demands could be met due to lack of funds from the Government —Central and State —and from the income of the Panchayat.

Common Property Resources

The common property resources available in this Panchayat include three ponds, namely Kodankulam, Karappankuttai, Innarikuttai, the Panchayat office building and two TV rooms. The ponds are used by the public for bathing the cattle, for water for the cattle and for watering the wet lands. These common property resources are maintained properly by the Panchayat with the support of the villagers. The villagers have planted trees on the roadside and village temple porambokes. The Panchayat also helps to plant trees on the roadsides and in temple porambokes.

Auditing

Shahilabanu feels that the present system of auditing once in three months is good because it helps in correcting mistakes, avoiding difficulties involved in preserving the bills, and also in remembering the category of work and the related bills. She also feels that it will be better if the auditing is done by one office, either the BDO's office or the District Collector's office.

Corruption

Shahilabanu was strong in her view that corruption cannot be eradicated, because it starts right from the Village Panchayat and goes up to the district level. If officials are not bribed, they raise more questions and the accounts are not settled. Even for the Panchayat work the Vice-President demands a certain percentage. So, corruption has become part and parcel of daily life in Panchayat activities.

Special Features

1. Shahilabanu became President because this Panchayat was reserved for SC women,
2. Her family members were educated and did social service, and

3. Mr. Nanthakumar, the Vice-President, had already been the President for two terms.

Even though she is the President, the people are made to think that Nanthakumar is the President of this Panchayat. When the research team visited the village, we saw a name board in the house of the Vice-President, proclaiming Nanthakumar the President of this Panchayat.

CASE – 15

MANJAMPATTI GRAM PANCHAYAT
MADURAI WEST BLOCK, MADURAI DISTRICT

Socio-Economic Condition

Mr. P. Alagar, the President of Manjampatti Village Panchayat, is a lawyer by profession. He is thirty-nine and belongs to the SC Parayar community. He lives with his wife and three children (two girls and one boy) in a nuclear family. He lives in the colony house allotted to him. He does not have any other assets. After his studies he joined the DMK Party. For the past seven years he has been serving as the local unit secretary of the DMK Party. In this position he had the opportunity to mingle with other members of the DMK Party irrespective of caste. Due to this the majority of the people understood his leadership qualities and extended support to him. Moreover he is the legal adviser of the Ambedkar Youth Committee in the village. Since 1993, he has been serving as the legal adviser and encouraging the activities of the Committee members.

His professional experience is utilised by the DPI, the party of the SC community. The office bearers of the DPI used to engage Alagar for their cases even though he belongs to the DMK Party. His free and close movement with other caste Hindus helped him to win the confidence of the majority. He attends the traditional Panchayat which settles disputes. The traditional Village Nyaya Sabha is convened as and when need arises and deal with problems like divorce, property disputes and also other personal disputes. The disputants pay an amount to the traditional Panchayat, which is meant for the Panchayat and not for the members.

Socialisation

His association with the DMK Party was the first step in his public life. The DMK Party's pro-*Dalit* stance and its motto of uplifting Dravidians attracted him towards the party. Even though his father belonged to the Congress Party, he joined in the DMK as he did not like the Congress Party because it perpetuated feudalism in public life whereas the DMK attracted the youth and provided space for the youth in the party and gave party positions.

As the secretary of the local unit of the DMK Party he had many opportunities to help the party members in their personal affairs. As he is an advocate he enjoys additional respect from his own party members as well as other villagers. People are in need of his services one way or the other. Because of this he moved closely with members of various communities and different parties. This helped to develop his leadership qualities.

Village Setting

Manjampatti is a small Panchayat having only one hamlet, namely Seegupatti. It is a multi-caste Panchayat but the majority of the people belong to the SC. The second dominant community are Moopers and the others are Naidus, Gounders, Kallars, Konars, and Pillais. There are about 850 families belonging to the SC and 670 families belonging to other communities. The village is located at the foothills of Algarmalai. Alagar said that earlier the village belonged to only the SC community and that, in course of time, the caste Hindus of nearby villages purchased lands from the SC community and established settlements in this village. Now only about 25 SC families possess lands in the village and the rest of them are agricultural labourers.

A traditional Village Committee in the name of Mariathaikaravarkal is functioning in this village. There are six members representing the six major communities. The leadership of the committee is vested with the Gounders. They are a minority in population but the major portion of the land holdings are with them. This Village Committee meets in front of the Amman temple. It discusses public affairs like celebration of temple festivals, settles disputes between communities and deals with any other common matters. The meeting site of the Village Committee has been improved by the Panchayat. A cement concrete pavement covering the area where the Village Committee meets was provided by the Village Panchayat. The Committee requested the Panchayat in this regard and the Panchayat obliged.

There is an unwritten rule in the village that no caste should form any association. Hence there is no caste association. Almost all political parties are functioning in Manjampatti Village. The AIADMK and the DPI are the vibrant parties, in which a number of the youth have been mobilized. The political parties are active only during the elections. Otherwise they do not show any interest in public activities. There is no conflict or clash among the caste groups. Even if a small difference of opinion is visible among the caste groups the Village Committee analyses the issue and ensures peaceful settlement between the parties. So the communities maintain peace and harmony.

Village Economy

The main occupation in the village is agriculture. Paddy and sugarcane are the major crops cultivated here. There are coconut and mango gardens. The Vaigai river provides irrigation water to the village. Apart from agricultural activities, the landless poor families engage in the production of coconut palm leaf thatches. A considerable number of poor people are employed in the construction industry.

The majority of the landowners are caste Hindus. The caste Hindus of higher order had trapped the SCs and acquired their land at a cheap rate, knowing the potential of the land in that area. People belonging to the SC, without knowing the implications, sold their lands and now on the same lands they are working as farm labourers. It is all so because the SCs had neither proper leadership nor awareness of development issues.

Recruitment Process

When the Panchayati Raj elections were announced, interest picked up among the various communities. But the position of President of Manjampatti Village Panchayat was reserved for the SCs. The caste Hindus could not file their nomination but the majority of them wanted an educated person as President. So the DMK cadres and the members of the Ambedkar Youth Committee (AYC), asked Alagar to file his nomination. At the same time there were three other SC candidates who also filed their nominations. Alagar belonged to the Parayar community whereas the three opponents were Pallars. Though the Pallars are comparatively more in number than the Parayars, the Pallar votes were divided and hence they were defeated.

The DMK cadres and the members of the Ambedkar Youth Committee joined together and canvassed for Alagar, distributing handbills. Alagar promised the people several facilities. His age, education, political background and social contacts spoke well for him. He won the election by a margin of 58 votes. The major expense was for the printing of posters and that was met by the Ambedkar Youth Committee and the DMK cadres. The Ambedkar Youth Committee members were also his close relatives and so they canvassed very seriously.

Village Profile

There are six Ward Members in this village, and three of them belong to the SC community. Of these six members four are men and two are women. The approach road leading to Manjampatti is two km long. It is a blacktopped one. Along the sides of the road there coconut trees planted by the Panchayat. There are two tanks, of which one tank is the

Panchayat's and the other one is a PWD tank. In the Panchayat tank also coconut trees are planted. Altogether there are 300 trees. A worker is employed for guarding the trees. A tree planting programme was executed more than a decade ago and now the income from these coconut trees is Rs. 25,000 for every three years. Fish cultivation is done in the PWD tank but the income is not shared with the Panchayat.

Perception of Panchayati Raj

Alagar has sufficient knowledge about the Panchayti Raj system as his father served as a member of the old Panchayati Raj system. He said that in the old system there was no space for people's participation and the President functioned arbitrarily. He explained some of the salient features of the New Panchayati Raj System like reservation of seats for women and SCs/STs, decentralisation of power, resource mobilisation, Gram Sabha and so on. Alagar criticised the absence of linkages among the three-tiers of the Panchayat system and the operationalisation of the MLA and MP Area Development Funds, which are just a duplication of the Panchayat's work. The joint signature system generates conflict between the President and the Vice-President. The Vice-President has his own priorities based on caste and political considerations. The allocation of group houses is not done properly. Only by political/official influence one can avail of the group house scheme. Alagar argued that, to ensure equity to the oppressed community of the SCs, there should be a separate allocation within the total money allocated under the MLA and the MP funds for the SC community. Otherwise the fund will be utilised only for the benefit of the caste Hindus. The Gram Sabha is misused by the supporters of the defeated candidate and so it has to be regulated. With his experience as lawyer Alagar found that the Panchayat could play a role in jurisprudence relating to civil cases. Any summons served to local persons in civil cases should be entrusted to the Panchayat, so that any misuse of power and authority by Police personnel could be prevented.

Development

The government plays a vital role in development in general. A large number of schemes implemented by the government have brought about progress directly and indirectly. The success of any development programme is dependent on the participation and cooperation of the people. Development means improvement in the per capita income. There are many small farmers in the village. Almost all of them depend on the system of irrigation. They don't have adequate money to invest in deepening of wells for irrigation. If the government gives financial assistance to these small farmers irrespective of caste they can improve their agriculture.

Rearing of milch animal is a successful venture in this village as there is adequate grazing land in the village but the villagers are selling the milk to private traders. Alagar suggested that if a cooperative society is established the people will get more benefited than at present. There are several orchards in the village where varieties of fruits are being grown. There is a scope for establishing a fruit based industry in this village.

CASE – 16

MATHIYANUR GRAM PANCHAYAT
THIRUNAVALUR BLOCK, VILLUPURAM DISTRICT

Socio-Economic Background

Mr. Dhandapani is the President of Mathiyanur Village Panchayat. He is aged thirty-three, is a degree holder and he also has a diploma in Cooperation. He lives with his mother. He is married and has a daughter who is of one year. He owns 7 acres of dry land. Recently he sank a borewell and decided to convert 2 acres of dry land into wetland. His house is tiled, electrified and has individual tap connection. During his college days, he was influenced by his teacher, whose advice was very much useful for his life. Hence he started engaging himself in social service activities in his village. Primarily he was concerned about the poor, particularly the marginalized. He used to visit various government offices and identify the schemes available for the poor. He took steps to bring such schemes to the people in his village. In the meantime, the Panchayat elections were announced. His friends encouraged him to contest. There were two opponents but they were not so familiar to the people as Dhandapani. Moreover, Dhandapani did not project any party in his election campaign. He promised the voters that he would try to get the available schemes to the villagers. Without much expense he won the election. Youngsters of all communities supported him.

Political Socialisation

The DMK Party leaders and their dedication to Tamil had attracted him since his college days. Hence he joined the DMK Party after the Panchayat election, in the year 1996. He has been serving as the village unit secretary of the DMK Party from 1999 onwards.

His Perception of Panchayati Raj

During the election to the Panchayat, Dhandapani came to know the importance of the Panchayati Raj system through newspapers. But he tried to understand all the details of the new system. After the election, he understood the salient features like reservation of seats for women and the marginalised, Election Commission, Finance Commission, District Planning Committee and Gram Sabha. The three-tier system and its administration and accounting procedure have been learnt gradually. The training given by the Gandhigram team under a DANIDA scheme helped him to understand more of Panchayati Raj. People's participation and local leadership are realized through the Panchayati Raj system.

On Politics

According to Dhandapani, politics is nothing but the sharing of power. The ruling party is very powerful as the officials extend more cooperation if the Presidents is from the ruling party. The higher level representatives like the MLA and the MP give more attention to Presidents from their party. The political parties fail to come together for mutual understanding and cooperation at the village level. Very rarely do they stress a common demand in the Gram Sabha meetings.

Perception of Development

To Dhandapani education and employment are essential for development. Needed information has not yet reached the common masses. The government must give awareness to the youth and the women on how to develop their skills to find opportunities to improve their economic condition.

Perception of Gender

Now-a-days the womenfolk are showing interest to come out of the house gain public exposure. The SHG is a key factor in this regard. They are shedding petty issues and coming together to discuss issues of development. Wage discrimination still continues but ill treatment in the family is now reduced.

Perception of Village Economy

Agriculture and animal husbandry are the main sources of the economy. The landed gentry improve their life standard as profitable cash crops like sugarcane are being grown. The landless, by hard labour, earn very little. As wages are more in cities, the very poor migrate to cities like Bangalore and Chennai and earn money. They return and purchase lands. The youth in former days did not show interest in physical labour. The trend has changed now. They engage themselves in various kinds of manual work and earn. The Government must give credit facilities to those who comc forward to start self-employment activities. If proper guidance and facilities are given to them, the majority of the poor will come up.

Perception of Social Justice

In Dhandapani's village, there is no incidence of untouchability. Basic amenities to all is the indicator of social justice. For more than 30 years, the families of the SC colony suffered as there was no electricity connection. After Dhandapani became President he was able to fulfil their basic needs. He feels it is social justice.

Village Setting

It is a multi-caste village. The SCs are the majority community. Vanniars, Yadhavas and Reddiars are the other castes living in Mathiyanur Panchayat. Pachavelikuppam and Illupaiyur are hamlets where Vanniars and Reddiars are the majority castes.

In each community, there is a system of traditional leadership known as *Nattamai*. The Nattamais of all the castes look after the celebration of the village festivals. Four festivals, namely Thaipoosam, Chittirai, Karthikai and Adi are celebrated in the village. All these festivals are celebrated by the SCs separately. The Vanniars, Yadhavas and Reddiars join together and celebrate the Chittirai festival. The contributions for festivals are collected separately and spent separately according to the community.

There is no caste based association. But there are the PMK and the DPI mobilised by the Vanniar and the SCs respectively. The DMK is the dominant party and the next is the AIADMK. The TMC and the CPI(M) are also functioning. A few youngsters have now joined together and become members in the CPI(M) as they consider the CPI(M) a non-caste party representing all communities. The leaders of the local units of all the political parties attend the Gram Sabha meetings. The DMK and the AIADMK cadres try to get government schemes. All the parties join together to demand road facility to temples as well as the fields. As the distance is two km, there was no provision to use the Panchayat fund. When Dhandapani explained this to the people, it was decided to cover one km first and that the balance could be covered in another instalment. There are four SHGs, one for the SC women and three for the BC women. They attend the Gram Sabha meetings. They have not yet availed of the revolving fund as these groups were formed only recently. There is no milk society, cooperative bank or other economic institutions. The youth run a Democratic Youth Federation. Some keep Cine Fans Associations, but they are not active.

Common Property Resources

There are three tanks and five ponds. Among the three tanks one is a PWD tank and the other two are Panchayat Union tanks. There are six tamarind trees and recently four shade trees were planted in the Panchayat office campus and the school campus. Only one pond is located near the village wherein it is proposed to plant trees. In the PWD tank, a large extent of the land has been encroached upon. About four persons have encroached and are cultivating the land. About 10 persons have encroached upon the poramboke land and are cultivating. There is a health sub-centre functioning well. Though the nurse is not staying there, she visits all the hamlets daily and honestly does her duties. There are three schools, one primary, one secondary and one Adi Dravida Welfare Primary School. There is a Village Education Committee and a Parent-Teachers Association. The district is covered under the DPEP. Dhandapani participates in the meetings of the Parent-Teachers Association and the Village Education Committee. He visits all the three schools in the Panchayat, meets the teachers and asks about their needs.

He participated in the School Day celebration and helped to distribute prizes to those who scored ranks from standard one to standard eight. The Headmaster reported about the DPEP activities and the grant received under the project and the purchase of furniture for the school. As per the request of the teachers, water supply connection was provided to all the schools, and repairing work was attended to on the floor of the classrooms which were in a damaged condition. A sum of Rs. 3,000 was spent from the Panchayat fund. Under the DPEP, one additional school building was constructed and under the EAS two buildings were provided, each costing Rs. 1.60 lakh.

His Performance

Dhandapani convenes the Panchayat Council meetings promptly and all the nine Ward Members regularly attend the meetings.

They bring their respective ward problems to the Council. He explains the financial details. The Vice-President belongs to the BC. He expects to do the work in his ward by himself and, to avoid any friction, this has been accepted. Among the four women Members, only one belongs to the BC. She participates well as she is educated. Education is very much necessary to the people's representatives, according to Dhandapani. The Gram Sabha meetings are also properly conducted. Around 125 to 150 members attend the meetings. To encourage more attendance, Dhandapani meets each Ward Member in their respective wards and asks them to bring in their ward people to the Gram Sabha. If only the Ward Members are interested, more people could be mobilized, according to Dhandapani.

House Tax Collection and Other Income

There are more than 700 houses in the Panchayat and they are mostly huts. The total house tax collection is Rs. 5,900, the professional tax around Rs. 4,000, and the stamp duty Rs. 15,000. As there is no fish cultivation in the tank due to non-availability of adequate water, there is no income in this respect. But the grass grown in the tank is auctioned for Rs. 3,000 per year as it is very useful for the huts. Under the Social Forestry Scheme an one time grant of Rs. 3,000 was received. As the majority of the population belong to the SC, the JVVT grant to Mathiyanur is substantial and has been received four times: Rs. 90,000, Rs. 1,00,000, Rs. 1,10,000 and Rs. 1,18,000. The Panchayat has received Rs. 40,000, Rs. 52,000, Rs. 1,10,000 and Rs. 44,000 in four years as SFC grant. The 10th Finance Commission Earmarked Fund was Rs. 5,000 and Rs. 25,000.

Programmes Carried Out

Improvement of the approach road to the graveyard in all the three villages was undertaken under the JVVT. About Rs.75,000 was spent in this regard. A retaining wall and two culverts were constructed at a total cost of Rs. 80,000 under the JVVT. Street maintenance was done at a cost of Rs. 13,000. Cement concrete roads at different places were laid. The total cost was Rs. 2,30,000.

Generally the SFC grant is spent on administration. But through careful expenditure, a savings is effected every year. From the savings the following three items of works have been undertaken :

1. Streetlights new to the colony area to benefit 300 families – this 30 year long need was fulfilled at a cost of Rs. 40,000.
2. Pipeline extension to two streets at a cost of Rs. 10,000.
3. Streetlight (7 Nos.) at a cost of Rs. 22,000.

By properly monitoring the motorpump maintenance the Panchayat avoided expenditure and so there was a savings in the SFC grant.

Resource Mobilization

Under the MLA Fund allocation, a metal road of 300 metres at a cost of Rs. 1.00 lakh was laid. Dhandapani requested the TWAD to sink a new borewell and to provide a motorpump. The TWAD spent Rs. 80,000 for these facilities. One hand pump was provided from the MLA Fund. The President and the Union Councillors jointly took efforts to improve the village. They met the Union Chairman and obtained funds for providing three handpumps, three buildings for three ration shops, 100 metres of cement concrete road and one revetment to prevent the erosion of road by rainwater. As the District Councillor's election was under dispute, the elected person did not function. Hence he could not be approached to avail of any help from the District Councillor's fund.

Though the MP belongs to MDMK, Dhandapani meets him frequently and requests him to help his Panchayat. The MP is kind and complies with the requests. He has sanctioned one bus shelter and one library building. The library building is available but there is no librarian. Hence the Panchayat newspapers and the books of the Ayyan Thirvalluvar Library are kept in the Library building for public use. Dhandapani has requested the authorities to provide funds for equipping the library with more books.

Drinking Water

Adequate attention has been given to providing drinking water. Earlier there were only 27 taps but now there are 48 taps. Eight individual tap connections were provided earlier. The persons who availed of the connections did not pay the water tax due for many years. They did not also pay the enhanced deposit. It has been decided to issue notices to these persons and if they fail necessary steps will be taken to regulate the same.

Monitoring of PDS

There are three public distribution system (PDS) shops in the village. Dhandapani periodically visits them and enquires about the quota and the allocation. If there is any shortage he talks with the Civil Supplies officials who are at Ulundhurpet. The officials explain that, in general, about 50 to 60 families are not living in the village or not availing of the ration rice and hence the quota has been reduced.

Sectoral Linkages

Dhandapani regularly visits the Union office, the THADCO office and the Social Welfare Board office to do necessary follow up on the requests of the public. He maintains good relationship with the officials of various Departments. He gets full information on all the schemes pertaining to each Department and makes use of them for many villagers. House site pattas have to be obtained for about 50 SC families and 60 MBC families. The site has been procured by the government. He met the landlords and persuaded them to part with the needed land and convinced them that the people would remember them for ever. Dhandapani frequently visited to the TWAD office for sinking a new borewell and building an OHT at a cost of Rs. 3.0 lakhs and they have been completed.

The PWD officials were contacted and the Panchayat has submitted a demand for desilting and maintenance of the tanks. They prepared the estimate. The Union tanks were desilted at a cost of Rs. 1.50 lakh. The Agricultural Engineering Department has desilted ponds at a cost of Rs. 2.50 lakh. With proper follow up on the DPEP scheme, adequate teachers for the school were appointed. With the help of health officials, a health camp was organized. A THADCO loan was availed of for 30 eligible individuals and the Panchayat ensured regular repayment also. Twelve TRSP toilets were provided under DANIDA and the Panchayat proposes to avail of more latrines. It was discussed in the Gram Sabha.

His Vision

Dhandapani wishes to aim for a high school as there is need and the necessary pupil strength, but he has learnt only recently that Rs. 80,000 has to be paid by the public. As this is a huge amount which cannot be mobilized immediately, he has talked to all the community leaders to plan for a fund raising and to pay the total fund required for upgrading the school. He proposes to avail of the government scheme for milch animal rearing as it is really profitable for poor families. He wishes to improve the agricultural activities as some farmers have lost interest in cultivation. He also wishes to help young men to get employment in the industrial sector.

CASE - 17

MELANETHUR GRAM PANCHAYAT
MANAMADURAI BLOCK, SIVAGANGAI DISTRICT

Socio-Economic Background

Mrs. Rakku, the President of Melanethur Village Panchayat, is aged 38, and has studied upto the eighth standard. She hails from the SC community. She owns 5 acres of land with a pumpset. Her family is a joint family; her father is living with her. Three daughters, aged 19, 16, 11 years, are studying. She takes keen interest in educating her children as she did not get the opportunity to continue her studies. Only after becoming the

President of the Village Panchayat she realised that necessity of education to all. Her husband is a farmer. She owns a house in the field and it is electrified but no toilet facility is available in her house. Rakku's marriage was a child marriage at the age of 13 years. She married a person who worked as a labourer on her farm. Though both of them belonged to the SC community, the bridegroom was economically poor. But understanding his honesty and hard work, she chose to marry him at an early age as she had lost her mother and was engaged in household work.

Being slightly educated, she used to help him to read and write and she also conducted tuition classes for the poor children. Village women were helped by her activities which earned a good name for her among the villagers, particularly the women. But these services did not satisfy her. When an NGO proposed the assignment of organising the poor for welfare programmes, Rakku enthusiastically came forward to take up the responsibility. For about 5 years she was actively engaged in organising a women's Sangam, educating them to understand various problems is their life, helping them to avail of schemes pertaining to the poor. In the meantime, she improved her leadership qualities by attending various training programmes and meetings organised by the NGO.

At the hamlet of Kakkudi, she served as the animator in the Non-Formal Education Programme, without getting any monetary benefit. She organised Sangams for both men and women. In course of time the NGO paid a honorarium to her. Her husband is less educated than her, but he respects her and encourages her in her activities. He accompanies her when visiting offices. But he never commands her. She conducts all discussions with officials by herself without her husband's help.

Recruitment

The villagers did not take the Panchayat elections seriously as there was inadequate awareness among the people. But the NGOs prepared their SHG women as candidates in a number of villages. Likewise in Melanethur the NGO advised Rakku to contest in the elections.

There were two other candidates in the fray. One was sponsored by the DMK Party and the other one by another NGO. The local DMK cadres compelled Rakku to withdraw her nomination. But she refused to do so as it was the fundamental right of every individual. Melanethur being the main village, the villagers mobilized themselves and opposed Rakku, who hails from a hamlet. They threatened her when she visited the villages for canvassing. But she refused to bow down and was prepared to face any challenge. The favoured candidate hailed from the same community and she was politically strong with the DMK behind her. The villagers of the small hamlet of Kakkudi accompanied and helped Rakku to canvass for votes. As there were nine hamlets, canvassing was done even during the night. Several times, the opponents threatened Rakku and her team. Yet she won the election by a margin of 62 votes. Her social service activities, her simplicity and her plain speaking character attracted the voters. Her identification with the NGO activities was also a reason for her success.

In general the issues highlighted by the people during the Panchayat elections are drinking water, road improvement, new streetlights and individual loans. Rakku told the voters that she would devote her time to bringing welfare schemes to the villages as she has been already involved in these activities as animator in the NGO. In the election campaign she used handbills and wall writings. She spent Rs. 10,000 for the election. The NGO supported her in the election. Their staff specifically oriented her for the canvassing. Her association with the NGO which sponsored her candidature has been further strengthened after the election. The local Youth Association extends help in maintaining sanitation during the village festivals. When an NSS camp was organised with the help of the NGO, the local youth lent their services to the college youth. The participants of the NSS camp did *shramdhan* and planted 90 coconut saplings. The NGO is running an ITI in which about 10 students from Melanethur got admission at the recommendation of Rakku. Moreover the poor students were given a fee concession also. The NGO staff are helping and guiding Rakku in the execution of her responsibilities.

Village Setting

In Melanethur Village there are people from various communities, namely SCs, Nadars, Vellalars, Maravars, Kallars, Konars. The SC is the majority community. The Nadars have their caste association. The youth of all castes have associations. There is also an NYK in the village. There are 18 SHGs of which 9 are sponsored by the NGOs and the rest are organised by the village women themselves. The monthly savings among the SHGs vary some groups save Rs. 25 per month, others save Rs. 50 per month and a few groups save Rs. 10 per month. But all collect 3 per cent interest. The youth organize sports like *kabadi* and cricket. There are associations in the names of cine actors like Rajnikanth, Vijayakanth and Sarathkumar. The NGOs function-ing in the village are SMSS and PERD. But the latter one is not active. Irrespective of castes the NGOs organise poor families and create awareness among them.

Temple

Under the jurisdiction of Sivagangai Samasthanam, a Sivan temple is administered in Melanethur. The festival of the Sivan temple is famous in this area. It is a week long celebration. Earlier the SCs could not participle in pulling the car. But, for the past five years, they have come and pulled the car along with the other castes. The caste Hindus could not do anything as the SCs are in the majority. But the BCs are not happy about this. Untouchability is being practised in the village. The SC labourers used to sit outside and get their feeding. But the labourers belonging to the BC and the SC work jointly on farms. There are two churches for Christians. There is no conflict between the Hindus and the Christians. Apart from the Sivan temple, there are Mariamman temple, Bathrakali temple and Malaitheivam temple. All castes come to the Mariamman temple. In Bhatrakali and Malaitheivam temples the *poojaris* belong to the Maravar and the Kallar community. The SCs are permitted but rarely visit. There is no cooperative body in Melanethur.

Political Parties

All political parties, namely the DMK, the AIADMK, the TMC, the Congress, the CPM, the CPI, the Puthiya Tamizhagam and the MDMK are found in the village. The DMK and the AIADMK are the dominant parties. The DMK Party insisted on the withdrawal of the nomination of Rakku during the election as the women's wing convener of the DMK Party was also in the fray. As Rakku refused to withdraw, the DMK Party people fostered a feeling of enmity. But, after the election, Rakku never showed any favour to anybody. She administered the Panchayat honestly and so the DMK Party men understood her and supported her in the Panchayat administration. They have now come forward to extend all their support to her and to select her unanimously in the next election. Her efforts taken for solving the problems in the provision of water supply have impressed the political parties. Village youth, irrespective of party affiliation, readily approach her. They even give her a lift on their bicycles. Politicians advise her readily and discuss the Panchayat activities with her.

Her Perception of Panchayati Raj

Earlier she didn't know the full details of the Panchayati Raj but she believed that a lot of welfare work could be provided to the villagers through Panchayats. Now she understands the full significance. Once streetlights would not function for months together due to non-availability of the people's representative. But the defects in the streetlights and water supply pipeline are immediately attended to by the Panchayats after the election. The Panchayat administration is like administering a family. Availability of funds is very important to meet various demands and so all the members in the family must make efforts to improve the finances, particularly from the common property resources. The people have not yet realised the importance of their participation and the politicians are interfering in the Panchayat activities. The selection of beneficiaries is influenced by the Councillors.

Perception of Development

Basic amenities must come first. The schemes and programmes of the government must reach the real beneficiaries. Living conditions and standard must be improved. Employment opportunities for poor landless people will improve their economic standard. All the activities of NGOs, the government and SHGs must be coordinated.

Perception of Village Economy

Due to increase in the cost of inputs, agriculture is now-a-days non-profitable. Employment in the agriculture sector is now shrinking due to drought, availability of agricultural machines and equipment in the villages. Village industries, small scale industries and cottage industries are essential for rural development.

At least around 10 to 15 persons have migrated for want of employment or business, and those who left the village are somehow or the other earning and improving their life.

Perception of Social Problems

Alcoholism is the main problem in the village. When efforts are taken to prevent the sale, the drunkards and the illicit distillers join together and the police do not regard it as a problem at all. So she could not stop the sale of alcohol.

Perception of Polity

The ideologies mouthed by various political parties are very much attractive but nothing will materialise if the parties do not give adequate attention to development issues. The performance of political parties is measured from the local units' activities.

Perception of Gender Issues

Society still maintains discrimination against women. The women are expected to adjust to the inhuman activities of a drunken husband. Education and employment opportunities are for men in India. It is expected that the reservation in the local bodies for women will change the status of women. There is a cultural hardship for women. If a man stays overnight due to unexpected circumstances it does not matter but, if a woman stays back, society will comment on her character. At this even a family which encourages her public life will feel hurt. But the present day female generation is far better than the earlier generation and she has the hope that women's status is improving steadily. The political parties must come forward to entrust positions/responsibilities to women in their party. Further more awareness, more training and more opportunities to women are necessary, she suggested.

Perception of Common Property Resources

There are 12 *ooranis* (tanks) in which the community holds a state. The fishing rights are auctioned for a nominal amount. The ooranis are protected by the community and the fish caught by the community are pooled and distributed to all the families of all castes. The Panchayat can take over these tanks but enmity will develop among the villagers and so Rakku has not taken any action in this regard. A graveyard is provided to each community. The threshing floor site has been encroached upon by individuals and the Panchayat's action to remove the encroachment did not succeed due to lack of support from the Revenue Department.

There is a stage meant for public activities like dramas during the festival days. There is a building referred to as Technical Centre in Melanethur but there is no record to verify the origin of the building and it is lying waste. The Panchayat proposes to make use of the same for women's activities.

Her Performance

Rakku improved her leadership by attending all meetings organised by the NGO and the Government authorities and by reading newspapers and the journal *Panchayat Seithi*. With this background Rakku administers the Panchayat competently.

There are three Wards in the nine hamlets in Melanethur. Totally there are nine Ward Members of whom four belong to the SC community. The Panchayat meetings are held every month, but the women Members, both SC and BC, do not show interest in attending the meetings. The husbands of the female Ward Members used to come and describe their wards' problems. Sometimes they even affixed their signatures instead of their spouses. The government officials in general do not take any serious note of this.

The male Ward Members bring various issues to the Panchayat and demand solutions. Generally Rakku manages them by explaining the details of the work carried out. Once there was a dispute over the selection of a site for providing a public water tap. Then, with the help of staff of the VAO, she selected a suitable site after verifying the records. All major issues are discussed with the community leaders. The public expect the President to come to the police station to protect them when they face trouble. She usually obliges them. But she does not to go the police station to help any drunkard. The Panchayat President has to take up social leadership also. Family problems and personal problems are also brought to the notice of the President. Rakku tries to settle all the problems brought to her. Political interference is always a problem. When 15 group houses were allotted recently, the ruling party local secretary stepped in to collect money from those who wished to get a house. The officials also tried to delay the finalisation of beneficiaries as they also expected money. She used to share all these problems with all without any hesitation. She explained in a public meeting in the presence of the then Minister that the selection of beneficiaries for certain schemes by officials was not properly done.

Gram Sabha

The participants raise questions menacingly but the President has to patiently reply to all the questions. Once there was an objection to the measurement in a road work when the expenditure was read out in the Gram Sabha meeting. Earlier this complaint had been verified by the Block officials and found to be false. So the same complaint should not have been raised in the Gram Sabha. But the concerned individuals again tried to raise the issue. At that time, the women members of the SHGs jointly opposed the complaint. The Gram Sabha meetings are respected by villagers. During the agricultural season, the attendance at the Gram Sabha meeting will be poor as the poor would be engaged in agricultural activities. Politicians try to show their public interest by shooting several questions during the Gram Sabha meetings. Their attempts are to mislead the public that they could do better service to the people.

Her Experience with the Panchayat Clerk

A person from the BC is the Panchayat Clerk. He fails to understand that he is an employee and that the President is a people's representative. He has not learnt simplicity and humility. He has openly disrespected her leadership several times. Yet she believed him. Only later she discovered that he had misappropriated the funds collected as house tax. The money was paid by her to avoid any problems. Finally, she dismissed him. Now she has employed her daughter as clerk and she is learning things slowly. As she knows all the details of record maintenance they are managing. The members did not oppose her when she proposed her daughter's name for Panchayat clerk. They advised her to employ her as she is educated and unemployed.

Interface with the Police Official

Due to the atrocities committed by individuals who used to take alcohol and who used to brew alcohol some prominent individuals lodged a complaint in the police station. The police came and asked the Panchayat President to name the individuals who are involved in the preparation of liquor. She refused to give the list as the police would misuse it and they will only get money from the distillers. But she told the police that brewing and selling of alcohol is going on everywhere. She was threatened by the thugs and she complained to the police. The police reassured her.

Committee Formation

Water and Sanitation Committee, Welfare Committee, Education Committee, Public Distribution Vigilance Committee are the various committees formed. The members do not have interest in public life. They expect the President to do all things.

The members of the different committees will show interest if they get sitting allowance, wage compensation, power and authority in their roles.

Tax Collection

The pending house tax has been collected fully. Auditing has been done and there was no major objection. The EOP, the Deputy PDO and the BDO periodically visit the Panchayat and verify the accounts and give necessary guidance in this regard. The house tax has been assessed freshly and an additional amount of Rs. 10,000 has been received by this revision.

Gender Issues

Even though Rakku is one of the elected Presidents under the Panchayati Raj System, the male Presidents of nearby Panchayats considered her a weak person as she is a woman. So they tried together to challenge the rights and authority of Melanthur Panchayat in respect of the PWD kanmoi (lake). The Kilanethur Panchayat President and villagers encroached upon the PWD kanmoi and demanded the whole benefit from the kanmoi. They disturbed the auction proceedings. As the matter became serious, a public committee was formed. Traditionally the rights have been vested with Rakku's village, but the two male Village Presidents of Kilamettur and Ayankuruchi tried to browbeat her since she is a woman. They tried to influence the Revenue officials to prove by the records that the right did not with Melanethur. At this juncture Rakku declared that she would set herself afire if the officials deviated from the original records. After this, the auction was conducted but the share due to Melanethur has not yet been credited in the account of the Panchayat.

Interface with Councillor

The Councilor felt hurt when Rakku, on her own, obtained sanction to construct a bus shelter for passengers from the Union Fund. Further, under the Union scheme, a Rs. 40,000 worth culvert was proposed for Melanethur. Rakku tried her best to get it, but the Councillor questioned her interference in the Councillors' work. The role and responsibilities among the representatives of the three-tiers are not properly spelt out and so there is unnecessary misunderstanding.

Social Sector

As good relationship is maintained with the VHN, she used to periodically meet Rakku and inform her about the health issues. Young women's meetings are held to create awareness on RCH activities. Special meetings are arranged for disseminating information on AIDS and sexually transmitted diseases; preventive camps are organized and the Panchayat has helped in these activities by making the necessary propaganda and arrangements. The sub-health centre is functioning in a rented house and the Panchayat made efforts to get a *pucca* building. A water tap has been provided to the school and preparations have been made for providing a tap to the high school also.

Panchayat Office

It is a neatly constructed building but the environment is not maintained clean. The President spends most of her time at the Panchayat office. The records are kept here but the clerk did not come regularly. She herself was doing the clerical work. She has decided to contest again as she has successfully administered the Panchayat in a balanced way. She is confident that she will get votes from all communities.

Activities carried out in Melanethur

The Panchayat has got Rs. 28,256 in the year 1997-98 and Rs. 42,936 in the year 1998-99 as SFC grant. During 1997-98, it got Rs. 12,848 under the JVVT. But there is an increase in the JVVT allocation for the year 1999-2000: it is Rs. 71,551. In the year 2000-2001 under JGSY there were two grants of Rs. 50,790 and Rs. 50,780.

Under JGSY, construction of TV rooms, road improvement (metalling), road maintenance, construction of bathing ghat and blacktopping of road were the major activities undertaken by the Panchayat in the past four years. Streetlights, public taps, approach road maintenance, public sanitation, handpump maintenance, tank renovation and paying of electricity bills were the major expenses in addition to establishment expenses. Attention is given to fulfil the felt needs of the people in respect of drinking water. Individual connection have been provided to 22 households. More streetlights (89 tubes and 2 sodium vapour lamps) have been provided. Toilets built under CRSP (120 Nos.) and lighting in the graveyard area have been provided.

CASE – 18

MUDIKANDANALLOOR GRAM PANCHAYAT KEERAPALAYAM BLOCK, CUDDALORE DISTRICT

Socio-Economic Background

Mrs. P. Senthamil Selvi, the President of Mudikandanalloor Village Panchayat, is 48. She has studied upto the ninth standard and belongs to the SC community. She belongs to a nuclear family. Her occupation is agriculture and she possesses one acre of dry land and but there is no regular income from this land. She has her own house and has equipped it with all facilities including toilet, electrification and individual tap connection. Her husband is a retired Health Inspector and gets a pension of Rs. 5,000 per month. This amount of Rs. 5,000 is their only source of income. She is not affiliated to any social institutions but she has an affiliation with the DMK Party, because her husband is attached to it. With regard to party activities she is involved in them at the local level.

The total population of the village is 2625, of which males are 1245 and females are 1420 and in the SC category males are 513 and females 528. The total Ward Members are six, with 4 males and 2 females. This Panchayat has different caste groups but the majority are SC. The others are Vanniars, Chettiars, Vellalars, Muslims, Carpenters, Irular, Naidus and Yadavas. This Panchayat has 525 households, of which 40 are group houses, 25 *pucca* houses, 30 tiled houses and the others huts.

The Panchayat has one OHT and the capacity is 1 lakh litres of water. There are 35 public taps. Besides, 6 persons have individual tap connections. There are 18 handpumps available in this Panchayat. With regard to health and sanitation, there are no proper drainage facilities. Besides there is no public toilet facility in this Panchayat, but 103 persons have constructed individual household latrines. There is no health centre in this Panchayat, but every Wednesday the Village Health Nurse comes and takes care of children, particularly for immunization.

The total length of roads is only 2 km in this Panchayat. This Panchayat has metal roads and cement roads for 100 metres and 260 metres respectively. This Panchayat has one *balwadi*, three noon-meal centres, and two primary schools with toilet facilities. But no higher education institution is available in this Panchayat. It is available in nearby Setthiathoppu. There are 74 books available in the Ayyan Library and people take the books home to read. Two bus shelters are available, one in the SC area and the other in the BC area. Previously the graveyard was encroached upon but now the graveyard has been enlarged to one and half acres by removing the encroachment. The encroachment were removed using officials and traditional leaders.

The following facilities are not available in this Panchayat: market, butchery shed, community hall and cinema theatre. The Panchayat has a Youth Association formed by the NYK. There are no caste and women's Sangams as registered organisations. There is no common land in this Panchayat but a few individuals have encroached upon the lands around the lake. The major source of irrigation is borewell and the major crops are paddy and sugarcane. About 300 families are engaged in milch animal rearing. They have formed two milk societies and the milk is sent to Setthiathoppu (about 400 litres everyday). Besides there are 100 families engaged in rearing goats. A veterinary centre is available in Setthiathoppu. With regard to politics, since 1975, the DMK Party has been dominating this Panchayat, because in 1975-96, 100 houses were constructed under a THADCO scheme during the period of the DMK rule. Hence the people are loyal to the DMK Party.

Recruitment Process

There are no basic facilities in this Panchayat. So Senthamil Selvi contested in the Panchayat elections. In 1986, she started a milk society with women members. For this reason the women's groups supported her and elected her Panchayat President. Three candidates contested in the election against her. But she defeated them by a margin of 148 votes. During the canvassing Senthamil Selvi assured the public that she would provide all basic facilities. During the election friends and relatives and local youngsters supported her. Besides, she spent Rs. 5,000. Further the SC people cooperated effectively. These were the reasons for her success.

Perception

Senthamil Selvi has little awareness of the features of the 73rd Constitutional Amendment Act. She knows only that a three-tier system had been established in the New Panchayati Raj System. She believes that the New Panchayati Raj System should be oriented more to rural development activities. In her view the educated can perform effectively because they know the rules and regulations of the Panchayat Act. Sanitation and primary education play a vital role in village development. Development does not mean merely providing basic facilities. It should enable the people to earn their livelihood. For better people's participation the basic amenities have been provided. The government has provided and allotted funds, launched economic programmes, constructed public toilets, health centre and veterinary centre and provided Public Distribution Scheme (PDS) and housing facility to the rural poor. Agriculture is the major component of village economy in this Panchayat, because women's groups were trained under the DANWA programme. Many are engaged in coolie work. People are not interested in village industry. They mainly concentrate on agricultural work. Some people have migrated to other states like Kerala and Gujarat for employment. Women are not discriminated against because they are working equally with men, but the wages they get is less. There are seven SHGs formed in this Panchayat. All the groups are engaged in dairy farming and earning money. Very often the SHGs conduct meetings discuss their problems and find solutions also. In this way women could be empowered through SHGs. With regard to common property resources, there are 40 coconut trees and one lake. From the coconut trees and the lake the Village Panchayat gets some income. Caste discrimination is slowly disappearing in this area. As literacy increases the parochial tendencies will wither away. Senthamil Selvi developed leadership qualities by attending training programmes, particularly in SIRD, DANIDA and at the Block level. Her husband always gives motivation and inspiration. Besides, she regularly reads Tamil newspapers.

Performance

In 1996-97 the following items of work were carried out in Mudikandanalloor and the hamlet of Shanthi Nagar. TV room and blacktopped road were provided in Shanthi Nagar under the JVVT scheme; 20 group houses and linkage roads were constructed in Mudikandanalloor under IAS and DDP Scheme; in 1997-98 steps in pond and graveyard road retaining walls were constructed under JVVT schemes. Maintenance core of bus shelter and nutrition were undertaken in 1998-99, three culverts were constructed in Mudikandanalloor under JVVT Scheme; a bus shelter was completed under JVVT scheme; one handpump was replaced in Mudikandanalloor under the Tenth Finance Commission Scheme; in 1999-2000, a drainage system, two culverts and individual toilets, besides two group houses, and a cement road were provided under the JGSY, IAS and Union general fund; one OHT was constructed under TWAD Scheme.

By using the SFC grant, the following items of work have been carried out: maintenance of graveyard road, and construction of steps in pond, installation of sodium vapour streetlights, handpump and maintenance of roads and streets.

In 2000-2001 the following items of work were carried out from JGSY, SFC, TRSP, and equalization fund and Panchayat Union general fund: a 100 metre cement road at a cost of Rs. 1 lakh in Mudikandanalloor, a 60 metre cement road under JVVT and purchase of sports materials. Encroachments have been removed for the purpose of creating a playground; 40 *katcha* houses were completed under JGSY with toilets. In TRSP Scheme, a toilet was constructed for the Adi Dravida Welfare School. Another toilet was constructed for the *balwadi.* A 100 metre cement road was laid from the Panchayat Union fund. These are the various items of work for Panchayat development in the past 5 years.

Seven committees have been formed but they are not functioning effectively. Senthamil Selvi paid her own money for others' house tax for getting the matching grant but still that tax has not been collected from the public. The house tax amount has been raised as follows :

Huts	Rs. 5.50 to Rs. 11.00
Tiled houses	Rs. 11.00 to Rs. 22.00

Other than the tax items, the resources mobilised are as follows: auction of fisheries, coconut trees (70) and tamarind trees (4). The Panchayat gets Rs. 4,000 to Rs. 5,000 as income per year from the above sources.

The government grant details are as follows :

(i) SFC grant per year	Rs.1,12,000
(ii) JVVT grant per year	Rs. 88,000
(iii) Earmarked fund	Rs. 10,000

Accounting and auditing pose no problem because all problems at official levels are sorted out. Auditing has been completed for four years.

There are six Ward Members who regularly attend the Panchayat meetings. Very often they discuss the basic amenities, *i.e.* streetlights, water supply and sanitary conditions. Besides, the Women Members demand electricity facility to all houses and culverts in certain places. As for Gram Sabha meetings 180 people attend regularly, of whom 60 are females and 110 are males, 80 per cent from the SC community and 20 per cent from the BC communities. In Gram Sabha meetings people always demand loan facility and group houses.

Assumed Duties

Senthamil Selvi has taken much effort for environmental sanitation in various ways, including conducting public meetings. She says that public toilets are essential for village sanitation. There is no specific system for the removal of drainage water. To improve school enrolment, Senthamil Selvi has provided motivation, inspiration and also prizes for school children. Toilets have been constructed and both teachers and students have been using them very well.

The Panchayat is situated near the road and maintained well. The maintenance of records is not clear. Senthamil Selvi visits the Panchayat office four times a week but the clerk attends office daily. Mobilising community support for Panchayat development is very difficult because there are illiterates. They do not understand the Panchayat's situation and the income and expenditure of the Panchayat. Even in Gram Sabha meetings, the people do not participate with interest. People's participation is essential for rural development activities. The details of activities carried out under different schemes are given below :

JVVT Work Details

1997-98

Income		*Expenditure*	
	Rs.		Rs.
Previous Amount	500.00	Steps for lake	35,000.00
Interest	276.00	Retaining wall	14,000.00
Through	1,24,984.00	Graveyard road Maintenance	27,847.00
		Final balance	48,913.00
	1,25,760.00		1,25,760.00

(*Contd.*)

1998-99

Initial balance	23,880	Final balance	4,817
Income	1,55,925	Expenditure	1,74,988
	1,79,805		1,79,805

1999-2000

Through District-Collector	34,874	For culvert	76,690
		For cement	5,200
District Collector	42,992	For drainage	16,000
Through Panchyat President	809	For culvert	15,140
		Final balance	15,412
Interest	78,375		
Initial balance	4,817		
	83,192		83,192

From JVVT fund, steps for canal, retaining wall and maintenance of roads to the graveyards were provided in the year 1997-98. In 1998-99 no work was done with JVVT fund. In 1999-2000 the following some items of work were done from JVVT fund, *i.e.* culverts, cement yard and drainage system.

Details of Earmark Funds

1998-1999

Income		*Expenditure*	
	Rs.		Rs.
Through District Collector	13,100	Funeral Assistant	5,400
		TV Room	1,500
Through Panchayat President	100	EB Charge	1,168
		Final Balance	5,082
	13,200		13,200

1998-99

Through District Collector	3,443	Funeral Assistant	4,500
Interest	560	EB Charge	3,367
Initial Balance	5,082	Hand pump maintenance	500
		Final balance	718
	9,085		9,085

(*Contd.*)

1999-2000

Through District Collector	12,660	Funeral Assistant	4,000
Through Panchayat President	4,960	Office maintenance	8,000
		TA for president	1,300
Interest	32	Final balance	5,070
Initial balance	718		
	18,370		18,370

From earmarked funds, the following items of work were done, i.e. funeral assistance, maintenance of TV room, payment of EB charges, handpump maintenance and office maintenance.

Income and Expenditure

Details of Mudikandanalloor Panchayat, Keerapalayam Block, Cuddalore District:

1997-1998

Income		*Expenditure*	
	Rs.		Rs.
Previous Amount	100	Salary	13,030
House tax	2,083	Family Security Scheme	150
Professional tax	3,462	Newspaper	784
Auction of trees	2,619	EB charges (streetlights)	3,235
Drought Relief Fund	9,712	Streetlight spare parts	6,437
Interest	83	TA	3,750
SFC grant	81,487	Sitting fees	1,925
Other sources	47	Other sources	200
Other sources	345	Equipment	1,680
Initial balance	16,636	TV maintenance	862
		Note	600
		Hand pump maintenance	52,850
		Road maintenance	7,980
		Other maintenance	1,783
		Final balance	21,308
	1,16,574		1,16,574

In 197-98, the SFC sanctioned a grant of Rs. 81,487 while the other sources of income were very low. Further Drought Relief Fund was also given to this Panchayat. The major expenditure was as follows:

1998-1999

Income	Rs.	Expenditure	Rs.
House tax	3,284	Salary	19,210
Library	267	TA for Panchayat president	3,600
SFC grant	1,38,108	TA for Panchayat assistant	3,480
Professional tax	4,800	Court expenditure	3,600
Auction form trees	21,307	Funeral Assistant	2,000
		Streetlight maintenance	4,113
		Written items	171
		Road maintenance	13,050
		Sitting fees for President	2,450
		Newspaper	570
		Electricity charges	6,532
		Fund changes	29,023
		.Bonus	725
		Family Welfare	180
		Graveyard maintenance	12,661
		TV maintenance	6,006
		Hand pump	15,069
		New handpump	31,567
		Steps	9,403
		Final Balance	7,297
	1,70,657		1,70,657

In this year SFC grant was sanctioned at a high level while compared to the previous year. The house tax was also increased. The major expenditure was for maintenance of graveyard and handpump.

1999-2000

Income	Rs.	Expenditure	Rs.
SFC grant	1,61,055	Salary	40,070
Stamp duty	18,009	TA for President	10,200
House tax matching	3,600	TA for Panchayat assistant	1,800
Professional tax	4,690	Funeral assistant	800
House tax	8,804	Stationary	1,480
Auction from trees	3,200	Handpump maintenance	9,877
Other sources	32	Family welfare	570
Initial Balance	7,297	Street light maintenance	30,292
		EB charge	12,539
		Road maintenance	23,000
		OHT maintenance	18,080

(*Contd.*)

	TV maintenance	800
	For drainage	28,000
	Final balance	890
2,06,747		2,06,747

The SFC grant has gradually increased from 1996-2001. Stamp duty has also increased. The major expenditure was for maintenance of streetlights, handpump, OHT and roads.

CASE – 19
KAKKOOR GRAM PANCHAYAT MUTHUKULATHOOR BLOCK, RAMANATHAPURAM DISTRICT

Socio-Economic Background

Mrs. Poomayil is the President of Kakkoor Village Panchayat, which is one of the 46 Village Panchayats in Muthukulathoor Union. She is a literate woman, having studied upto the ninth standard. Her age is 38 and she belongs to the SC Pallar community, which is the dominant one in Kakkoor Village.

Her husband is an ex-serviceman and now works as a security guard in the State Bank of India, Paramakudi, earning a monthly salary of Rs. 5,785. Her family is a joint one as her father-in-law and mother-in-law are living with them. She lives in a *pucca* house owned by her. It is electrified and toilet facility is also available. Her husband possesses a scooter. They have six acres of land. She has three sons and one daughter. Her eldest son, after his school final, did not continue his studies and the others are studying in the local area.

Married at the age of 17, Poomayil lived outside the village. Along with her husband, she lived in military quarters in New Delhi, Secunderabad, Jalandhar and Kashmir. This exposure changed her personality. Earlier she was very much reserved and incapable of interacting with men. But, after visiting all these places and living with different communities, she became courageous, and never minded sitting near men during the bus travel.

After the retirement of her husband, they settled down in her village. Her village is a multi-caste one. But her SC Pallar caste is the dominant caste. The caste Sangam, named Devendrakula Vellalar Sangam, has been strengthened year by year since the 1970s by the efforts of her village elders. The community families used to meet once a month and collect Rs. 10 per week per family. The collection is done by a committee. A building worth Rs. 2 lakh has been constructed recently from the common fund collected by the caste association. Her husband, even during his service in the military, was engaged in public work and Sangam activities whenever he came to the village on holidays. Moreover her husband's family is a big group. Her in-laws and their families are also living in Kakkoor. After the retirement of her husband, he could devote more time to public services. When the oorani (tank) water was misused, the Village Committee regulated the same and ensured the availability of water to everyone during the summer. In these activities, her husband used to mobilise the support of the youth belonging to other castes also.

Recruitment

With the above background, Poomayil contested in the Panchayat elections. The family members decided to make her contest in the election as it was reserved for women. They proposed her name because she is sociable, kind and helpful to all other family members and because she is educated. Her father-in-law, being a member of the Tamil Maanila Congress Party, mobilized the support of the party cadre. A former opposition leader from this area also advised Poomayil's family to field her and agreed to extend his party's support to her in the election. There were five candidates including Poomayil in the race. But Poomayils family was confident of winning the election. So they fielded Poomayil.

Apart from SC Pallars there are caste Hindus, Muslims and Christians also in the same Panchayat area. Konars are the next dominant caste followed by Thevars, Muslims, Chettiars,

Vellalars, Asaris and Sakkiliyars. Poomayil's family belongs to the dominant caste. Moreover they enjoy the support of the Tamil Maanila Congress, particularly that of the then opposition leader in the State Legislative Assembly. He was an MLA. He came to the village and convened a meeting for her.

The opposing candidates were from Thevar, Muslim and Konar (Yadava) communities. They believed that they would get the support of their own castes. Poomayil, along with the village elders, family members and TMC party supporters, mounted a rigorous campaign. She and her husband jointly went from door to door canvassing for votes and assuring the public that she would bring all development schemes to this Panchayat. Those belonging to other castes also extended support to her. They also joined the campaign. The other candidates spent a lot of money, and they bribed the voters. But, in the stiff competition, Poomayil won by a 245 votes margin. About Rs. 40,000 was spent for the election campaign.

Village Setting

Caste Association

Prominent castes like Pallars, Konars, Thevars and Vellalars have caste associations in Kakkoor. Each community has its own committee to discuss the problems of concern to the caste members. But only the SC Pallars have a well established caste association. The caste leaders developed the consciousness among the people that only through a united community people can get better services and facilities from the government. The SC community members had differences of opinion among themselves on a variety of issues. Educational opportunities, employment opportunities other than agriculture, are the major contributing factors for the slow but steady improvement of the socio-economic conditions of the SC community. Moreover, traditionally, the SCs of Kakkoor were not put into any subjugation in the name of caste. They enjoyed good status among the other communities due to their numerically dominant position and also they are the *poojaris* of the Muniappasamy temple and Nachiamman temple.

Temples

In the Muniappasamy temple both Thevars and SCs worship and celebrate festivals but, separately. But the *poojari* is from the SC community. In the Nachiamman temple which is the deity of the Yadava community, the *poojari* is from the SC community. A portion from the offerings like Pongal and mutton rice have to be given to the *poojari*. In this way the SC community of Kakkoor did not suffer due to untouchability.

The Christians of Kakkoor were once converted from the SC community. All sects of Christians, Roman Catholic, Protestant and Pentecostal are living here. They also have different churches for worship. The Muslims have a *dargah*. Apart from these, there are the Vinayaga temple, the Murugan temple, the Amman temple and the Akniraja temple. The SC Cobbler community has its own Jakkamma temple where only this community worships and others do not visit. There is no issue like Muthal Mariyathai (first respect) as all castes commonly celebrate the festivals like mulaipari. For the Muniappasamy temple celebration all the communities contribute including Christian and Muslims. Likewise during the celebration in the *dargah*, Hindus also donate liberally.

Youth Association

The youth of the prominent castes have their youth wing. They distribute sweets, exchange greetings and involve themselves during the marriage of their members. Most of them are united irrespective of castes for sports activities. They contribute and purchase sports equipment and conduct sports activities.

Cine Fans Associations in the name of cine stars Vijayakanth, Rajinikanth, Prasanth and Kamalhasan are also active in the village and they conduct several social and cultural programmes.

Registered Milk Society

There are two registered milk societies but one is not sound while the other one is functioning well. There is a primary agricultural cooperative credit bank also.

NGO

World Vision of India is the NGO functioning in this area. Apart from women SHG activity, the NGO is helping the community in education, common facilities like desilting of oorani, cleaning of OHT, water supply and streetlights.

School

Two Union primary schools, one TELC primary school, one Government high school and two *balwadis* are functioning in the village.

Public Distribution System

The ration shop is functioning in a rented building.

Graveyard

There are five graveyards separately for five communities. Communities like Asaris, Chettiars and Pallars hold funerals on the bank of the oorani.

Women's Association

There are three SHGs sponsored by World Vision of India. Apart from savings and micro credit, the members of the SHGs engage in social development activities. They were able to stop gambling in public and the sale of arrack in the Panchayat area, but with great difficulty.

The Relationship between the Panchayat and the Village Institutions

All the village institutions have in one way or the other been useful and helpful to the Village Panchayat. The NGO is very much associated with the Panchayat. Several items of welfare work are being carried out by the NGO. The youth and the women attend the Gram Sabha meetings. In consultation with caste association leaders, the Panchayat work is carried out amicably. Their opinions are well taken by the Panchayat.

The President is the Chairperson of Parent-Teachers Association through which whole village community was mobilised to upgrade the middle school into a high school. A local resident donated five acres of land for the school. Philanthropists from the Muslim community donated for construction of the building and the compound wall, and the villagers contributed for purchasing furniture. Three teachers are employed by the PTA from the contributions of students which is Rs. 3 per head per month. The Village Panchayat plays a key role in these activities. A watchman is also employed. The entire functioning of the school is due to the initiative of the community.

A Reference for Caste Rivalry

Though there is no open rivalry among the various caste groups in Kakkoor Panchayat area, the SC and the Thevar communities entertain suspicions towards one another. When some outsiders, particularly of the Thevar community, developed a feeling that the SC community is dominating in this area, they attempted to stop the sanction for the high school to this Panchayat. They feared that if any caste rivalry develops their wards in the school would be the vicitims of the conflict since the SCs are the majority. But the rest of the communities of this Panchayat joined with the SCs to get the sanction for the school. With the help of the MLA and the opposition party leader they successfully got the school upgraded into a high school. Now students of all communities, including Thevars, are studying in the school. In the past six years no untoward incident has happened.

During the assembly elections, a dispute between two young men of Thevar and SC Pallar communities became an issue. A case was registered in the police station. However, a peace committee was constituted and the problem was settled amicably.

During 1996-97, when the statue of Muthuramalinga Thevar at Muthukulathur was damaged, tension prevailed in all villages.

But, at Kakkoor, there was no problem. The President and her community leaders openly announced that the issue did not occur in their village and the leaders of all the communities advised restraint. In spite of this propaganda, a few members of the Thevar community asked the police to provide protection and so a police DSP came to verify the situation. After learning of the action of the President, the DSP appreciated it and asked her to ensure peace among the communities. Nothing happened at Kakkoor. This adherence to law and order even during a time of tension earned a good name for the President and her family members. Due to this they now enjoy a proximity to Police and Revenue Department officials.

Political Parties

All political parties function in Kakkoor. The DMK and the AIADMK are the two dominant parties and others such as the TMC, the BJP, the PMK, the MDMK, the Puthiya Tamilagham, the Dalit Panthers, the Makkal Tamildesam, the Tamil Munnetra Kazhagam are all present in the Kakkoor Panchayat area. Petty issues develop among these parties such as removal of the notice of one party by the other. But these disputes are solved peacefully. There is no permanent building for any political party. The party office bearers used to give their opinions on Panchayat activities. They are well taken while taking decisions.

Village Economy

Farming is the main occupation of the majority of the people and they possess land, mostly rainfed. About 150 borewells are available for irrigation. They grow cotton, chilly and paddy as the main crops. Ragi and millet are also grown in rainfed areas, but not to a large extent. In most of the years, due to the failure of the monsoon, the villagers suffer and they do not get sufficient employment opportunities. All the families rear milch animals. The IRDP loan has been availed of by more than 100 families, but most of them do not repay the money. So the milk society is not functioning properly. In Kakkoor all the communities rear goats. Now the youth are not coming forward to continue this traditional practice of goat rearing. They try to get visa and seek employment abroad. Cutting of karuvelan (wood tree) and preparation of charcoal is a good business. Poor families are engaged in this trade. Brick kiln is another source of employment.

Her Performance

Poomayil understood that only by bringing various schemes to the villagers she could earn a name. Hence she used to establish good rapport with the Union officials. Her openness and direct talk with officials are very useful in maintaining good relationship with the officials. She was able to mobilise funds from the Union for various activities like provision of Panchayat building, desilting of ooranis, provision of handpumps and installation of a ring well.

As the MP belonged to her party, she got Rs.2.75 lakhs for the construction of the building for the newly upgraded Government high school. From the MLA Fund she got Rs. 1.50 lakh to lay roads. In spite of repeated meetings with the District Councillor, she could not get any fund from him. The District Councillor favoured Presidents of his caste.

Samathuvapuram

It was proposed to construct a Samathuvapuram in the village of the Union Chairman. But sufficient space was not available there. Upon learning of this, Poomayil, in consultation with her community leaders, contacted the ex-MLA, who belonged to her community. The ex-MLA contacted a Muslim representative who had settled abroad and influenced him to part with his lands which were lying waste in Kakkoor. In this way she prepared the groundwork and contacted the Adi Dravida Welfare Officer who was responsible for identification of a suitable site for the Samathuvapuram.

In the meantime, the members of the Thevar community opposed the sanction of the Samathuvapuram in the fear that the area already dominated by SCs would further be consolidated by the SCs. But the ex-MLA and the then Opposition Leader helped in establishing the Samathuvapuram in Kakkoor Village.

The President took this issue to the Panchayat medai, the monthly meet with the District Collector and assured that the construction would be completed without any problem. Out of 100 houses, 25 houses were constructed by Poomayil. The work did not bring any profit. Instead she suffered a loss of Rs. 1000 for each unit. In spite of that she did not feel sorry as the balance amount was settled by the Union administration whereas another contractor who got the construction work of 25 houses could not complete them within the allotted amount. He had to borrow money for construction from a private money lender. The undue delay pushed the contractor into a crisis as payment of about Rs. 3 lakh was pending.

Public Distribution System (PDS)

When the distribution of essential commodities became a problem due to more number of cardholders and lack of adequate quota, Poomayil took steps to bifurcate the shop into two and ensured the prescribed quota to the eligible people. There was no complaint as the employee in the rationship was a local person in service for more than 15 years. He understood the village well and never favoured anybody unduly. The shop was functioning in a rented building. Poomayil took steps to get sanction for a new building.

Activities Carried out by the Panchayat

As the roads were in a bad condition, attention was given to improving all the roads. Metalling was provided in 3 roads for 900 metres at a cost of around Rs.1.35 lakh. When drinking water was not available, an open well was dug at a cost of Rs. 1.00 lakh. A culvert and a small bridge were built. Gravelling of a mud road was undertaken. Under JVVT, 150 metre length of cement concrete road was provided at a cost of Rs. 1.40 lakh. When 20 group houses were allotted to Kakkoor, the selection of beneficiaries was done in the Gram Sabha and with the involvement of the beneficiaries, all the 20 houses were constructed by Poomayil herself. Two TV rooms with platform were provided in two hamlets.

By frequent visits to the TWAD office and by continuously raising the drinking water problem in Panchayat media, Poomayil got the TAWD to provide a water tank and pumping motor to Kakkoor at a cost of Rs. 1.10 lakh. All the work except those of TWAD were executed by Poomayil. Her husband looked after the contract work. Her relatives were engaged in the construction activities. Her unmarried sister helps her in looking after the family and so she has time to regularly visit the Panchayat Union and other offices in connection with the Panchayat activities. The construction of buildings is not very profitable but she gets 5 per cent profit after giving commissions to the officials concerned at the rate of 5 per cent.

Panchayat Administration

Poomayil convenes the Panchayat Council meetings regularly. Out of 9 members, 6 are male and 3 are female. Five members regularly attend the meeting. The rest are engaged in business or private employment and so they do not attend regularly. The meetings go on smoothly. The Vice-President is a lawyer by profession, very cooperative with Poomayil. He never demands any commission. The Gram Sabha meetings are also convened regularly. There is good response from the public and around 150 to 200 members regularly attended the meetings. The income and expenditure statement is read out by the Vice-President or by an elderly member who is a teacher by profession. The SHG women and youth voice various demands in the Gram Sabha meetings. They raise a volley of questions. Poomayil replies to all the questions.

Tax Revision

The house tax was raised from Rs. 5 to 11 for huts, from Rs. 11 to 22 for tiled houses, and from Rs. 22 to 44 for *pucca* houses. Earlier the shops were taxed at random. Now Rs. 44 is collected as tax. Now the house tax receipts come to Rs. 7,800. Earlier it was only Rs. 3,800. The fishing rights were not properly auctioned. Poomayil herself paid the minimum amount and allowed the people to take the fish free from the tank. The house tax is not fully collected before the stipulated period. But the due balance after collection is paid by Poomayil herself so as to get the matching grant from the government. Poomayil does not know about the formation of committees and their functions. She used to refer only to the Peace Committee which has been in place in the Panchayat traditionally.

She used to meet the nurse during her visits and help her in mobilising children for immunization. The nurse's quarters was in a damaged condition. In spite of repeated petitions and personal meetings, the health officials did not repair it and so the nurse was not staying in the quarters. Earlier the nurse stayed there and attended to all deliveries. When a theft occurred in her quarters, the nurse vacated it and got a transfer. The new nurse is not as duty concious as the previous nurse. Poomayil has to supervise her and ask her to attend to her assigned duties. The Panchayat office is in a new building, electrified, well furnished, with toilet and water facility. The records are kept at the Panchayat office. The Panchayat clerk is a B.Com. graduate and so knows about administration. There are two OHT operators and one sweeper.

The Panchayat has 68 tubelights, 16 sodium vapour lights and 36 bulbs as streetlights. But due to low voltage, the tube lights are not functioning properly. There are 14 public taps in the village and 16 taps at the Samathuvapuram. Due to the failure of the monsoon, drinking water shortage is being experienced. Moreover the water in general is not of good taste. So people prefer the oorani water as it is of good taste.

Village Common

There are 4 ooranis out of which two serve as drinking water sources. There are two kanmois in which trees are grown under the Social Forestry scheme and once in three years about 5,000 to 6,000 rupees are earned by the Panchayat from these. There are three threshing floors which are very much useful. There are 10 tamarind trees grown by private parties in Panchayat poramboke. They pay Rs. 5 per tree to the Panchayat.

There are encroachments in Pillayarkovil thidal and at Karupasamy koil area and in one oorani. They are enjoyed by individuals belonging to the Thevar and the Konar communities and they could not be evicted as they have the patronage of the government. The temple area encroachments enjoyed by a Thevar could not be evicted since caste rivalry would emerge. Most of the encroachments are mainly in Revenue poramboke. If these are given to the Panchayat, they will be looked after properly by the Panchayat.

Perception

1. Regarding Panchayati Raj, Poomayil feels that in the New Panchayati Raj System, funds are directly devolved from the Government and the reservation for women is a good opportunity for womenfolk. The three-tier system is not helpful as the village people's felt needs are not properly looked into by the upper tiers.
   Poomayil used to get assistance from her husband when she received communications from various offices. Her husband's encouragement and guidance are the basic sources of her strength and her success.
2. Regrading development, Poomayil suggested that the government must come to the rescue of farmers and landless labourers by introducing more schemes to generate employment opportunities through agriculture.
3. The SHGs need more encouragement and training facilities for improvement of skills and capacity so that they can produce some marketable articles during the off season.
4. With regard to politics, the political parties give respect to women Presidents as their services are needed for canvassing votes from among women. If the reservation is not provided, the political parties will not turn to the women.
5. Women's status has now improved due to the SHGs and their public activities. But alcohol addicted men resorting to wife beating in rural areas is widely prevalent. The bankers do not release the revolving fund

sanctioned to SHGs as most of the members are defaulters of IRDP loans. Family economy is not under the control of women. Both men and women must think of development. If men are drunkards and unemployed, the earnings and savings of women will be wasted.

Future Plan

Poomayil has decided to contest again in the Panchayat elections as her husband is encouraging her and the TMC party is also encouraging her. As her family's regard has improved among other communities she has a bright chance. The other caste groups who appreciate Poomayil and her family's decent involvement in public activities will continue to extend support.

CASE - 20

PALI GRAM PANCHAYAT
ULUNDURPET BLOCK, VILLUPURAM DISTRICT

Socio-Economic Background

Mr. Thanga Viswanthan, aged 35, the President of Pali Village Panchayat, has studied upto the 10th standard. He is unmarried and lives with his mother and his younger brother. Belonging to the SC, he owns one acre of dry land and his brother runs a provision store. His house is a hut, electrified, only now provided with a toilet. His late father was a former Member of Parliament. His mother is a pensioner on account of his late father.

Political Socialisation

After finishing school, Thanga Viswanathan closely associated himself with the local DMK Party men. Most of the villagers are the supporters of the DMK Party. In the year 1986 he participated in the agitation organised by the DMK Party in protest against the domination of Hindi language and he was imprisoned for 47 days. Then he became the Vice-President of the youth wing at the Union level in the DMK Party.

With the encouragement of elders, he learnt to meet officials and was introduced to MLAs and high level functionaries of the party. When the Panchayat elections were declared, he was asked by the party to contest. There were four candidates and of them two were more educated than him and the other two were older to him. In spite of all this he won by a margin of 170 votes.

He visited all the households and he was accompanied by the youth and the supporters of the party. Though he belonged to the DMK, the party did not give much attention to the local elections. Instead they mobilised votes for the other two-tiers since that phase of the election was on party basis. The higher level functionaries contested only for the higher level bodies. Hence they could not spare their time for the local election. His victory was achieved mainly because of his social service activities in the village.

Village Setting

It is a multi-caste village but the dominant community is the SC. There are more than 500 SC families in the Panchayat area. Vanniars and Udayars are the next dominant communities in the Panchayat. Konars, Chettiars and Potters are also living in the village. There are three settlements in the Panchayat, Pali, Colony, Pali new Colony and Seikh Hussain Pettai. About 150 Muslim families are living in Seikh Hussain Pettai. There is a mosque in the Pettai.

As there are two primary schools and one high school, most of the villagers are educated. Particularly among the SC community a large number of persons are well educated and employed in good positions. In this way the village of Pali has attained a reputation. There are teachers, lawyers, Central and State government employees, drivers, conductors in the village. The former court Judge, Justice Swamithurai, who is now a member of the State Human Rights Commission, belongs to Pali village. He still helps and guides the villagers.

Religious Institution

Natraj temple, Pillayar temple and Mariamman temple are the big temples. There are a number of smaller temples belonging to various sections of the SC community. The SC community is grouped into several clans and families. There are differences within the SC community.

Political Parties

The DMK is the predominant party. Next to the DMK, the AIADMK is the popular party. There are other parties, namely the MDMK, the CPI and the TMC. The DMK gained popularity and the party employed individuals to influence the villagers to support the DMK. Moreover, there was one representative from the village who contested in the Assembly elections from the DMK Party. The constituency was a reserved one. As the opportunity was given to Pali village, the villagers fully involved themselves in the DMK Party's campaign for the success of their own village candidate as MLA. But unfortunately he was defeated. But in this process, the DMK party consolidated its influence over the villagers irrespective of caste and class.

Village Economy

Agriculture is the main source of income. There are about 100 irrigation wells, of which 20 have electric pumps and about 20 farmers use oil engines. Paddy, groundnut, and sugar cane are the major crops grown in the village by the farmers. Black gram is the main crop in the dry land. Two tanks are rainfed: one is a PWD tank and the other is a Union tank. There are 3 ponds under the Panchayat.

The PWD tank is very big, with an area of 250 acres. About 75 per cent of the villagers own land and most of them are small farmers. Due to non-availability of adequate rainfall the tank is not full. Milch animal rearing is also a practice in the village. There is a milk society but now it has become defunct due to inefficient management by the elected board of directors. There is maladministration also. There are seven SHGs functioning with the guidance of two NGOs, namely SEED and the Ramakrishna Ashram. One group hâs availed of the revolving fund. There is no comprehensive information from the NGOs or the groups. The SHG members attend the Gram Sabha meeting. The SHGs guided by the Ramakrishna Ashram have proposed to start milk vending through the Ashram. The NGOs and the SHGs do not make use of the Panchayat properly. But the SHG members are now acquiring awareness through group activities. The youth are not properly organised so far. Recently the Ramakrishna Ashram conducted a meeting for the youth and advised them to form an association. The youth frankly comment on the activities of the Panchayat and the Departments of the Government. Once a contractor used sub-standard quality material in the construction of a school building which was discovered by some young men. The contractor was warned and asked to set right the construction. Then they reported the problem to the Panchayat President. He met the contractor and the deficiency was corrected. There is an Ambedkar Youth Mandram but it does not engage in any serious activities.

Thanga Viswanathan, with the help of the SCs, formed a committee to install Ambedkar's statue. With great effort the statue was brought from Vellore. As the preparatory work was not yet completed, the opening ceremony has not yet been conducted. It is delayed due to lack of adequate money. Thanga Viswanathan is persuading the SC youth to extend their support to the fund raising.

Scheduled Caste *vs.* Backward Caste

Even though there is no serious dispute between SCs and BCs, the BCs opposed the selection of a site for the PDS in the SC colony as it is far away from the other end. In the meantime, the PDS was functioning in a rented building at Seikh Hussain Pettai. When the fund was allocated for the construction of a *pucca* building, the building was constructed at Seikh Hussain Pettai itself as it is considered common to both SC and BC. There is one part-time PDS functioning in the Panchayat building itself. Every month on two different days the commodities are distributed in Pali main village and in Seikh

Hussain Pettai, as there are 450 cards and 350 cards earmarked for the respective outlets.

In general the villagers are very much cooperative. But some families belonging to the SC have sent petitions against the President out of envy. The officials conducted an enquiry and found no mistakes in his administration. Youth leadership is still not yet recognised in the village. Hence the elders used to find fault with Thanga Viswanathan without any real basis.

His Perception of Panchayati Raj

The provision for reservation for women and *Dalits* and for independent power and responsibility to the Village Panchayat is a very good arrangement according to Thanga Viswanathan. He understands the various dimensions of Panchayati Raj. He used to read newspapers and books to understand the Panchayat and government activities. His close association with officials was very much useful to tackle the Vice-President and the clerk when they failed to cooperate. The clerk was dismissed and the Vice-President was replaced successfully. It is only by reservation that an SC became President in Pali. So far only BC Presidents have administered the Panchayat.

On Development

More schemes to improve agriculture, irrigation sources and to provide employment opportunities are essential to bring about progress in rural areas. The SHGs are getting awareness but economic activities are not introduced to them. It is only by sustainable productive activities that the villagers can augment income and improve their economic standard. There should be elders and opinion makers in the village and through them the government schemes could be availed of and guidance could be received to plan life in the rural areas.

On Social Justice

The attitude of BCs towards the SC has not yet changed. Some of the creamy layer among the SCs do not respect the poor SC families. It is by showing solidarity that untouchability can be removed and not by the enactment of laws. No affluent SC family is interested to live in the villages along with other poor SC families.

His Performance

Thanga Viswanathan is very regular in conducting Panchayat meetings. There are nine Ward Members. Of them six are men and three are women. Almost all of them regularly attend the meetings. The women Members used to raise their voice to get facilities for their wards. In general the women Members took their role seriously and tried to outwit their male counterparts so as to get recognition from the people. As for the Gram Sabha, around 75 to 100 members used to attend but women's attendance was always very poor. In spite of preparatory work to mobilise more number of participants, the villagers who engage themselves in agricultural activities do not give importance to attending the Gram Sabha. The general public from Hussain Pettai, the Muslim area, do not attend the Gram Sabha, but the Members representing their ward attend regularly. The maintenance of tanks and other farm related activities have been frequently questioned in the Gram Sabha meetings. The President had to explain the follow up measures taken by the Panchayat. Due to the Gram Sabha, the work carried out in each ward is known to the public and so the villagers question why their ward is not provided with certain facilities. At this juncture the President explains the funding system and how various types of funds are allocated to the Panchayat. The Gram Sabha is slowly picking up after SHG members started attending and, in course of time, it will be a good forum.

The functioning of the health sub-centre was not proper. People asked the Panchayat to report the problem to the Health Department officials. After several complaints, the nurse was transferred and a new nurse was posted. She is doing well but not staying in the centre. The electricity supply was disconnected to her quarters without any notification even to the Panchayat. The sectoral departments do not consider the Panchayat as the responsible institution in this regard. But, if they need any help for organising camps, they come and ask for help from the

Panchayat. The Panchayat has not yet gained adequate power and hence this type of disregard is experienced.

Panchayat Income and Expenditure

The average annual income is around Rs. 2.0 lakh only. The major source is the Finance Commission (grant of Rs. 1,71,094). The next source is stamp duty share (Rs. 25,474). The house tax collection is very limited (Rs. 3,863). The expenditure items are payment to EB (Rs. 50,000 per year), on water supply maintenance (about Rs. 20,000), on street maintenance (Rs. 40,000). Apart from this there is establishment charges, salary, TA and stationery (Rs. 20,000) per year.

Scheme Work

Under JVVT allocation Rs. 45,000, Rs. 74,000, and Rs. 1,32,000, under 10th Finance grant Rs. 14,000 and Rs. 17,000 have been received. In the year 1996-97 the EAS was directly given to the Village Panchayat. At a cost of Rs. 4.0 lakh 1.6 km of BT road was provided. Graveyard approach road maintenance was undertaken at two places at the total cost of Rs. 35,000 and concrete cement passway to drain out rainwater across the road was provided at a cost of Rs. 30,000. A cement concrete road at a cost of Rs. 74,000 was also provided.

The MLA was kind enough to sanction a grant for a threshing floor. To purchase a new motor for improvement of water supply, around Rs. 1,35,000 was spent. The MLA belongs to the President's party and he maintains good relationship with him.

The MLA further sanctioned Rs. 1.0 lakh for the provision of a cement concrete road. The District Councillor and the Union Councillors have also allocated their grants to the Village Panchayat. Cement concrete road was provided for 135 metres at a cost of Rs. 1,75,000 from their funds.

Group houses (20 numbers) were constructed. Thanga Viswanathan visits Ulunthurpet Union office everyday and so he is able to complete all the works in time with their advice and consultation. He himself executes most of the work, and there are some profits and losses too.

Record Maintenance

He used to verify all the records regularly and without his knowledge the clerk cannot do anything. The audits are completed without any major objections. Officials expect money but they do anything for money.

Sectoral Departments Activities

Thanga Viswanathan organised a medical camp, an Animal Husbandry medical camp, an AIDS awareness campaign, and a cultural programme and awareness camp on small savings successfully. But, to organise all these programmes, he had to spend his own money.

Administration

There are one clerk and four OHT operators in the Panchayat. The clerk did not do his duties properly. He was a post-graduate and he clashed with the President, who warned him and then, in consultation with the officials, dismissed him. The villagers had the practice of connecting a pipeline to the main line to draw water without authorisation. After giving a warning, Thanga Viswanathan disconnected all the lines and regulated the water supply. Individual connections are now streamlined and the amount due is also collected. He organised awareness camps to create awareness about the CRSP and DANIDA toilet schemes among the people but they did not respond positively. Under IRDP, 17 beneficiaries availed of loans and properly utilised them as per his advice.

Thanga Viswanathan is happy that he improved the drinking water supply: 50 public taps are provided, 13 HP are made available. He provided 70 streetlights, 10 sodium vapour lamps and they arc properly maintained. Cement concrete road and group houses were provided.

His Leadership

Due to his position as President, Thanga Viswanathan is able to move with the officials and political leaders. He was one among the core team which tried to bring a college to Ulundurpet. In spite of the concerted efforts they could not get a Government college or a private college. It is a felt need of the people. Money is essential to maintain respect in public life. Thanga Viswanathan does not earn anything but has a debt of Rs. 1.0 lakh. He does not yet have a *pucca* house. Yet he finds pleasure in serving the people.

His Vision

The village has certain traditional regulations and Thanga Viswanathan wishes to sustain them. He wants to give assistance to the educated youth to get employment in private or government sector. He wants to get the maximum output from the farm sector and by this he wishes to make his village a model one.

CASE – 21

PERUMALAGARAM GRAM PANCHAYAT KORADECHERY UNION, THIRUVARUR BLOCK

Socio-Economic Background

Mrs. Punitha Magalingam, the President of Perumalagaram Village Panchayat, is 42. She completed her school final. She is married and has two sons and one daughter. She belongs to the BC Vellalar community. Her family is nuclear. She lives in her own tiled house. The house is in the Thanjavur style with big and spacious halls and needed facilities. Her husband is a farmer owning 10 acres of wet land. He is also engaged in brick kiln industry. They own a tractor which is looked after by her son.

Recruitment

Punitha Magalingam faced stiff opposition, as four women contested against her. Out of them two were from the SC and the others from the BC. The SC women were fielded by the SC community. They ensured the support of the SC people to the SC candidates by obtaining promises from them. Punitha did not have any political background but her husband is the secretary of the local DMK unit and a close associate of Mr. Stalin, the Mayor of Chennai. He is also a former President. The Village Committee decided to ask her to contest in the election. In a stiff competition, with the help of the DMK youth, the friends of her sons and her family, Punitha canvassed in the village. The DMK Party cadres helped in the canvassing. At first she did not evince any seriousness in the canvassing as she did not have experience. But, after understanding the people's expectations, she went to all the streets, met the people and sought their support. By continuous campaign, personal meetings and door to door campaign, she was able to win the election by a margin of 500 votes. As the result was an unexpected blow to the SC community, the members of the SC community resorted to violence and they broke the tubelights in the streets. The members belonging to the SC used to join together and show their strength by resorting to strikes in the farming activities. During the Parliamentary elections, they joined the Communist Party of India. Further the landless labourers of the SC community struck work unexpectedly on Punitha's farm. They completed the harvest but did not come to bundle the harvested paddy. Due to their illegal strike, Punitha suffered a heavy loss.

About 25,000 was spent for the election by way of printing notice and poster, engaging public address system and meeting the food expenses of the supporters. The DMK Party cadres openly sought the support of the public on behalf of Punitha. Further most of the caste Hindus supported her, as her husband was the President of the Village Welfare Association. The two candidates of the SC community split the SC votes. This was a factor responsible for Punitha's success. The defeated candidates took the contest seriously and even after the election they did not talk to her. But as President she could not entertain any enmity and so she voluntarily talked to them.

Village Setting

Perumalagaram is a small village having one hamlet, namely Krishnakottakam. In the main village of Perumalagaram, caste Hindu communities like Vellalars, Konars, Kallars, Padayatchis and Isai Vellalars live. Scheduled Caste families also live there. In Krishnakottakam only SCs and Vellalars are living.

The Vellalars and the SCs are the major communities in this Panchayat. Most of the caste Hindus are landowners and the SCs are landless labourers. They are member of Communist parties. The Scheduled Caste people and the Vellalars have Village Welfare Associations separately. The Welfare Association of Perumalagaram Village meets once a month. Issues related to agricultural activities are discussed in the meetings. The wage disputes in the agricultural operations are also discussed. At the time of the discussion on wage disputes, the representatives of the SC community used to come over there. Temple celebrations and family problems, other common problems like sanitation, streetlights and drinking water supply distribution are also discussed in the Welfare Association meetings. The Village Welfare Association has a new President as Punitha's husband relinquished his position because of an understanding with his wife during the Panchayat election. The Vice-President of the Village Panchayat is now holding the position of the President of the Village Welfare Association. The Village Welfare Association used to communicate with the Panchayat and government officials on common causes.

Village Temples

Mahamayee, Ayyanar, Sivan, Perumal and Vinayakar are the deities in the village temples earmarked separately for the above gods. Except in Mahamayee temple in all the temples the *poojari* is a Brahmin. The SC community struggled against the monopoly of the caste Hindus over the processions of deities during the celebrations. They succeeded in their attempt by getting one day of procession for the SC community. There is no untouchability in practice. The SC people are free to visit the temples and conduct Ayyappan *Poojari* etc. inside the temple. It is observed that the SCs are consolidating their unity and are always on vigil. Any minor disrespect to anyone of them is considered disrespect to their whole community.

Youth Association

The youth of Perumalagaram Village do not have a separate association for themselves but they join the youth of Koradachery, the nearby town and engage in youth activities like sports, attending political meetings and helping the community during temple celebrations. They do not have any orientation in Panchayat activities.

Caste Association

When the Vellalars took the initiative to form a caste association, Punitha's husband discouraged them by pointing out that it is a small village and that all caste groups are living together without any enmity and hence it is unwarranted.

The SC community does not have any caste association, but, as a community, they are consolidated. They induce their Ward Members to represent their problems to the Panchayat. They participate in the Gram Sabha meetings with the intention of knowing how much money has been spent for the SCs in the Panchayat.

The Self-Help Groups

There are many SHGs but Punitha's could not give the details. One SHG of a caste Hindu community used to meet her to use a common place for their women's group activities. The SC people have one SHG. They requested her to permit them to hold their SHG meeting in the Panchayat hall. The SHG women do not show interest in attending the Gram Sabha meetings. They engage in savings activities rather than understanding the village Panchayat. Once an SHG reported the illegal sale of alcohol and by telephoning the police authorities and with the help of women, Punitha was able to stop it.

The Political Parties

As all the SC people joined the CPI it is the dominant party in the village. The DMK is the second largest party. The AIADMK and the TMC Parties are also present. Unfortunately, in the DMK Party, the majority of the members are landholders and in the CPI all the members are agricultural labourers. Hence the DMK is regarded as the enemy of the CPI.

The office bearers of all the political parties used to informally meet Punitha's husband and share their opinions on the Panchayat activities. The husband used to report their feelings to his wife. Their opinions are well taken by the Panchayat.

Perception of Panchayati Raj

To Punitha if the Panchayati Raj System is sustained local leadership will emerge and people will be empowered. The reservation for women and decentralized planning are the major features of the Panchayati Raj System. She used to read the Act as she owned the book. Besides, from the communications periodically circulated by NGOs involve who themselves in Panchayat activities, she used to get details about governance. After her association with the Women Presidents Asociation, she has gained a lot in terms of leadership.

On Development

Development could be achieved through the initiative of individuals instead of depending on the government. The government providing necessary infrastructure facilities is basic to development. Health, education, transportation, irrigation source maintenance are the major steps leading to development. The present day Village Panchayat does not have development orientation as it acts as the agent of the government.

On Village Economy

Agriculture is the main occupation to more than five hundred families in the village. Due to continuous increase of the cost of agricultural inputs and wages, the farmers could not get any profit. So the poor families, irrespective of caste, should be given due assistance, particularly those of the SC community. The farmers who possess irrigation wells produce cotton also along with paddy. Gingelly, green gram and black gram are also grown.

Animal husbandry once provided good income to the villagers. Now it is declining. About a decade ago, Punitha's family possessed more than two hundred goats. But due to non-availability of shepherds and fodder they sold the goats. Moreover the traditional fodder plants are not grown due to the degradation of the environment. The agricultural practice has also changed from manure to fertilizer and so cattle rearing is now not practised seriously by the farmers. In spite of this handicap about 200 families still rear cattle. The youngsters, after education, do not get employment in the village or even in nearby towns as there are no big industries to accommodate them.

On Social Justice

Reservation and other special treatment have been extended to the SCs to improve their socio-economic life, but there are a large number of very poor families in other castes also. Hence the government should give attention to all the poor irrespective of caste.

On Gender Issue

Gender equality is not yet realised in villages but the status of women is improving after the reservation introduced in the local bodies. The SHG is a good approach for empowering women. But they need political orientation. The Association for Women Presidents is a milestone in the process of changing the mindset of bureaucrats. Men are now-a-days encouraging women's participation in public activities, but they have not come forward to share the day-to-day responsibilities of the women. Unless there is a change in the role perception, gender equality is only a slogan. Punitha's husband encouraged her and educated her in Panchayat administration, conducting of Gram Sabha meetings and drafting of resolutions. "Comparing my earlier life of a housewife, I am very happy to observe a positive change in my husband's mind as well as the minds of my sons after I became President," Punitha said. When canvassing for the assembly elections, Punitha actively participated in the campaign. This involvement brought her a name in the party circles.

On Polity

As her parents were the supporters of the Congress Party, Punitha did not like the DMK, but now she is serving as the women's wing convener of the DMK Party. The political ideology of any party could be implemented only when the concerned party assumes the power of government. At present there is a tendency among the people to support a party which gives more populist schemes to the people. People do not give much importance to the ideology of the parties.

Panchayat Activities – Panchayat Meeting

There are four Wards and nine Members in the Panchayat. All these Members regularly attend the meetings scheduled every month. The SC Members, both men and women, used to influence the other Members for allowing more benefits to the SCs. After attending a training programme and from self-learning, Punitha used to explain the importance of the Ward Members in educating the people about the significance of the New Panchayati Raj System.

The Ward Members expected more from the Panchayat as Punitha's husband is a key person in the DMK Party who could contact Ministers and bring needed help to the villagers.

Gram Sabha Meeting

As the Gram Sabha is a statutory forum, the Panchayat could do a lot of things through the Gram Sabha. When the aided school management delayed the appointment of a sanctioned additional teacher, the secretary of the school was asked to come to the Gram Sabha and explain his problem in front of the people as the public demanded action against the school management. After the Gram Sabha meeting, the management appointed one more teacher but the running of the school is not yet up to the people's expectation. In another meeting the non-availability of a toilet in the school was discussed and then with the donation by the teachers, a toilet was provided. It was possible to achieve these because the concerned parties took serious interest in the deliberations of the Gram Sabha. The SHG members attend the Gram Sabha meetings but the SC women's group is yet to show interest in attending. But the SC men and the youth attend. The number of participants in the Gram Sabha meetings is usually 150 to 160. If they find any mistake in the work executed by Panchayat they readily criticize it. After the reading out of the income and expenditure statement, a few used to raise their voice but all things are smoothly handled. The Panchayat administration is proper. Punitha used to verify the accounts and the 31 forms and the rest of the details are looked into by her husband. As the husband is helping in accounts maintenance, there is no fear of any mistakes. The Panchayat items of work are carried out mostly by the President and the Vice-President and contractors are avoided. She even encourages the Ward Members to take responsibility for executing the work to be carried out in their wards but they do not come forward to spend time for these activities.

Work Carried Out

A variety of items of work are carried out in Perumalagaram Panchayat. The major sources of funds are JVVT, EAS, SFC and Village Panchayat fund. In the year 1997-98, a bathing ghat, a culvert and metalling of a road were provided under JVVT at a cost of Rs. 1.57 lakh. Handpump and the arrangement for covering the OHT were done from Panchayat funds. Under EAS one kitchen shed and three TV rooms were constructed.

In the year 1998-99, 15 group houses were constructed, a *pucca* building for the PDS was constructed under EAS, two

OHTs were provided and a platform and retaining wall were provided near the public well. Altogether the cost was around Rs. 16.77 lakh. By approaching the Member of Parliament sanction was received for the construction of a community hall at a cost of Rs. 5.00 lakh. During the year 1999-2000 more importance was given to improving the road facilities. Blacktopping of road was carried out in the SC area and the bazaar area. Altogether around Rs. 11.55 lakh was spent on improving the roads from the SFC allocation. Under CRSP 5 individual household latrines were provided and all are in use. Women's sanitary complex is under construction with the help of the District Collector. Under JVVT, metalling of road was carried out and 5 SC poor families were provided houses. From the Panchayat fund a retaining wall was provided to the village tank at a cost of Rs.0.77 lakh. During 2000-2001, a cement concrete road, an additional bathing ghat and a culvert were provided. Apart from these activities, Punitha Mahalingam helped the poor in getting other benefits from various schemes.

Issues Regarding Common Property Resources

There are four tanks in the village and out of the four two are under the control of influential individuals. Punitha has not succeeded in retrieving the tanks from the individuals though she went up to the District Collector. It is a pending issue.

The coconut, tamarind and fuel wood trees are under the control of the Panchayat but the Village Welfare Association takes charge of them for a small amount and reaps large benefits. Only Rs. 1,450 from trees and Rs. 840 from fishing were earned by the Panchayat in the year 1999-2000. The Village Welfare Association re-auctions its rights. It is nothing but establishing the control of the traditional Panchayat over the formal Panchayat.

Normally 20 per cent of the Panchayat income is spent on electricity bills. (There are 163 streetlights, 3 TV centres for which electricity expenditure has to be incurred). The income from the house tax is only Rs. 10,000 to Rs. 12,000 as there are more number of huts in the village for which more tax could not be demanded.

Providing adequate drinking water is a problem in the hamlet of Krishakottakam. When the villagers met the Vice-President he directed them to Punitha without explaining the non-availability of funds in the Panchayat. As the people suffered a lot, a handpump was provided from her personal money.

Accounting and Auditing

As her husband is fully monitoring the accounts Punitha is free from fear. The extension officer of the Panchayat regularly visits, goes through the records and gives his guidance in the maintenance of the records and there is no serious objection raised by the auditing officials. Regarding the commission to officials, all the dealings of the officials are with her husband and so she does not know exactly how much is paid as commission to the officials.

Activities in Social Development

When the women's sanitary complex was sanctioned, it was on condition that a share should be given by the Panchayat. But, due to lack of funds in the Panchayat she could not make a promise. The District Collector made arrangements for the construction of the women's sanitary complex. Arrangements were made by the Panchayat, when a cultural troupe visited the village, to propagate public sanitation. The village health nurse visits regularly though she comes from a long distance of 7 km. There is good contact between the President and the nurse. Out of the 3 OHT operators employed in the Panchayat, one is a lady. When 20 coconut saplings were planted on the banks of the village tanks, the villagers did not cooperate to protect the same. The fencing was damaged and grazing cattle ate away the saplings.

Panchayat *vs.* Police

To prevent the sale of illicit alcohol the police seek the help the Panchayat to organise public meetings etc., but when complaints are made against the menace of gambling, the police do not take any action. If any dispute due to alcoholism is reported the police do not come to take action. They just make a show that a meeting is held in the presence of the Panchayat President. The number of youngsters who fall in the trap of alcoholism is increasing steadily. When an individual encroached upon the vacant site in front of the temple, other individuals, in protest against the encroacher, occupied other spaces available. Then a complaint was lodged with the Police. The policemen came, but did not take any action against the encroacher. The other persons voluntarily removed their plants in protest. The encroacher had earlier encroached upon a public land and later sold the public property. Punitha reported that the Revenue Department is normally the most corrupt Department and it will do and undo things for money. The Panchayat has no links with the Revenue Department.

Her Future Plan

Her family members anticipated some problems when a woman runs the Panchayat, but things have moved smoothly. There has been no problem in the Panchayat. The tenure is getting completed successfully. Punitha expressed her desire to contest again but her son advised her not to contest and said that other women can take up this responsibility. After assuming the responsibility, from the association of women leaders, she understood more about women empowerment and the problems in the process. And so she would work for women whether she contests or not. But through the Panchayat a lot of things could be achieved, particularly for women.

CASE – 22

POLUKURICHI GRAM PANCHAYAT
CHENTHAMANGALAM BLOCK, NAMAKKAL DISTRICT

Socio-Economic Background

Mrs. P. Kannamma, the President of the Polukurichi Village Panchayat, belongs to the Sakkiliyar SC caste. She is a Hindu of

47 years. She has studied up to the 9th standard and lives with her husband, son and daughter-in-law. Her husband is working as sub-registrar in Tiruvannamalai District, and her son has studied B.E. and is searching for a job. The daughter-in-law is working as a teacher. She owns a tiled house with electricity, toilet facilities and individual water tap connection. She is a housewife, not doing anywork apart from the Panchayat work.

Her father was a contractor and took up many items of work in the Panchayat and he carried out many development activities. Hence the people of this village Panchayat knew him very well and through him people knew her. There is another factor which helped her in the Panchayat election, namely her past social service done to the people. She used to help the people to get certificate from Government offices, benefits from service organisations and loans from banks. Her father established a good rapport with the Gounder caste people which helped her to get more votes.

Socio-Political Environment of the Village

The population of this Panchayat is 6,821. Of them 3,518 are males and 3,303 are females. There are three hamlets, namely Polukurichi, Kuttavangampatti and Narasingaputhur. Polukurichi has 1,709 families, Kuttarangampatti has 151, and Narasigaputhur has 140. There are four wards and 9 Ward Members in the Panchayat. Among them one is a woman.

There are 1,250 houses in the Panchayat area, of which 200 are *pucca* houses, 1,000 are tiled houses and 500 are huts. Sakkiliyars, Pallars, Parayars, Gounders, Chettiars, Vanniars, Muslims, Muthurajas, Barbers and Dhobis are living in the Panchayat. There are five wells, eight overhead tanks, 18 handpumps, 85 public tap connections, 10 motors, 4 primary schools, 5 noon-meal centres, one high school, 166 streetlights, 3 TV sets, 2 ration shops, one police station, one post office, one primary health centre, one Central Cooperative Bank, one nationalized bank, one Housing Cooperative Society and one Milk Cooperative Society. The Panchayat has given 45 individual house water tap connections.

One half of the agricultural land is being cultivated through well irrigation and 35 per cent of the remaining land is rainfed. Farmers cultivate paddy, tabacco, banana, turmeric, onion, sugarcane and some cereals. All the political parties have their units in the Panchayat and of them the DMK and the AIADMK are dominant in terms of strength. The youth have Cine Fans clubs. Women have four SHGs.

Recruitment

There were five candidates in the election. Four persons contested in the election against Kannamma. She won the election by a margin of 350 votes.

Development / Democracy

Development, according to Kannamma, is nothing but leading a healthy decent human life with needed basic facilities without affecting nature. People should have livelihood security and they should be independent. They should have social respectability. Development could be explained not in terms of money but in terms of the conditions in which people live and how happy they are. Kannamma complained that women's health is not taken care of by the women themselves. This matter she gathered from the ANM. This perception led her to work for women's health. She has a plan to provide protected drinking water to all. Further she has determined to focus more on oilseed production through agriculture instead of growing crops by mining water. She has a dream of establishing tiny and cottage industries to make use of the waste to produce saleable products. Some of the families from this Panchayat shifted to other states like Kerala and Karnataka for doing agriculture and building work. If the government started small and village industries and cottage industries in the villages they could have avoided this kind of large scale exodus from this Panchayat. The government should take necessary steps to start village industries and cottage industries in order to prevent the migration from the villages.

Performance: Monthly Meetings

Nearly all the Ward Members participate in the monthly meetings of the Panchayat. Particularly the women and *Dalit* members actively participate in the meetings and ask the President to meet the basic needs of their wards. The women Panchayat Ward Members exert pressure on the President to provide the basic amenities to their wards. Kannamma moves closely with all the Ward Members and clearly explains to them the income of the Panchayat and the financial position. She assures them that, on the basis of this income, she would distribute the work to the Wards. All the Panchayat work is divided among the Ward Members on the basis of their urgent needs. There is no quarrel between the President and the Ward Members and the meetings are conducted very smoothly and cordially.

Gram Sabha Meeting

Around 200 people participate in the Gram Sabha meetings. Kannamma takes serious steps by printing notice and distributing the same to all the Ward Members and village elders. They are pasted in public places of the villages like hotels, petty shops, corners of the streets, tea shops and distributed to the SHG members. She arranges mike announcement in all the villages. The President herself personally invites the SHG members to attend the Gram Sabha meetings.

Around 30 *Dalit* women attend the Gram Sabha meeting and they demand basic facilities, particularly loan facilities. The SHG members attend the meetings and ask the Panchayat to arrange for loans to start small trade in the village itself. After the formation of SHGs women member's participation has increased.

The Ward Members attend the Gram Sabha meeting without fail. There is a general feeling among the people that the demands expressed to the President through the Gram Sabha have not been met and that there are a number of items of work being carried out in the villages which are not the felt needs of the people. But the Panchayat carries out such work because the government has given money for the same through schemes. People feel that it is a wastage of public money. This is the main reason for the poor attendance at the Gram Sabha meetings.

Government Programmes

In the year 1995-96 they got an earmarked grant of Rs. 94,000 and 10th Finance Commission grant of Rs.83,000. The amounts have been spent for laying roads, constructing small bridges, maintenance of drinking water wells and streetlights. In 1996-97 JVVT fund of Rs. 72,000 was spent for road work. In 1997-98 the shandy income of Rs. 48,000 from auction, Tenth Finance Commission grant of Rs. 2,00,600, JVVT fund of Rs. 4,22,900, Million Wells Scheme grant of Rs. 1,89,000, and Indira Housing Fund of Rs.5,40,000, were spent for construction of small bridges, formation of new street roads, construction of group houses, public latrines, additional school buildings and check dam. In 1998-99 State Finance Commission amount of Rs. 1.35 lakh, shandy auction income Rs. 0.54 lakh, Tenth Finance Commission grant of Rs. 1.35 lakh, JVVT amount of Rs. 2.285 lakh and Indira Housing Fund of Rs. 3.20 lakh were spent for extension of streetlights, formation of roads and construction of small bridges, construction of public latrines, laying concrete road, construction of colony houses and household latrines (36 Nos.). In 1999-2000, they got Rs. 5.44 lakh from the State Finance Commission, shandy auction income was Rs. 0.55 lakh, income from house tap connection Rs. 0.40 lakh, JVVT amount Rs. 2.04 lakh and all this was spent for extension of streetlights, purchase of new electric motor, laying of roads and construction of bridges, and extension of drinking water pipeline, construction of public latrine, laying of concrete road and construction of household latrines.

Linkage with other Departments

Kannamma moves well with the Social Welfare Department to get guidelines and marriage loans for the villagers. She approaches bank officials to get revolving funds for the SHG groups and the Highways Department for getting blacktopped roads laid. She often visits the BDO's office and the District Collector's office by which she taps all the resources for providing basic amenities to the villagers. When she visited the other sectoral Departments one or two times they did not pay attention to her words. After her repeated visits they were made to listen to her words and to extend all possible help to the Panchayat. This is her experience with the sectoral Departments.

Linkage with Other Tiers

Whenever she met the Union Councillor or the District Councillor she used to ask them to do some work for her village. The Union Councillor allotted some money for the construction of bridges for the village. Kannamma feels that there is no link among the three-tiers and that it is not good for the Panchayat system. She pointed out that it is difficult to contact the District Councillor and get some work done.

Linkage with People, Problems and Schemes Implemented in the Village

Kannamma was a social worker before she became the President of Polukurichi. So she is known to the people. She used to discuss with the people their basic needs. At the time of formation of roads, construction of small bridges or removal of encroachment she used to inform the people. A problem arose when she had to evict an encroacher in the village Natham at the time of the extension of the pipeline. The drinking water pipeline crossed the footsteps of the house. The house owner did not allow to demolish the footsteps. She approached the house owner and explained the importance of extending the pipeline. The Ward Members also explained the importance of this work and finally they convinced him. In each and every case the people resist because they have strong notions on each and every issue.

Perception about Panchayat

Kannamma knows about the New Panchayati Raj and its implications. She feels that reservation of seats for women and *Dalits*, Gram Sabha meetings, planning from below and people's participation are the key features of the new dispensation. Gram Sabha and reservation for women are both important in the Panchayati Raj institution. Reservation of seats for women would empower the women's leadership qualities and women could achieve freedom, and women could participate in the decision-making process. This was made possible only through this new system.

The Village Development

She underscored the basic needs of the rural areas, namely food to the poor, employment opportunity, good education, health facilities, water to drink. These needs have to be attended to by the Panchayats.

Human Rights

Since the President belongs to the SC, human rights violations are not permitted, particularly in the temples, tea stalls, and working places. The SC people move with other caste people freely.

Public Property

All common properties are well protected and they are enriched. Encroachments have been removed. Steps have been taken to develop common properties to get income from them. There is a lot of scope for generating income from the common properties.

Socialisation Process

At the time of the election Kannamma contested as an independent candidate, and, after the election, she has not joined any party because the people of this village supported her not on the basis of any party but on the basis of her family background, and the social work done by her in the village. If she had contested in the election on the basis of party, definitely she would have been defeated by another candidate. She is beyond political clutches.

Auditing System

Every three months the local officials do the auditing and correct the mistakes, if any, in the bills. Officials educate her as to how to write the accounts and submit the bills. So, this system is helpful and useful to the Panchayats. The officials of the BDO's office are very cooperative and helpful to clear the accounts. This system is good.

Formation of Committees

Kannamma formed two committees, namely Peace Committee and Vigilance Committee. Five members have to look after the JGSY work and inform the Panchayat about the progress of the work. She had no problem in the formation of the committees and in allotting the work to the committees. The Peace Committee looks after the social issues and settles disputes between the caste groups, if any. By and large the people maintain peace and harmony.

General Information

1. Since her husband works in the Government he reads the GOs and informs her about them and he helps her to get the Government programmes.
2. She has formed SHG groups, gone to banks to get revolving funds for the groups and started small trades for the groups.
3. Kannamma has advised the SHG groups to take up social issues, particularly women's issues.
4. She had gained experience earlier of how to move with officials and get things done in the Government offices. This was very useful after she occupied the President's post.

CASE – 23

RAMARPURAM GRAM PANCHAYAT AGASTHEESWARAM BLOCK, KANYAKUMARI DISTRICT

Socio-Economic Background

Mrs. Mary Jerald, the President of the Ramarpuram Village Panchayat, is a forty-year-old lady from a Christian family background. Educated up to the PUC, she is able to move on her own LML Trendy and is a member of a joint family. Her husband works in the Agriculture Department of the Kerala Government. Her elder son is studying in an engineering college and her daughter is doing her 12th standard. Her family's economic background provided the opportunity to think of public service. Being educated and hailing from a respected family Mary Jerald was well known among the villagers. She is independent and confident of doing her work on her own. She is also committed to public service. A woman with abundant love towards children she was also able to undertake the Panchayat activities.

Village Setting

Ramarpuram Village is located north of the Thovarai Panchayat Union. There are 7 hamlets scattered around, with Ramarpuram as the main village. The total population of the Panchayat is 3,478. Of them 1,697 are men and 1,779 are women. The SC and ST put together constitute 404 families. The total number of voters in the Panchayat is 2,437, which includes 1202 males and 1,235 females. The estimated total population resides in 1,075 households.

Facilities Available in the Panchayat

Sl. No.	*Details of Facilities*	*Number*
1.	TV rooms	7
2.	Community hall	1

(*Contd.*)

(Contd.)

Sl. No.	*Details of Facilities*	*Number*
3.	Libraries	3
4.	PDS	1
5.	OHT	5
6.	Handpumps	31
7.	Open wells	9
8.	Public taps	65
9.	Individual taps	186
10.	Streetlights	28
11.	Primary schools	3
12.	Higher secondary school	1
13.	Teacher training institute	1

There is no social problem in Ramarpuram Panchayat except the consuming of illicit liquor by which most of the money is being spent by the poor men. The two major religious groups in the village are Hindus and Christians and there are four places of worship respectively for both the religious groups but till now the Panchayat has not experienced any conflict between the two groups.

Perception of the Leader

Mary Jerald does not belong to any caste organisation or political party. She is a regular reader of newspapers and viewer of TV and widely travelled in India and abroad. She was determined to do some service to the people. She started the practice of helping her village people to receive benefits from the Government programmes before she became the Panchayat President. She realised the importance of service when elections were announced for Panchayats. The motto behind her contest was mere service. By spending Rs. 10,000 for the election she got elected by the margin of 65 votes. The family was instrumental in her becoming the President of the Panchayat.

The Panchayat

The Ramarpuram Panchayat comprises of 5 Wards with 9 Members. Of the nine one is from the SC that too a male and the others belong to BC and among the BC ones, there are three women. The Panchayat is dominated by the female population. The Panchayat office is located in the main village in a new building inside a complex with a PDS shop and a community hall. The members of the Panchayat are cooperative. The officials also cooperate with the Panchayat and the Panchayat has taken the lead in implementing various schemes and progarmmes. The Panchayat meetings are conducted regularly as per the norms.

The Details of the Meetings

Year	*No. of Panchayat Meetings*			*Total*
	O	S	E	
1996-97	3	—	2	5
1997-98	14	1	—	15
1998-99	13	—	3	16
1999-2000	10	1	—	11
2000-2001	9	1	—	10

The attendance during the Panchayat meetings is 100 per cent and it is rarely that one or two members are absent. For the Gram Sabha meetings the Panchayat gets 10 per cent quorum. Only 2 special Gram Sabha meetings were conducted. SC and ST women show much interest in attending the Gram Sabha meetings. As they are conducted in front the Panchayat office, the members find it easy to attend the meeting and discuss the items on the regular agenda issued by the State Government. They take at least two hours to discuss all the items on the agenda. During the Gram Sabha meetings there is no conflict.

The Performance

Mary Jerald, who does not have any political background, was able to perform her duties as the President of the Panchayat very well because of her independent decision-making, family support, cooperation of the officials and colleagues. She maintains cordial relations with the higher level political representatives also. As the District Panchayat Chairman belongs to her area, she could make use of the funds allotted to the District Panchayat. The first thing she assured the people was to solve the drinking water problem. She sank a new borewell and deepened wells. Thereby needed water was supplied to the people. The major items of work done by her are:

Year	*No. of works*	*Total (Rs.)*
1996-97	5	2,77,000
1997-98	7	4,57,893
1998-99	15	18,60,320
1999-2000	29	21,80,420
2000-2001	9	6,79,340

MP-LADP-MLA-LADP-NNT

On an average Mary Jerald was able to mobilize four lakhs of rupees every year through various schemes for rural development activities. In the year 1996-97 she mobilized Rs. 3,00,000 and in 1997-98 Rs. 4,50,000. She mobilized resources through the MP. She admits that service is not an easy task. She moved back and forth to get the schemes implemented in the villages. Yet another achievement of her was that she collected 100 per cent house tax in her Panchayat and was able to receive more funds as matching grant and the pending items of work have been completed with this money.

Mary Jerald, on receiving an application, a decision on the spot and determines the action, if necessary, and the beneficiary is taken her to the appropriate office on her scooter and the things are got done. The secret behind her success is her exposure to the outside world and her independent thinking. She has no fear or hesitation to approach anybody for a public cause. Further she is always open to criticism and correction. She is always caordial to all and she never antaganises people.

As for women's empowerment Mary Jerald feels that women are to be educated first and they must be provided with liberty to take decisions and the family has to support them. Economic independence will help women leaders and training is a must in the initial phase as the procedures are complicated. They will take time to learn. She faced audit objections and only during the last month training was provided that too at the fag end of her tenure. So timely training and support will help to make the Panchyat leader a perfect and effective manager of the Panchayat.

CASE – 24

SARUKKALAI GRAM PANCHAYAT PARAMAATHI BLOCK, NAMAKKAL DISTRICT

Socio-Economic Background

Mrs. P. Papu, the President of Sarukkalai Village Panchayat, is 35 years old, an SC woman of the Sakkiliyar caste and a Hindu by religion. She knows only to affix her signature. Even that she learnt from her daughter. She does not know how to read and write. She lives with her husband, two sons and one daughter. She lives in a colony house, having electricity but not having toilet facilities and individual tap connection. Her husband and she are engaged in agricultural activities as labourers since they have no land.

She has been working in a farm owned by an upper caste family. Since that particular upper caste (Gounder) is dominant they have decided to elect her as their candidate unanimously. The main decisions are taken by the Vice-President of Panchayat who belongs to the Gounder community. All the Ward Members, the Vice-President and the President are unaniomously elected in this Panchayat.

Socio-Political Environment of the Village

According to the 1991 census the population of this village is as follows. There are six hamlets in this Panchayat.

1.	Charkkali	127	606
2.	S. Pudupalayam	183	666
3.	Karungalipatti	150	241
4.	Kottakalpalayam	38	186
5.	Salappalayam	26	103
6.	Chinna Kattupalayam	10	49
		534	1,851

There are four wards and six Ward Members in the Panchayat. One SC male, and three males from BC and two females from BC are members of the Council. This Panchayat is situated 18 km southwest of Paramaathi Panchayat Union. There are 120 concrete houses, 512 tiled houses and 8 colony houses in the Village Panchayat. This Panchayat consists of different caste groups, namely Gounders, SCs, Barbers, *Dhobis* and Chettiars.

Facilities in the Village

Sl. No.	*Nature of Facility*	*Numbers*
1.	OHT	5
2.	Open wells	17
3.	Tanks	2
4.	Handpumps	21
5.	Public taps	51
6.	Streetlights	37
7.	Sodium vapour lights	1
8.	Television sets	3
9.	Blacktop road	1
10.	Metal road	9
11.	Public toilet	1
12.	Primary schools	3
13.	High school	1
14.	ANM health centre	1
15.	Ration shop	1

Recruitment

The President and the six Ward Members are selected by the village people without any election. This particular President Papu was selected for Village Panchayat President as she was working in the village on a Gounder's farm. In this Panchayat the DMK, the AIADMK, the TMC, the Congress, the Puthiya Tamizhagam all have their party units. Among the parties the AIADMK Party is very strong in terms of strength. The youth have Fans clubs to have fun and to do some service.

Panchayat Activities

Papu is not involved in any activities and all the village development activities are carried out by the Vice-President of this Panchayat.

Expenditure for 1995-96

Sl. No.	*Items*	*Amount of Expenditure (in Rs.)*
1.	Salary and allowance	6,308.00
2.	Stationary	110.00
3.	Miscellaneous	1,417.00
4.	Streetlight maintenance	1,570.00
5.	Electric pumpset mainte-nance	19,126.00
6.	TV & Radio maintenance	2,822.00
7.	Road and Bridge mainte-nance	4,700.00
8.	Library maintenance	599.00
9.	Electricity Charges	24,031.00

Expense Statement for 1995-96 to 1999-2000

Sl. No.	*Year*	*Rs.*
1.	1995-96	75,373.00
2.	1996-97	80,269.00
3.	1997-98	1,73,418.00
4.	1998-99	1,92,553.00
5.	1999-2000	2,45,526.00

The village has marriage hall, Panchayat office, public latrine, Kalai Arangam and OHT.

Perception Panchayat

Papu does not know anything about the Panchayat and the Panchayat activities. She has gone to the Namakkal District Collector's office for training and she has not gone to any other place in connection with her post. All the Panchayat activities are done by the Vice-President. She is only a rubber stamp Panchayat President.

Village Development

She pointed out that basic facilities like drinking water, sanitation, roads, streetlights, employment to poor people and school facilities are to be provided to the people. In the village local resources have to be used and cottage industries have to be started for the purpose of creating employment opportunities in the village.

Human Rights

Human rights are being violated in this village. One can find segregation and discrimination in the village temple and in the working places. Papu herself has suffered this. She is the President of this Panchayat but she is not able to enter the village temple.

Public Property

Certain public properties are protected by the communities themselves. Some of the public lands have been encroached upon by influential individuals. This kind of encroachment could not be evicted. The dominant caste takes the decision and the others have to follow.

Socialisation Process

In this Panchayat the President and the Ward Members are unanimously elected by the villagers. The Vice-President of this Panchayat carried out items of work like laying road, maintenance of drinking water, tank, electric motor and public latrine.

Involvement in Panchayat Work: Panchayat Administration

The President of this Panchayat does not know what work is carried out in the Panchayat since all the Panchayat activities are carried out by the Vice-President. The President of this Panchayat is merely affixes signature. All the Panchayat activities are carried out by the Vice-President with the help of the villagers.

Tax Collection

House tax and professional tax collected every year without any dues. The house tax collected in the years 1995-96, 1996-97,

1997-98, 1998-99, 1999-2000 was Rs. 1,967, Rs. 1999, Rs. 2057, Rs. 2057, Rs. 2375 respectively. The Professional tax collected in the years 1995-96, 1996-97, 1997-98, 1998-99, 1999-2000 was Rs. 7,548, Rs. 11,802, Rs. 12,038, Rs. 14,817, and Rs. 13,590 respectively. They increased the house tax in the year 1999-2000. Upon this the people remitted the house tax without any objection.

Government Grant

The Government grants available are State Finance Commission grant and JVVT grant. The details are given below:

The State Finance Commission's Grants

1997-1998	Rs. 11,324
1998-1999	Rs. 12,000
1999-2000	Rs. 18,009

JVVT Grants

1997-1998	Rs. 93,000
1998-1999	Rs. 33,235

The funds were received from the government and used for providing basic facilities like drinking water, streetlights, colony houses, road facilities etc. But the funds are not given in time, and hence completion of the work, measurement sanction the instalment clearance are not done in time. Due to this reason the work was delayed.

The Panchayat has constructed marriage hall, public latrine, drama hall, OHTs (5 Nos.), colony houses, and done maintenance of streetlights, sanitation, extended the public drinking water system and the public distribution system (ration shop).

Auditing System

The present system of auditing and accounts procedure is very helpful to the President as well as the Panchayat clerk, because all the bills are cleared quickly and, if there is any doubt in the bills, it will be raised and sorted it out quickly. The annual audit is usually carried out in the month of February or March. It is a routine task and the accounts are finalised. At that time the President has to bear the food and diesel expenses of the audit officials.

The officials are always cooperative and help in writing the accounts and submitting the accounts.

Gram Sabha

The President of this Panchayat makes arrangements to conduct the Gram Sabha meeting and present the Panchayat accounts and get concurrence for the work done so for and work are going to be carried out. They assess the needs of the people on the basis of their needs. Then they prepare their plan. All the work is done by the Vice-President of this Panchayat. Even the Gram Sabha meeting and the monthly meetings are organised by the Vice-President.

Nearly 100 to 150 members assemble in the Gram Sabha, but only some participate in the Gram Sabha. Particularly *Dalit* women's participation is poor. After the introduction of SHGs the women's participation has increased. The members of the SHGs ask for basic facilities for their living area. If there is any question asked by the people in the Gram Sabha meeting, the Vice-President answer the question. The President may listen to what is discussed.

Monthly Meetings

All the six ward members participate in the meetings. Some Members may be absent in one or two months due to personal or emergency work. This meeting is also actually conducted by the Vice-President. He is the person who handles all the Panchayat work in the Panchayat. The Ward Members of the Panchayat raise their voice about their ward people's basic needs. They share the work among themselves. In the meeting the Vice-President points out the sanctioned amount and work carried out.

Forming of Committees

The President does not know about the committees formed in the Panchayat. No committees have been formed in the Panchayat.

Observation by the Research Team

This innocent poor President still lives in a colony house with a single light with her husband and three sons. The eldest son, after completing higher secondary education, is engaged as a daily wage labourer in a mill when he gets employment for 10 days in a month. Due to poor economic condition she has borrowed money to educate her second son who is studying +2.

The President is so innocent that she could not make use of the services of her Panchayat clerk for writing an application for her son to submit it to the MLA (who was visiting the Panchayat) to get any job in the Panchayat or the school. The study team could witness her poverty. She could not spend even a rupee to purchase a sheet of paper to write an application on and so she tore off a sheet from the notebook of her son.

When the research team visited her for an interview she said that she is the President for name's sake only and on records but she knows nothing about the Panchayat. In the Panchayat Council meeting, the Panchayat pays Rs. 50 as sitting fees and the Vice-President conducts the meeting. Similarly, in the Gram Sabha meetings also, only the Vice-President responds to the questions raised by the Gram Sabha members. She will be only a spectator like many others. She is so innocent that she could not get the post of Panchayat clerk available in the Panchayat for her son. She said she just signs the records and that she knows nothing and also does not involve herself in any Panchayat activities.

CASE – 25

SARUTHUPATTI GRAM PANCHAYAT PERIYAKULAM BLOCK, THENI DISTRICT

Socio-Economic Background

Mr. N. Ramachandran, the President of the Saruthupatti Village Panchayat is 63 and has studied up to the 7th standard. He hails from the Parayar SC community and lives in a joint family with his eldest son, daughter-in-law, one grand-daughter and one grand-son. Agriculture is his main occupation and his family owns $1\frac{1}{2}$ acres of land with well irrigation. The family lives in a *pucca*, electrified house, with individual water tap connection and without toilet facilities. His son is working as a conductor, his daughter-in-law is working as a teacher, and his grand-son and grand-daughter are studying in the 5th and the 2nd standard respectively. The family has all modern household facilities from two wheeler to TV set.

Village Setting

The village is situated on Theni-Dindigul road in the northern part of Theni at a distance of 8 km. The Panchayat has a total population of 5,860. Out of them 2,980 are males and 2,880 are females. There is no hamlet in this Panchayat. There are nine Ward Members. Among the nine Members six are males and three are females. Three males and two females are from the SC, three males and one female are from the BC. There are 345 *pucca* houses, 561 tiled houses, 492 huts and 183 colony houses in the village. SC Paraiyars are the majority community in this Panchayat and the other communities are Pillais, Chettiars, Asaris, Naickers and *Dhobis*. All are living in the same village.

The youth have Cine Fans associations for Vijayakanth, Rajinikanth, Vijay and Prasanth. They help the Panchayat at the time of Gram Sabha meetings. There are six SHGs in the village. They also take part in the Gram Sabha meetings and articulate their demands.

Village Economy

In this Panchayat the majority (700 to 800 families) of the people are engaged in agriculture activities. The major (60%) portion of the lands are dry lands. The remaining (40%) lands are getting well water to cultivate paddy, sugarcane, cotton, and in the garden lands, cholam, millet and kambu are produced. Nearly 100 people go over to Theni everyday by seeking employment in the construction industry as mason and helpers and painters. A few families are engaged in making bricks in the roadside areas.

Nearly 100 to 150 families get income from the animals. They buy heifers and sell them after they yield. From this they earn money and support the family.

Common Property Resources

There are three tanks in the village. To avoid soil erosion trees are already planted on the tank bunds and the Panchayat gets income from the trees. On the roadsides 39 tamarind trees which yield Rs. 1,500 every year as income to the Panchayat and the tamarind trees on the highways yield Rs. 5000 per year. In the tank areas the auction of fisheries yields Rs. 500 per year.

Village Temples

There are three temples in this village. One is for the Pillai caste, another one is for Chettiars and the third for SCs and Naickers. Roughly two hundred years back the SC community got permission to celebrate festivals in the temple and obtained a Vengalapattayam from the king. So every year, three days' celebrations are done by the SC and for another three days by the BC community. There is no caste conflict in the village. Since this temple is common to both castes, caste Hindus and the SC community, they do not quarrel. Both communities celebrate the festival in a harmonious way.

Political Parties

In this village all parties have their units. There is no separate building for the parties. Political parties work actively only at the time of elections. After that there are no serious political activities. Parties are not vibrant or effective as the caste associations are dominant in social activities.

Recruitment

When Ramachandran contested in the Panchayat election his own caste leader (Nattamai) also contested. But a few elders from the Pillai, Naicker, Asari and Chettiar castes supported him because his brother belongs to the Congress Party and he is an important person in the village. As President of this Panchayat in the past, his brother carried out many development activities in the Panchayat. So, people knew the family and they felt that they will work for the welfare of the people.

At the time of canvassing he gave promises to the people that he would give priority to drinking water, drainage and colony houses to the people. He won the election by a margin of 702 votes. His family background was responsible for his success. The election was smooth and there was no hostility. The political parties played no role in the election.

Perception of Panchayati Raj

In New Panchayati Raj System the Gram Sabha is an important component, whereby power is given to the people. All the items of work are carried out in the Panchayat with the consent of the Gram Sabha. Reservation for SCs and women is another important feature in New Panchayati Raj System. The SHGs can be equipped well through the Panchayat and arrangements can be made for loan facilities to them. The present fund allocation to MLAs and MPs to develop the constitutency is not good. It breeds corruption. Everyone in the representative system will demand the same. The Gram Sabha demands certain facilities but schemes carried out in the villages through various allocations have not fulfilled the demands. To spend money for any scheme, the Panchayat should get approval from the Gram Sabha.

There is no linkage among the three-tiers of the Panchayat system. In the earlier Panchayat system, the Panchayat Presidents were members of the Panchayat Union, but now there is no linkage between the Panchayat and the Union. In the earlier Panchayat system the President got schemes from the BDO and did the work in the villages. People did not know anything about the scheme, the amount or what type of work was carried out. The work was going on. Now it is an institution of self-governance.

Development/Democracy

Ramachandran has carried out many items of work every year. In the year 1996-97 he spent Rs. 10,000 for extending the pipeline. In 1997-98 he spent Rs. 94,000 for extending the pipeline. He constructed a TV room for Rs. 20,000. A small bridge was constructed at a cost of Rs. 1,38,000. In the year 1998-99 another extension of the pipeline was carried out at a cost of Rs. 53,000 and extension of streetlights was carried out at a cost of Rs. 11,000. In 1999-2000 year extension of new pipeline work carried out at the cost of Rs. 90,000 and new small bridges were constructed at a cost of Rs. 21,000 and road metal spreading was carried out at a cost of Rs. 51,000. Household latrine construction was also carried out at a cost of Rs. 20,000. Under the Namakku Naame Scheme the Naicker caste group collected one-fourth of the amount required and a metal road work was laid in their area. In 2000-2001 the PHC doctors visited this village and conducted a medical checkup.

Panchayat President Opinion about Village Development

According to Ramachandran a village should be provided with 100 per cent drinking water facilities, employment opportunity to all the unemployed, and health facilities for all in order to develop. It is true that no village in India will have all these facilities. It is possible to achieve the results within the available means. When the work of extension of the pipeline was carried out in the streets, it was found that people had encroached upon the area. With the support of the Ward Members, the SHG members made the encroachers to vacate the area. Ramachandran frequently asks the health worker to attend to the needs of the pregnant women and lactating mothers.

Human Rights

The majority of the people are from the SC community having lands for more than three generations, and many people are employed in Government departments. These will help the SC people to maintain their status in the village. In public places like ration shop, temple and tea shops human rights are safeguarded. There is no caste discrimination in the village.

Socialisation Process

Ramachandran's family was originally oriented towards the Congress Party. At the time of the election he contested as an independent candidate. After the election he joined the TMC Party because he has been in the Congress Party from the beginning. Leader Moopanar came out of the Congress Party and started Tamil Maanila Congress Party. Now he is in the TMC Party.

NGO Link

In this Panchayat there is an NGO called SIRPI working for the upliftment of the poor. This NGO is engaged in forming women SHGs and giving guideline on small savings, health care, and self-employment. Nearly six SHGs are formed, and small savings are going on in the groups. The group members started their accounts in the banks and shortly they will get the revolving fund. The NGO staff members spread awareness among women regarding health, age at marriage etc. The NGO staff members take steps to get loans to start coir making. The products could be sold in the Theni weekly market.

Committee Formation

Ramachandran formed a Parent-Teachers Association, Peace and Appointments Committees. Except the Parent-Teachers Association, the other committees exist only on paper. In the head PTI committee, the headmaster, the teachers, parents, the Panchayat President and the Ward Members are members of Parent-Teachers Association.

Ramachandran discussed with school teachers the cent per cent enrolment of students in the school. He asked them to make special efforts to enroll *Dalit* students as they are employed as farm child labourers.

Involvement in the Panchayat Activities/Work

Ramachandran properly follows the rules and regulations of Panchayat administration. While giving any Panchayat work to a contractor, the prescribed procedure is followed and he ensures the quality of the work. He cited an incident. When the drinking water pipeline was being extended, the contractor used ordinary pipe, people brought this to his notice and he immediately ordered the contractor to change the pipe. Another event also happened at the time of the pipeline extension. To extend the pipeline, the encroachers were asked to vacate their encroachment to extend the pipeline across a common property. They refused to oblige. Immediately he asked the Ward Members and the SHG women leaders to intervene. Acting as a community they have removed the encroachment.

Collection of Tax

Ramachandran collects the house tax and the professional tax every year with great difficulty. He increased the house tax in the year 1999-2000. After increasing the house tax, he has collected the house tax fully. The government has provided the matching grant.

Accounts and Audit Procedures Adopted in the Panchayat

Ramachandran admits frankly that he does not know about accounts. The Panchayat clerk maintains the accounts and gets the signature from him (the President). The present system of auditing is a good one. Once in three months officials verify the accounts and inform if there is a lapse. This system is good to get the bills cleared in time.

Monthly Meetings

Meetings are convened regularly for which notices are given to Members in time. Female Ward Members present themselves in the monthly meetings and demand their needs. The President promptly shows the income and expenditure statement and allotts the work on the basis of needs. In the monthly meetings there is no quarrel among the Members. The meetings go on well.

Gram Sabha Meeting

Information relating to Gram Sabha meetings is sent through bit notice and drum beater. Ramachandran personally invites the village caste leaders, Ward Members and NGO staff members. Ramachandran suggests that the Gram Sabha meeting can be convened twice a year. The Presidents and the Ward Members are afraid of meeting the people in the Gram Sabha because they have not fulfilled even a few demands of the people resolved upon in the earlier meeting. People directly scold the Presidents and the Ward Members for this. So the government has to take necessary steps to increase the Panchayat fund and convene the Gram Sabha meetings two times a year.

In the Gram Sabha meetings *Dalit* women used to take part and voice their needs like drinking water, employment for women and loan facilities to SHG group members. Female participation has increased after the formation of SHGs.

Facilities Available in the Village

Sl. No.	*Nature Facilities*	*Quantum*
1.	Panchayat office	1
2.	OHTs	4
3.	Public water taps	69
4.	Individual tap connections	245
5.	Handpumps	14
6.	Open wells	2
7.	Motor pumps	4
8.	Noon-meal centre	3
9.	Primary school	2
10.	TV rooms	4
11.	Streetlights	134
12.	Temples	3
13.	Harijan Welfare School	1

A unique income generating activity is carried out in this village. People purchase heifers and rear them. The moment they yield they dispose of them at a good price. This is a trade for them. People come from many places to purchase milch animals from this village. The villagers earn several thousands by this trade.

Communal harmony prevails in the village as they have devised a mechanism to celebrate the temple festivals. Normally communal harmony is disturbed mainly during temple celebrations. The village elders have devised a mechanism by which both SC and caste Hindus celebrate the temple festivals in two different periods, though the temple is the same. For one full week it is the affair of the caste Hindus to celebrate and the next week it is the responsibility of the SC people to celebrate.

CASE - 26

SEKKANUR GRAM PANCHAYAT
VELLORE BLOCK, VELLORE DISTRICT

Socio-Economic Background

S.R. Natarajan, the President of Sekkanur Village Panchayat, is 62 years old. He is unmarried, and has studied upto the 8th standard. He belongs to a Scheduled Caste. He is living in a joint family with his elder brother, the brother's wife, son, daughter-in-law and grand-son. His main occupation is agriculture. They have 8.5 acres of land of which 5 acres are garden land with well irrigation and the remaining 3.5 acres are leased out to his relatives. This family lives in a *pucca* electrified house with toilet, drinking water and tap connection facilities. His brother is a retired jawan. His brother's son is working in a private company and earns Rs. 3,000 per month. Natarajan performs the Panchayat activities and also looks after the family's agriculture.

Recruitment Process

Natarajan belongs to the DMK Party since 1964, he has been acting as the village party secretary and he has been always faithful to the party. In the years 1965 to 1970 he was the Vice-

President of the Village Panchayat and worked for the welfare of the people and earned a good name in the village. There are nearly fourteen caste groups in the village, and among them the SCs are the majority. There are Vanniyars, Aruthathiyars, Muddaliars, Naidus, Muslims and a few minor caste groups in the Panchayat. The other caste groups supported him and hence he won the election. Two candidates contested in the election against Natarajan. They were not the either influential or important persons in the village. Natarajan won in the Panchayat election by a margin of 380 votes.

He has been working for his villagers from 1964, and has helped the villagers in getting government loans, ration cards, and a few other things. He mingles with all the communities with love and affection as a community member.

Moreover he was the Vice-President of the Panchayat in the years 1965-70 and President from 1986 to 1991. During these periods he worked for the welfare of the people. He carried out many welfare activities. He was a member of a cooperative society, the President of the Noon-Meal Vegetable Buyers Cooperative Society, a Director of a Land Development Bank, a member of the District SC Welfare Board, and a leader of the Panchayat People's Welfare Committee. These positions helped him to carry out development activities in the Panchayat. All these factors enabled him to get the support of the people in the Panchayat election and get elected in the year 1996. At the time of canvassing he printed a bit notice and asked the people directly to extend their support to his candidature by citing his past performance in the Panchayat. Based on his past service and his promises the people extended their support to him to win the election. He spent Rs. 5,000 for the election. Though the other candidates had spent more they were not able to win the election. After the election the candidates who contested in the election have not maintained any enmity and they have extended support to him in all the Panchayat activities.

Village Setting

Sekkanur Panchayat consists of three hamlets. There are 765 families, and the population is 3,295. The majority of the population is from the SC caste, the second largest community are the Vanniyars. The other communities are Arunthathiyars, Mudaliars, Naidus, Muslims, Pillais, Reddiars and Naickers and they are all minorities in terms of their strength. Besides these communities there are a few families of Asaris, *Dhobis*, Barbers and Yadhavas in the village.

There is an association for the SC community named Dr. Ambedkar Mandram which is run by the youth. During the festival time they conduct sports, give prizes to the students and children. The Vaniha Chettiars have their own association and this association celebrate the festival in the month of January. At the time of celebration they distribute sweets and food to the villagers. The President is the temple trustee of the Chettiar community.

The SC community youth and the Chettiar caste youth are attend the Gram Sabha meetings and requested to provide basic facilities to all the areas of the Panchayat. There are a number of Cine Fans associations, but Rajinikanth, Vijayakanth, Prasanth, Karthik, and Vijay are popular among the youth. The youth of the SC community back Prasanth Mandram. They celebrate the birthdays of the cine stars. There are two SHGs in the village. The groups are organised among the SC community. They are in the network of CRUD-Karunya NGO. The NGO creates awareness among women about the need for savings and how to utilize money properly for development activities. There is a good relationship between the Panchayat and the NGO.

Village Temples

There are ten temples in this Panchayat and among the ten, two are common to all the villagers. They are Kaliamman temple and Mariamman temple. The SC community participates in celebrating the village festivals. All the caste groups used to collect money for temple festivals except from SCs and minority castes. They used to donate things to the temple, or conduct any one of the cultural events at the time of village festivals. The Arunthathiyar community's deity is Maduraiveeran.

These temple activities unite the villagers and they celebrate the festivals jointly. These activities help the people to participate in the Gram Sabha meetings of the Panchayat, because the President of the Gram Panchayat is the temple trustee.

The political parties, namely the AIADMK, the DMK, the PMK, the TMC and the MDMK are functioning in the village. But the differences between or among the political parties have not given rise to conflicts among the communities. The local leaders of all the parties used to attend the Gram Sabha meetings. Natarajan is the DMK Party branch secretary of that village since 1964. He knows the party representatives like the local MLA and the MP. So the Anna Marumalarchi Thittam (AMT) was sanctioned to this Village Panchayat. Many people appreciated it and attended after the Gram Sabha meeting and voiced their grievances.

His Perception of Panchayati Raj

Natarajan knows about the earlier Panchayati Raj and the the New Panchayati Raj System. He was the Vice-President of the Panchayat from 1965 to 1970 and President in the years, 1986-91. In the old Panchayati Raj System there was no reservation for SCs and women. In the new system the President gets money from the Government directly, gets concurrence from the Gram Sabha or monthly Ward Members' meeting. He plans for the village development with the active participation of the people and on the basis of the plan work is executed. The periodical financial allotment to the Panchayat are the significant aspect of the new system. As for maintenance of records, no body guides the Panchayats. The Government sends orders which the Presidents do not understand. The Presidents need good training in administration and record maintenance. Natarajan attended training programmes organised by the District Collector's office, BDO's office and SIRD.

In the Gram Sabha meetings people's expectations are many and they ask for many welfare programmes but the Government allots a very limited funds to carry out welfare programme, and hence they are not able to satisfy the needs of the people. Natarajan is confident that in course of time, the Panchayat will be the right body to fulfil the basic needs of the people.

In this area agriculture, and chamber bricks are the main occupations of the villagers. The village economy can be improved only through agricultural related activities. If the government provides loans to the villagers for establishing brick chambers the villagers will get benefited. Another avenue is to improve the animal husbandry, since a lot of dry land cultivation is going on in their area and hence animal rearing is possible. Small and village industries should be encouraged and they will help the people to improve their standard of life.

Many people, during the off-season, and during the season too are engage in construction work, flower trade and brick chamber work. In order to support these, the Government must take necessary steps to provide proper training and financial assistance to the people. In agriculture, building work and other manual works, there is wage discrimination against women. Reservation is a new opportunity to women to enter public life. But it can be effective only if their husbands encourage them to perform their role.

Common Property Resources

There are Pettai poramboke, canal poramboke and tank poramboke in the Panchayat area. There are three tanks and a canal in the Panchayat. One tank is full of black babul trees and they are auctioned and the contractor has not yet cut the trees. Through this the income of the Panchayat has gone up by 2.5 lakh. The road poramboke trees give an income of Rs. 4000 per year, and the 2 *patta* trees give an income of Rs. 500 per year. From the trees auctioned in the year 1986-87 income of Rs. 76,000 has come only now.

There in another tank with an extent of 55 acres with black babul trees and they are safeguarded by the Social Forestry watchman and nearby villagers. The tank trees were auctioned for Rs. 5 lakh. The Panchayat share of Rs. 2.5 lakh has not yet been received by the Panchayat. Last year the remaining two tanks were desilted and deepened. Prosophis trees helps 10 to 20 families and they give fuel to the villagers. The naturally grown trees in the mayanam road, cart path and tank areas have helped the people to get their firewood.

Social Justice

There is no two tumbler system. Everybody is treated as equal in tea shop and temples. In the village temples people can pray to the god and goddess but the SCs are not allowed to come inside the temples (Mariamman and Muthalamman). The Arunthathiyar community is also not allowed inside the temple. Caste Hindus used to visit the SC temple and the Arunthathiyar temple. They are allowed inside these temples.

Socialisation

Since Natarajan held positions in the old system from 1965 to 1970 and from 1986 to 1991 and as President during 1996-2001 he knows the old and the New Panchayati Raj System. He regularly reads newspapers, like Thinakaran, *Murasoli, Thinamalar, Thinathanthi* and magazines, like Thugloq, Kumutham and the monthly magazine *Tamilarasu*. Moreover he is an experienced elderly person in the party and the Panchayat he carries out all the Panchayat work through regular tenders. So he knows the Panchayat activities and works.

Performance: Panchayat Activities

When, he was the President of this Panchayat from 1996 to 2001 he carried out many development activities during that period. He provided streetlights and handpumps for all the people. He normally carries out work on the basis of the need.

During the current period he provided an OHT with a capacity of 60,000 litres at a cost of Rs. 9 lakh to Pettai. In the same way he provided another OHT with a capacity of 30,000 litres at a cost of Rs. 7 lakh to Periya Sekkanur and one more OHT with a capacity of 30,000 litres to Udayar Palayam village at a cost of Rs. 6,50,000. Handpumps have been provided to the Muslim street. Colony houses have been provided to the

Arunthathiyar people at Periya Sekkanur Colony at a cost of Rs. 1,20,000.

Latrines to 20 houses at a cost of Rs. 6,40,000 have been provided and to another 25 houses at a cost of Rs. 3,00,000 have been provided. A school building at a cost of Rs. 3,00,000, ration shop for Periya Sekkanur at a cost of Rs. 1,32,000, drainage for Periya Sekkanur at a cost of Rs. 1,50,000 have been provided. Extension of streetlights (50 Nos.) in the area of Periya Sekkanur Colony at a cost of Rs. 4,17,000 has been done. Retaining wall (2 Nos.) in Periya Sekkanur and Udayarpalayam at a cost of Rs. 65,000, small bridges to Periya and Chinna Sekkanur villages at a cost of Rs. 60,000 have been provided. Village roads have been blacktopped at a cost of Rs. 12 lakh.

Monthly Meetings

Every month Natarajan sends the committee agenda to every Member through the Panchayat clerk and gets signatures from the Members. He prepares an agenda paper separately and sends it to all the Members of the Panchayat. He adopted a new technique of using a separate sheet for getting the signatures. Then, at the time of the meeting, he gets their signatures in the notebook also. A printed notice is circulated to the Members regarding the committee meeting. All the Panchayat Ward Members participate in the meetings, particularly the women Ward Members, and voice their ward people's grievances regarding basic facilities. Since the President is from the SC, the Panchayat's SC members participate in all the meetings get some work for their ward. So far all the monthly meetings have been on well without any problem.

Gram Sabha Meetings

Natarajan prepares a bit notice and supplies to all the Ward Members to inform their ward people about the Gram Sabha meeting. The notice is pasted in important places in the village like hotels, tea stalls, petti shops, grocery shop, temples and savadis. On the Gram Sabha meeting the villagers are informed through a dum-beater. Natarajan invite the village elders personally.

In the Gram Sabha meeting, the Panchayat income and expenditure statement is read out by the Panchayat clerk, indicating what works was carried out, the total amount spent and the completed works. What work is going to be undertaken, amount to be spent and the time stipulation for the completion of the work. All these are discussed. In the question hour the Panchayat clerk and the Panchayat President answer the questions of the people. After the question hour, they get the suggestions of the members of the Gram Sabha and prioritise the items of work which are going to be carried out and get it approved by the Gram Sabha.

Accounts and Audit

Natarajan feels that the present accounts system (once in three months) is good because the accounts are verified by the BDO's officials who correct the mistakes, if any. He does not know accounts and their audit system, and the clerk takes care of the accounts and the audit. But sometimes Natarajan asks the clerk to explain the item and only then affixes his signature.

Collection of Tax

The house tax and professional tax collected in the year 1996-97, 1997-98, 1998-99, 1999-2000 were Rs. 6,119, Rs. 6,926, Rs. 10,206, Rs. 12,110 respectively. Up to this, there is no balance of house tax and professional tax. The house tax was increased in the year 1997-98 (50%). After the increase too house tax has been collected fully and the professional tax too.

Linkage with NGOs

Natarajan has a link with the Narayani Sithar Peedam and Karunya (NGO) carry out to some welfare activities in the Panchayat. The Narayani Sithar Peedam donated furniture to the school costing Rs. 1 lakh. The Narayani Sithar Peedam is a Hindu religious institution having funds and they are doing many welfare activities in the nearby villages particularly they have concentrating in children's education. Natarajan is a member of the Narayani Sithar Peedam. Karunaya concentrates in health aspects. Natarajan approached the NGO and got their help for the villagers to construct household latrine in their houses. The NGO constructed 60 household latrines in the village. At the time of festivals the Panchayat and the NGO cleans the village with the help of the villagers.

Linkage with Other Tiers

Natarajan has good contact with the other tiers—the Union Chairman, Union Councillors, District Panchayat Chairman and Councillors and he has got some programme from them for the development of the village.

Observation by the Research Team

Natarajan is unmarried and he has worked in the Congress Party in the beginning. Later he joined the DMK Party in the year 1964 and engaged in the Panchayat activities and became Vice-President of this Panchayat in the year 1965. Subsequently, he became the President and continued his service in the village. He worked hard and prevented the spread of caste clashes in the district. He concentrated much on preserving communal harmony. Hence, he was awarded a certificate to this effect. There is only one sweeper in the Panchayat and it is not possible to clean the village. So Natarajan engaged a sweeper on daily wages and removed the garbage in the village. The Panchayat office is kept open from 9 am to 1 pm and from 2 pm to 6 pm except on Sundays. Natarajan told the research team that there is a new pattern adopted in leasing out land. Usually out of the total cultivation, the land owner used to get two portions and the tiller take one portion, he has now changed the pattern. Now, out of the total cultivation, the land owner and the tiller have to take equal shares. This has been accepted. It is a revolution that he has effected in the village.

CASE – 27

SENGIPATTI GRAM PANCHAYAT
THANJAVUR BLOCK, THANJAVUR DISTRICT

Socio-Economic Background

Ms. V. Punithavalli, the President of Sengipatti Village Panchayat, aged 30, is a post-graduate with a B.Ed degree in addition. She has completed her M.Phil programme also. She belongs to the SC community. She lives with her parents and the family includes her married brother. Besides her, there are two sisters and one brother, all unmarried, and they constitute a joint family. The family owns 6 acres of wet land and 5 acres of dry land. The dry land is a common property belonging to her father's family. She lives in a tiled house of her own, electrified and having individual tap connection. The toilet is under construction.

Recruitment Process

Her father is a retired teacher who devoted his time only to his profession and did not involve himself in public activities. But the family is a cultured family. One of her brothers is a driver in a transport corporation. Another brother is a tailor. No one in her family thought of contesting in the Panchayat elections. But the villagers, mostly the youth belonging to the Tamil Desa Pothuvudamai Party, met her father and requested that she contests in the election. Mostly SC youth are members in this party. Some families belonging to the BC suggested to her to contest for the Union Council Ward membership. But the general public wanted a good educated woman President. Since many insisted, she felt that she could get the needed support.

The youth, who promised their support to her, organised public meetings and discussed common issues like basic amenities and issues related to farmers. They fully involved themselves in the election campaign. They spent their money to print wall posters and notices and they assured the public that good administration would be given by this candidate. There were five candidates and almost all of them contested on party basis. All the other candidates had no sound educational background.

Her supporters, mostly young men and women, visited hamlets and resorted to door to door canvassing. Street corner meetings were also organised and they focused on efficient administration in the Panchayat. In one hamlet, namely Melakad, there are 30 houses but no electricity connection and no drinking water facility. She promised them that she would take necessary steps to fulfil these felt needs. She won the election. She spent only Rs.10,000.

The major reason for her success was the whole hearted support of the village youth. Cutting across castes there was goodwill towards her family. The other candidates were not educated and were married women. People wanted an independent and educated woman to head the Panchayat.

Village Setting

In Sengipatti Panchayat there are five hamlets, namely Ayothipatti, Maniampatti, T.B. Sanatorium, Mela Elakkal and Othathern. It is said that Sengipatti is the mother village for 18 villages as the famous Mariamman temple is situated here. The SCs are the majority caste and besides them there are Kallars, Chettiars, Ambalams and Udayars also. There are Christians in the BC as well as the SC communities.

For each caste there is a committee which is traditional in character. It consists of Nattamai, Kariakarar, Odumpillai and Mappadi. Temple celebrations, marriage functions, settling of disputes and other customary and cultural activities are handled by these committees. The importance of the caste committees has declined after the institutionalisation of the Village Panchayat.

Women Sangam

There are nine women's Sangams in the Panchayat. All have bank accounts. They have not yet availed of bank loans and they have proposed to start dairy development. The women's Sangam members meet once a month. Along with micro credit, the women discuss public issues and take initiatives to solve them in order to improve their status. The young men extend support to the women in this regard. Due to this new trend, the significance of the traditional Village Committee and caste committees has now declined.

Farmers' Association

There is a well organised Farmers' Association which has a good relationship with the Department of Agriculture. They get farmers' loans, attend training programmes and make use of the various programmes pertaining to farmers. The New Kattalai Highland Channel covers 15 villages to the extent of 15,000 hectares. Punithavalli herself has undergone training organised by the Agriculture Department. The Farmers' Association members attend the Gram Sabha meetings and maintain good rapport with the Panchayat, offering various suggestions.

Other Associations

The youth group themselves under Rajinikanth, Vijayakanth and Sathiaraj Cine Fans' Associations. They organise sports and cultural events for the benefit of the youth and the public. The SC youth have joined together under the banner of Dr. Ambedkar. Most of them show interest in public activities.

A Primary Cooperative Agriculture Credit Bank is functioning in the village. The President of the Bank requested the Panchayat to open an account with the society. The PDS is run by the Agriculture Cooperative Society. Punithavalli visits and regulates the running of the shop.

Health Committee

Last year a Health Committee was formed in which three Ward Members and three others were enlisted as members. The function of the PHC was discussed in the meetings. The PHC is run by the Panchayat Union which gives a grant of Rs. 10,000 per year. The amount is utilised for the purchase of medicines/drugs for just 4 to 5 months. During the rest of the year, the doctor just visits the PHC. Punithavalli met the doctor and the Union Chairman in this regard but the situation has not improved. She suggested to enhance the grant meant for the purchase of medicines or convert the PHC into a Government health centre.

Religious Institutions

The Mariamman temple is famous, where, during the annual five-day celebration, the BC communities enjoy the right to organise Mandakapadi, *i.e.* each day's celebration is entrusted to a community belonging to the BC. After 1996 there has been no celebration as the SCs also demanded Mandakapadi rights. The issue has not yet been settled. But there is no denial of temple entry or worship. There are other village dieties, Ayyanar, Angalamman, Kamatchi and Bagavathi along with Lord Ganesh temples. There is no practice of two tumbler system or caste related riots. Intercaste marriages have been celebrated between Naidus and SCs.

Mahatma Gandhi TB Sanatorium

There is a TB Sanatorium under the jurisdiction of Sengipatti Village Panchayat but due to non-cooperation between the staff and the management, there are few patients. But for that there would be more number of visitors by which the village bazaar would always be busy.

Political Parties

The Tamil Desa Pothuvudamai Party is the dominant party. It is headed by the social activist of left ideology Mr. Maniarasan. The members of this party are mostly the youth who courageously muster themselves and solve many public issues. The other political parties are the AIADMK, the DMK, the CPI and the TMC, but they are not so active.

Public *vs.* Village Panchayat

When the public demanded widening of the village main road and its improvement, the Panchayat decided to do so and started work. As the VAO delayed the measuring of the width of the road for widening of the road the Panchayat was not able to undertake the road work. In spite of the villagers helping the Panchayat in pressurising the VAO, the response was not positive from the VAO. But in the case of street maintenance, there was absolute cooperation from the people and understanding among the dwellers of a street who helped in removing the encroachments and involved themselves with the Panchayat in successful completion of the street improvement work.

Her Perception

Being a highly educated young woman, Punithavalli feels that the Village Panchayat Presidentship is a good opportunity to serve the people. She understands that providing basic amenities is the duty of the Panchayat. After one year, she realised that the Panchayat has to work for social development and that it could be achieved. She welcomed the reservation for women and *Dalits* in the Panchayat system. Otherwise their entry in local bodies could never occur. Development could be achieved only after providing the minimum basic amenities. The SHGs could be involved in economic activities. Irrigation facilities in the villages have to be improved.

On Village Economy

The extent of cultivable agricultural land has shrunk due to non-availability of water for irrigation. Vast areas of land are lying waste and, due to lack of pasture land, animal husbandry is also declining. The village craftsmen are not getting recognition for their products. Around fifty people get employment opportunity in a nearby cement factory. Quite a number of families are engaged in charcoal manufacturing activity. Punithavalli suggests creating employment opportunities through cottage industries by using the available skills in the villages as the scope for agriculture has declined. The major issues in the process of development are lack of education, lack of awareness, mismanagement of family economy, laziness among the youth and poor skills among the artisans and masons. They expect doles and grants from the government. Alcoholism was controlled with the help of the village women and the community leaders. But it has resumed after the Assembly elections.

On Social Justice

The mindset of caste Hindus is not yet changed. Earlier the former President was invited for hoisting the national flag in the school. Now the Headmaster is not inviting her as she belongs to the SC. In spite of that, as Panchayat President, she has gained social status.

On Party

According to Punithavalli, making oneself powerful and supreme is politics. Instead of public welfare, most of the politicians are aiming for power. But, to work for the people, we do not require power.

On Gender Issues

In public affairs the opinions of women are not yet considered. Only women like elected women representatives and SHG leaders, who have got orientation in public activities, are getting recognition and their opinions are taken into account by menfolk. Providing higher education to girls is not part of the mindset of parents. Recently a higher secondary school was established in this Panchayat area. Till then the girls were not permitted to continue their studies after school final as they had to go over to other places for it. The management of the Vallam Women's Polytechnic, run by the Periyar Memorial Trust, organised a women's awareness programme and provided training to women, which has proved very useful to young women. Women need more support and facilitation from outside for their development issues. Steps have to be taken to sensitize the village community on gender. Political parties like the Communists and the Dravidian parties encourage their women's wings to engage in public activities.

Status of Common Property Resources

There are one tank under PWD, 5 tanks under the Union and 10 village ponds in Sengipatti Village Panchayat. The pasture land is encroached upon by individuals and a number of houses have been constructed there. Around 15 farmers encroached upon around 75 acres of common land. There is a Social Forestry land vested with the Forestry Department. Teak and cashew-nut plantations could be raised to earn more income as well as provide employment to landless labourers. There was earlier a weekly market in Sengipatti Panchayat. For the past 20 years it has not been functioning. Punithavalli took steps to re-establish the weekly market in a common place which had been encroached upon by an individual. But the Revenue Officials did not cooperate with her in removing the encroachment. If the Revenue Department is honest it can remove the encroachment and provide a lot of common lands to the Panchayat. By making use of the common lands, the Panchayat can get a lot of revenue. But, in the present corrupt revenue system, this will not happen. If the Panchayat takes steps, neither the Revenue Department nor the Police Department will cooperate. The Panchayat President will be the sufferer. Being a *Dalit*, she cannot touch even an inch of land and it will be made a point for conflict between the *Dalits* and the caste Hindus.

Socialisation and Leadership Process

During her girlhood days Punithavalli wanted to help in improving children's education. But it was only a dream as she did not know the ways and means to do it. But, after she became the President, she realised the significance of local leadership and its scope for improving the village community. From the beginning, she set in her mind that she is answerable to the people and so, at any place and at anytime, if anybody seeks her help as President, she was determined to do her best for them. So she studied the activities of various Departments and very carefully established rapport with them.

By engaging in monitoring and executing Panchayat work, she learnt a lot. Most of the work is executed by the Panchayat. Hence her direct involvement is needed to ensure quality at least, if not profit. In this engagement she has to stand in the midst of workers, clerks, officials and the general public. She cultivated the needed patience to give reply to the questions of the Ward Members and the public. She developed the orientation through attending the meetings and training programmes organised by the government. The TMC party contacted her parents as they are Congress people and the local leaders of the TMC encouraged her and requested her to become a member in the party. But she refused as she wanted to be apolitical.

Panchayat Activities

The convening of Council meetings and Gram Sabha meetings are to be handled properly. After she became President, one year rolled by without any achievement. In the second year she got awareness and struggled a lot with officials and the authorities. Only from the third year she could achieve what she intended to. One cement concrete road work was given to a contractor who was the benami of the President of the nearby Village Panchayat. As the contract work executed earlier by him was not of good standard she opposed the allocation of the work to him and pressed that the work should not be allotted to him. This issue was brought to the notice of the District Collector and the Collector questioned her knowledge of administration. The Collector did not know her educational qualification. When he enquired about her educational qualification and she replied boldly that she is a post-graduate with a B.Ed. degree and an M.Phil. degree, he verified the details and ordered that the work should not be entrusted to that contractor. The work was executed by the Department. The school toilet site was located very near the public tank. The work was given to a Union contractor. She came to know of it and objected to it. The contractor belonged to the DMK Party and so the officials were afraid to stop the order. But she prevented it with the help of the villagers and, at last, the site was changed.

During the year 1996-97, 20 group houses were allotted to Sengipatti and the selection process was done early. Under JVVT Rs. 1,27,000 was spent for various items of work like culvert construction, road work and one TV room construction. The SFC grant is Rs. 46,514 per quarter in a year. Concrete cement road, streetlight extension, construction of culvert, bus shelter, and TV room have been undertaken from this.

With the help of the MP and the MLA, water supply has been improved by constructing 4 new OHTs through comprehensive village water scheme. The details of the schemes available in Thiruvarur District because known to her when she met officials at a training programme organised by TNSWB. With much interest, she visited Thiruvarur where the concerned TWAD office is located and, through the MLA, got the allocation for new overhead tanks. Getting information is very important in administering the Panchayat as there are various sectoral Departments in the Government system.

Concrete cement roads are preferred by the public and so, in six streets, concrete cement roads were provided. She used to read various newspapers in the vernacular where more details of various schemes announced by the higher authorities, Ministers and the Chief Minister are published. She used to verify with the appropriate office and immediately try to avail of the same. Her parents encouraged her to function independently. The Panchayat clerk is very efficient in providing necessary guidance.

She regularly attends the Public Grievances Day and submits the resolutions of the Gram Sabha meetings. The desilting of four tanks was made possible by her frequently meeting the concerned authorities during the Public Grievances Day. The issue of non-payment of professional tax by the staff of the TB Sanatorium was not solved even though the District Collector was the Chairman of the Sanatorium. It was said that there is a lot of arrears in the disbursement of their salary and so the Panchayat could not collect the professional tax from them. Granting house site patta to 32 BC families and 32 SC families was made possible as she properly followed up the petitions. The allocation of site for the construction of a threshing floor was made by the VAO but the ruling party influenced the higher officials and transferred the VAO. Revision in house tax was effected in the year 1998. The earlier fixation was Rs. 2.20, Rs. 5.50 and Rs. 38.50 for hut, tiled house and *pucca* house respectively. It was revised to Rs. 5.50, Rs. 22.00 and Rs. 88.00 respectively. She explained to the villagers that it was the Government order and are hundred per cent house tax collection would get a matching grant from the Government. Auctioning of fish ponds could not be regulated as the local communities are involved in the transaction. She learnt maintenance of records and accounts and regularly verifies the records. Audits are completed without any major objection. In spite of her honesty in administration, the officials expect money to finalise the accounts. They could not demand it but she met their food expenses and gave money to them.

The Gram Sabha meeting was successfully conducted and she was able to mobilise more than 250 members every time. There are more participants from the SC community as they have the practice of organising youth Sangam and women's Sangam. There are only a few participants from the hamlets. The sources of Panchayat finance, the schemes and allocation of funds for each work are explained in the Gram Sabha meeting.

All Ward Members (BC 4 and SC 5) regularly attend the Gram Sabha meetings. The work executed in their wards is entrusted to them if they demand so. Out of 9 members 1 BC and 2 SC members used to execute the works by themselves. The protection of the tree saplings planted by the Forest Department is ensured through the Gram Sabha. The cattle menace in the plantation was controlled with the help of the villagers as it was referred to the Gram Sabha. Punithavalli's relationship with the Vice-President is smooth. He belongs to the BC. As he demanded his ward's work, the committee permitted him to carry it out. Members used to criticise the work if the people identified any mistakes in the work carried out in the villages.

Social issues like child labour exist in the village. Steps are being taken to stop this practice. But the parents are sending the children for employment as they need money for their sustenance. In the case of girls who failed in the school final examinations, to improve their standard, with the help of the youth association, coaching classes are conducted. Punithavalli gives much attention to the functioning of the noon-meal centre and the health sub-centre. With the help of the villagers, improvements have been made in the primary school. Toilets have been provided to three schools. A library is functioning well and the youth are visiting the library to read the newspapers. The Panchayat office building is not in good condition. Repairs are needed and so the records are kept in her house. She has decided to contest again and is determined to serve the community. She does not like to join any political party as, with just the help of the villagers, a lot of things could be done.

CASE – 28

SIVAGANAPURAM GRAM PANCHAYAT NILAKOTTAI BLOCK, DINDIGUL DISTRICT

Socio-Economic Background

Sri M. Periyasamy, the President of the Sivaganapuram Village Panchayat, is 68 years old. He has studied up to SSLC and worked as a teacher for 30 years and retired from service. He hails from the Pallar (Scheduled) caste, and lives in a nuclear family with his wife and son. Agriculture is his occupation. His family owns three acres of land with well irrigation. His family lives in a tiled, electrified house without toilet and water tap facilities. His wife is a teacher. He gets Rs. 3,000 as pension. His wife's salary is Rs. 5,600 and their agricultural income Rs. 15,000 per year. His son has studied up to +2 and he is looking after the agriculture.

Recruitment Process

When he was a teacher he used to help the people by writing applications, motivating the parents to send their children to school, and arranging to provide poor children notebooks, books, pen and pencil. He helped the poor to get Government loans from banks and Government Departments. These activities helped him to contest in the Panchayat President's election.

Another helpful factor was that those who studied under him (both male and female) requested their parents to cast their votes for him. Only one person contested against him in the Panchayat election, but he did not have any such service background. Periyasamy got the Naickers, Chettiars, Piramalaikallars, Agamudiars, Pillais, *Dhobis* and Sakkiligars to support him to win the Panchayat election by citing his service in the village when he was working as a teacher. During the electioneering he told the people that he knew all the details of the Government Departments, Government schemes and how to get things done in the Government offices. This attracted the attention of the voters.

Periyasamy won the election by a margin of 265 votes. His social work and the support of the majority of the castes were the main reasons for his success. The election was smooth and did not cause any friction. When he was working as a teacher he followed Thanthai Periyar's principles strictly. At the time of the election he contested as an independent candidate. After the election he thought that, to get schemes one has to get the cooperation of the ruling party, and so he joined in the DMK Party as it was the ruling party at that time.

Village Setting

The village is situated south-west of Nilakottai Panchayat Union office and 10 km. from Nilakkottai. There are 2,366 people, out of which 1,226 are males and 1,140 females. There are three hamlets in this Panchayat. There are five Wards and nine Ward Members in this Panchayat. Among the nine Members seven are males and two females. Two male and one female Member belong to the SC community. There are 428 tiled houses, 120 huts, 22 *pucca* houses and 70 colony houses.

The youth have Cine Fans Associations for Rajinikanth and Prasanth, and they help the Panchayat at the time of Gram Sabha meetings. There is an association for farmers, but it is not registered. The leading farmers attend the Gram Sabha meetings. There are three SHGs in the Panchayat, and the members of

SHGs attend the Gram Sabha meetings and demand drinking water, drainage facilities, streetlights and loan facilities for their wards and members. Jeevanthara well loan has been given to the SHG members.

Village Economy

Agriculture is the main occupation. Well and tank are the sources of irrigation for the lands. Banana, coconut, paddy, flowers and black gram are the agricultural products. In dry lands sorghum and millets are produced. There are more than 300 families engaged in agriculture. Nearly 100 men and women go over to Nilakottai for employment in the construction industry as masons and helpers and painters. A few families are working in the Villampatti mill. Many families are engaged in animal rearing to get income.

Common Property Resources

There are two small tanks and four ooranis (tanks) in the village. In the year 1991-92 they planted black babul under the Social Forestry Scheme. The villagers planted trees on the bunds of the tanks to prevent soil erosion. In the burial ground poramboke area they planted black babul, neem and vagai trees. The black babul trees planted in the tank under the Social Forestry Scheme (SFS), after the maximum period of seven years, were auctioned for Rs. 2,32,690 and 50 per cent of the auction amount (*i.e.* Rs. 1,16,345) is yet to be given to the Panchayat. Tree planting work was carried out in the tanks and burial ground poramboke areas to get income for the Panchayat.

Village Temples

Caste Hindus are living in Sivaganapuram village. There are three Hindu temples and the minority caste group people do not have a temple but there is a small place for their worship. The SC caste people are not allowed inside the caste Hindu temples. They can participate in and contribute to some programmes only. But there is no caste rivalry in the Panchayat.

Political Parties

The Congress, the DMK, the AIADMK, and the CPI are the parties functioning in this village. There is no separate building for any parties. During the election time the parties are activated and after the election there is no serious political activity. Parties are not vibrant as the caste associations are dominant in social activities.

Perception of Panchayati Raj

Periyasamy feels that the reservation for *Dalits* and women is very useful for developing these segments. The SHGs can be equipped well through the Panchayat and arrangements can be made for loan facilities to them. The Gram Sabha is another important factor to strengthen the peoples' participation. In the earlier Panchayat the President was a government agent to implement the work in the villages. Periyasamy suggested that the allocations under the MLA and the MP schemes should be based on the priorities proposed by the villagers in the Gram Sabha.

Development / Democracy

Periyasamy has carried out many items of work every year in this village. In the year 1996-97, under the JVVT scheme, three TV rooms were constructed at a cost of Rs. 48,000. Under the JGSY Scheme a blacktop road was laid in Sivaganapuram. Six colony houses were constructed under the Indira Memorial Scheme at a cost of Rs. 1,62,000, and from the 10th Finance Commission grant, the pipeline was extended and a retaining wall was constructed at a cost of Rs. 41,000.

In the next year 1997-98 under the JGSY construction of retaining wall, small bridge and threshing floor at a cost of Rs. 1,00,264 was done. Under the JVVT, blacktop road at a cost of Rs. 2,50,000, was laid. Under the Jeevanthara Scheme an open well was dug at a cost of Rs. 42,000. Under TWAD Scheme extension of the pipeline at a cost of Rs. 20,000, under JVVT scheme a road to the burial ground at a cost of

Rs. 38,000, from 10th Finance Commission fund extension of pipeline at a cost of Rs. 15,196, from Collector's fund extension of electricity and lights at a cost of Rs. 6,300 were carried out.

In the year 1998-99 under the JVVT Scheme three retaining walls and a threshing floor were provided at a cost of Rs. 97,000, and from the 10th Finance Commission fund a retaining wall and a new drinking water pipeline were provided at a cost of Rs. 63,790.

In the year 1999-2000 under the JVVT Scheme a threshing floor, a cement floor, retaining wall were constructed at a cost of Rs. 1,48,000. Twenty colony houses at a cost of Rs. 6,40,000, under Indira Colony House Scheme were constructed. Under CRSP Scheme five individual household latrines were constructed at a cost of Rs. 5,000, and from the Central fund blacktop road was formed at a cost of Rs. 2,60,000. From the Educational Fund the school building repair work was carried out at a cost of Rs. 14,000. Under the JGSY Scheme a cement road was laid in four places in the Panchayat area at a cost of Rs. 91,980. A small bridge was also constructed at a cost of Rs. 36,300. These are the items of work carried out in the five years.

Village Development

Periyasamy believes that, to develop a village, all basic facilities have to be provided to lead a decent human life and necessarily one has to create employment opportunity to make use of the human energy. People cannot be developed by giving benefits. At the time of construction of retaining wall the farmers association helped him to evict the encroachers in the odai poramboke areas.

Since he is a retired teacher he has requested the school teachers to increase the strength, attendance, and improve the quality of education. In the year 1999-2000, from the Educational Fund, he carried out repair work in the school. He attended the SHG monthly meetings and made arrangements to get a Jeevanthara well loan for the SHG members (2 members got Jeevanthara well loan). This will help the women to improve their life.

Socialisation Process

Periyasamy has followed Periyar's principles for the last thirty years. At the time of the election he contested as an independent candidate. After the election he joined the DMK Party because he thought Periyar's principles could be implemented only through the DMK Party. He has faced some challenges in the Panchayat and come out successfully only through the support of the DMK Party.

Committee Formation

Periyasamy formed Parent-Teachers Association. The Headmaster, parents of school children, the Panchayat President, the Ward Members and teachers are the members of the Association. At the time of the formation of the committee there was no problem. As a former teacher and he has concentrated on the school activities and improved the children's educational level.

Human Rights

The Panchayat President is from the SC community. Wherever injustice occurs in public places like ration shop, temple, well, he intervenes. In the tea stalls there is no two tumbler system. Earlier when the SC people entered the streets of the caste Hindus, they removed their chappals. This habit has been eradicated. Everybody is treated as an equal in public places.

Involvement in Panchayat Work

Periyasamy contracts for the Panchayat work in the name of others and carries out the same. This is with the intention of maintaining quality. In this regard there arose a problem between the Union Engineer and Periyasamy. The Union Engineer colluded with six Ward Members and restricted the Panchayat work. In the first two years Periyasamy was not able to carry out much of Panchayat work. Then he went to Chennai to meet the party members and got orders from the District Collector to carry out Panchayat activities for three months. He carried out the Panchayat work without any problem.

Periyasamy is interested in constructing a check dam and a retaining wall, because if water is stored in the check dam, the people will get water and at the same time, the water level will rise in the wells.

Road formation and clearing the bushes from the burial ground were done. Since it is an agricultural area Periyasamy constructed a threshing floor for all the villages. Cement roads to the villages was another work carried out.

Now Periyasamy has got the Union Councillor's fund of Rs. 27,000 to clear the supply channels of the tanks.

Monthly Meeting

Periyasamy conducted the monthly meetings regularly. The information was sent through the Panchayat clerk. The female Ward Members used to participate actively in the meetings. The women Members demanded drinking water facilities, health facilities and sanitation facilities, streetlight facilities and employment opportunities for women. For the last two years there has been no rivalry in the Panchayat meetings.

Gram Sabha Meetings

The Gram Sabha meeting has to be conducted four times every year. The meeting information is sent through bit notice and drum-beater. The Panchayat Ward Members are directly contacted. Periyasamy invites the village elders and the caste leaders in the village for the Gram Sabha meeting.

Nearly 100 to 150 people participate in the Gram Sabha meeting, and among the participants nearly 50 are women. *Dalit* SHG members attend the Gram Sabha meeting and express their needs like drinking water, streetlights, drainage facilities and Jeevanthara well loan.

Many resolutions are passed in the Gram Sabha meeting but funds are not enough to complete the work before the next Gram Sabha meeting. Periyasamy says that the government has to take necessary steps to increase the Panchayat fund allocation.

Tax Collection

Tax collection is important in Panchayat activities. Periyasamy collects the house tax and the professional tax every year with great difficulty. He increased the house tax by 20 per cent in the year 1998-99. He suggested that the government must take steps to facilitate remitting the house tax like the electricity bill.

Accounts and Audit Procedure Adopted in the Panchayat

At present once in three months the accounts are being checked. This system is good for the Panchayat because if anything is missed, it could be corrected from memory. Doubts could be cleared. This system helps the President to remember the incidents and give correct answers to the government officials' queries.

The accounts and audit system helped Periyasamy to prevent corruption. Usually he meets the food and refreshment charges of the visiting officials.

General Information about the Village

1.	Panchayat Building	-	1 No.
2.	Marriage hall	-	1 No.
3.	Community hall	-	2 Nos.
4.	Panchayat Union school	-	2 Nos.
5.	Motor room	-	3 Nos.
6.	TV room	-	7 Nos.
7.	Panchayat tank	-	2 Nos. (1. Alankulam 2. Sirukkulam)
8.	Public latrine	-	1 No.
9.	Oorani	-	5 Nos.
10.	Open well	-	2 Nos.
11.	Handpump	-	14 Nos.
12.	Electric pump	-	3 Nos.
13.	Public tap	-	25 Nos.
14.	Tubelight	-	46 Nos.
15.	Sodium vapour lamp	-	1 No.
16.	TV	-	6 Nos.
17.	Total houses	-	(a) *Pucca* – 22 Nos. (b) Tiled – 428 Nos. (c) Huts – 120 Nos. (d) Colony house – 70 Nos.

Income Statement

Sl. No.	*Details*	*Amount in Lakhs*				
		1995-96	*1996-97*	*1997-98*	*1998-99*	*1999-2000*
1.	House tax	0.040	0.030	0.030	0.030	0.050
2.	Professional tax	0.020	0.020	0.030	0.030	0.040
3.	Stamp duty	1.270	1.200	0.340	1.270	0.970
4.	Tree tax	0.010	0.090	0.010	0.010	0.020
5.	SFC grants	—	—	0.850	0.890	1.680
6.	House tax matching grant	0.060	0.020	0.050	0.050	—
7.	10th Finance Commission grant	—	—	0.850	0.850	1.680
8.	JVVT Scheme	—	1.140	1.190	1.190	—
9.	CRSP Scheme	—	—	0.030	0.030	—
10.	IAS Scheme (group house)	—	1.620	—	—	6.400

CASE – 29

SOODIYUR GRAM PANCHAYAT PARAMAKUDI BLOCK, RAMANATHAPURAM DISTRICT

Socio-Economic Background

Mrs. N. Kalimuthu is the President of the Soodiyur Village Panchayat. She is 42, married and has one son and one daughter who are studying in college and school respectively. Her husband is the secretary of the local unit of AIADMK Party. Kalimuthu belongs to the Thevar community (MBC). Her family is a joint one as her father-in-law is living with them. They own five acres of land and have their own house (now under construction). She is a literate, having studied upto the 3rd standard only.

Recruitment

There were three candidates including Kalimuthu contesting in the election. The others belonged to the Yadava community. To redress his disappointment due to his defeat in the earlier Panchayati Raj elections, Mr. Nagarajan, Kalimuthu's husband, fielded her as a candidate as the seat was reserved for women. Kalimuthu did not have any political orientation but she was one of the office bearers in a women's group. This helped her to reach a better position than the other two candidates. Further the services rendered by her husband to the public, particularly to SC community and his initiatives to bring irrigation water in time to Soodiyur were the main reasons for her success in the election.

Kalimuthu explained that the big farmers belonging to the Yadava community do not lend much cooperation to the others in respect of bringing irrigation water to Soodiyur as they could earn more by selling their well water to the needy farmers who belong to different castes. Further the big farmers of the Yadava community prefer to sell their well-water to the farmers of their own caste at a lower rate. The farmers of the other caste like Vellalars, Thevars, Kallars, Potters, Servais and Udayars, who are suffering a lot due to the non-availability of irrigation water from Virakanur Dam, have no other way than to depend upon the landowners who own borewells.

So Nagarajan mobilised all the farmers of Soodiyur, struggled with the PWD, and defying the orders of the PWD, they opened the shutters of the dam and let out water to Soodiyur *kanmoi*. Moreover all breaches in the channel on the way to Soodiyur were plugged by the villagers under the leadership of Nagarajan. So all the villagers except the Yadava community supported Kalimuthu in the Panchayat election and she won by a margin of 176 votes.

Kalimuthu belongs to the minority community of Thevars. There are only 25 Thevar families in Soodiyur whereas the

Yadava community has more than 250 families in this Panchayat. Kalimuthu was able to mobilise the support of all the other communities, particularly the SCs and she was able to defeat the other candidates. This proved that caste is not the factor but the character of the candidate that determines the success of the candidate in the local body elections.

Village Setting

Soodiyur is a multi-caste village where the Yadavas are the dominant community. The SCs come next. Other castes like Udayars, Servais, Thevars and Kallars are more or less equal in number. Only the Yadava community has a caste association engaged in mobilising their community for political gain.

There are three women's Sangams. The members meet once a month and discuss the health and the education of their children. Officials like the BDO used to come and discuss with the women members. The women's association members used to join together for a common cause like availing of transport facilities and desilting and maintenance of irrigation channel.

When the school teachers came late, the women took it as an issue. Now the teachers are hiring an auto and coming to the school in time. The issue was made serious only by the intervention of one of the women's associations. Kalimuthu, being a member of a women association, could easily share the issue with the other women members. A registered milk society is functioning in the village.

Village Temples

Sathurakiriyar temple and Irulappar temple are the two temples in which Thevars, Servais and SCs claim the right to worship. At other temples like Muneeswaran, Amman, Mariamman, Vinayagar all caste people worship but the *poojaris* for these temples belong to the Pandaram community. The Krishnan temple recently constructed is meant for the Yadava community only. All the caste groups are living together cordially and there is no rivalry among them. Moreover, in general, the SCs and Thevar help one another in their farming activities and untouchability does not exist. The Thevars and the SCs do not encourage castewise mobilisation. There are two hamlets, namely Soosaipparpattinam and Arulananthapuram in which the Udayar Christians and the Konar Christians live. There are four churches, two in Soodiyur and one each in Soosaipparpattinam and Arulanathapuram.

Village Economy

Agriculture is the primary occupation and around 100 families are engaged in farming. The major source of irrigation is a PWD *kanmoi* and irrigation water released from the Virakumar Dam which has a link with the Vaigai River. Paddy, chilly, cotton, banana and sugarcane are the major agricultural crops. Animal husbandry is the next source of income in which people of all castes are engaged. About 50 families from the Yadava community are rearing goats. There is a veterinary centre at Parthibanur Village, 7 km. away from the village. Employment opportunities are centred round agriculture and animal husbandry. Brick kiln and construction industry are the next source of employment.

Perception of Panchayati Raj

Kalimuthu did not know the salient features of the Panchayati Raj System. She thought that it is a Central Act and election is compulsory. She did not read the Tamil Nadu Act and was unaware of the Government Orders.

On Gender Issues

Kalimuthu feels that the social customs and traditions related to women are slowly getting transformed.

The women are giving importance to educating girl children. When the District Collector convened the Panchayati Medai, her husband accompanied her and represented the village problems to the Collector. As the Collector did not permit him to talk on behalf of his wife he allowed her to speak to the Collector. After that incident he never accompanied her to the Collector's meeting, but he encouraged her to attend. In this way the women are now shouldering new responsibilities in various walks of life. She felt very bad about her limited literacy and so said that by proper education alone women could stand on their own legs.

On Polity

The present day politics is male dominated. Kalimuthu is now serving as the women's wing convener of the AIADMK and has taken part in election campaign during the Assembly elections in her Panchayat and neighbouring villages. It was a new experience, but, as she did not fully know the politics, she just requested people to cast their votes for the AIADMK candidate. According to her, political empowerment is a long process and rural women need more education to shine in politics. The SHG is the basic unit encouraging women's participation in public life, but not all women in the SHG are showing interest in public activities. Local problems pertaining to women are now understood by women and gradually they will understand all the dimensions of politics. Men have to help the women for their emanicipation.

Common Property Resources

There are wastelands free from encroachment. The area earmarked for threshing is also free from encroachment. There are five graveyards and all are in use by the concerned castes. There are three *ooranis* but no water due to the failure of the monsoon. Bushes are found in the ooranis. Along with trees they will be auctioned by the Panchayat.

The villagers, in general, do not encroach upon the common properties, but near the Panchayat office, in a busy place, two tea shops are run by individuals. The Panchayat does not take any serious steps to vacate them as the teashops are needed.

Her Performance

Convening of Panchayat Meeting

The Panchayat Council meetings are conducted regularly and the members eagerly attend. The members show interest in knowing all the details of the accounting. They demand welfare work for their wards.

The illegal drinking water tap connection given before the establishment of new Panchayat system is an issue in the Panchayat meetings as about 60 such illegal tap connections had to be discontinued as per the order of the District Collector. The houseowners went to Court and got a stay against the order to discontinue the supply. The Ward Members suggested to meet all the houseowners and convince them to pay the deposit amount. In this way the Members are showing interest during the Panchayat meeting.

Convening of Gram Sabha

Kalimuthu's husband used to attend the Gram Sabha meetings and explain the Panchayat activities. The poor among the caste Hindus are now demanding group houses. When 20 groups houses were allotted, 18 SC and 2 BC beneficiaries were selected with the initiative of Ward Members who explained the condition of the proposed beneficiaries in the Gram Sabha. On another occasion, when only one unit to the BC was allotted, a very poor man who has been living in a hut for the past 25 years was selected without any hue and cry from the others. Women and service minded individuals are participating in the Gram Sabha deliberations. The SC men never feel any hesitation to voice their feelings in the Gram Sabha meetings. To mobilise the people, preparatory activities like printing notice, propaganda through public address system and door to door intimation are carried out. Though the venue is the premises of the temple situated inside the village itself, people do not attach seriousness to the Gram Sabha meetings.

The participants, apart from Panchayat activities set by the officials, discuss other issues like kanmoi maramatu and bringing of irrigation water in time. Provision of drinking water and streetlights are the main demands of the public and so necessary work is carried out in this regard. As the old OHT was under repair, it was demolished and, with TWAD assistance, a new OHT was provided. The public tap line was extended in the year 2000 at a cost of Rs. 20,000. Due to unexpected torrential rain, in the year 1999-2000, heavy damage was caused to streetlights and around Rs. 40000 was spent towards maintenance of the drinking water supply system and streetlights.

An approach road to the graveyard with a culvert was provided at a cost of Rs. 33000 in the year 1999. Gravelling work to the village road and the hamlet roads was carried out at a cost of Rs. 23,000. Under earmarked fund, a cement concrete road was provided at a cost of Rs. 46,000. So far twenty group houses have been given to poor families under *kutcha* house scheme. Ten families have been provided with Rs. 10,000 each for renovating their houses with fire proof roofs.

The JVVT allocation has steadily increased year by year. The allocation in the year 1997 was Rs. 7,500 and it was enhanced to Rs. 23,000 in the year 1999-2000. During 2000-2001 Rs. 34,000 was allocated to the village. Any major work was executed only after the receipt of the stamp duty as the Panchayat income from other sources was limited. When funds were available 40 sodium vapour lights were provided.

When the government sanctioned around Rs. 20 lakh for a watershed programme, the opponents of Kalimuthu tried to block it because it would win her a good name. But her husband made efforts with the help of the DRDA officials to convene the Watershed Association, in which representatives from each major community, namely Yadavas, Thevars, Servais and SCs are included. Kalimuthu became the Chairman of the Association.

But the formation of the executive committee became an issue as it is the empowered body to execute the activities. Kalimuthu's husband is an active farmer and as he works for the cause of the marginal farmers, most of the farmers wanted him to be nominated. So he was elected President of Watershed Committee.

Most of the felt needs of the people raised during the Gram Sabha meetings like provision of cattle pond, percolation pond, maintenance of inlet channel, desilting of *kanmoi,* additional borewell for irrigation were provided from the funds allocated under the Watershed programme.

President as an Empowered Personality

Kalimuthu's husband involves himself in public activities. He struggled with the PWD officials to bring irrigation water to the *kanmoi* and attended to repair work when the bank of big *kanmoi* was breached. He deals with such issues through the Panchayat.

Panchayat *vs.* Caste Association

The association of the Yadava community, the Emanuel Peravai and the Mukkulathor Peravai are the major caste based organisations functioning in the village.

The office bearers of Mukkulathor Peravai tried to make Kalimuthu withdraw her nomination as they had decided to field their own candidate. Though Kalimuthu belonged to the same Thevar community, she refused to oblige them. Her husband, who is a key member of the Peravai, disassociated himself from the Peravai. After this the Peravai did not function.

The Yadava Association planned to capture the Panchayat leadership. They used to raise unwarranted questions and level criticism against the Panchayat as they regarded the husband of Kalimuthu as their enemy. But she used to tackle everything patiently.

Panchayat *vs.* Traditional Village Committee

The Village Committee of Soodiyur is a dynamic one as it has got a lot of responsibilities. The maintenance of a 7 acre thidal is the major activity of the Committee. From the sale of grown fuel trees, the Committee could mobilise money. The sale proceeds are utilised to maintain the village temples, the in-let channels and to organise celebrations in the temples. The committee used to collect community funds from each family excepting those belonging to the SC community. As the husband of Kalimuthu is one of the members in the executive body of the Committee, the Panchayat activities are supported by the other members of the Committee.

The money of the Village Committee is deposited in the cooperative bank of Parthibanur, a nearby village. The secretary of the bank cheated the bank. In this misappropriation the Village Committee's deposit was also misused by the bank officer. The villagers held the Executive Committee responsible and asked them to return the Rs.1.50 lakh deposited with bank.

Her Activities in the Field of Social Development

Low cost toilets were provided to 85 families. Toilets and ground level water tank were provided to the middle school.

The immunization programme details were properly communicated to the public by the Panchayat. A medical camp was organised in the village.

A Youth sports centre was established and necessary equipment for outdoor games like Tennis and basketball were provided.

Auditing/Accounting

Kalimuthu does not know the details of accounts and auditing because it is a very big challenge not only for women Presidents but also for men. Nobody tells them the procedures. But everybody asks questions. The officials use it as a weapon. So she leaves it to her husband and he assists her in keeping the accounts properly and getting it audited.

She just visits the government office, meets the officials, submits the demands of the people and appeals to them. Submitting accounts and getting them audited are done by the clerk and her husband.

The Transformation in Her Life

Kalimuthu said that though her husband is shouldering most of her responsibilities, she is improving herself. Now she has improved her writing skill and visits government offices and shares the village problems with the officials independently. She meets the people without fear and replies to the queries raised in the Gram Sabha meetings and attends the Panchayat medai organized by the District Collector. Earlier she was only a housewife. But, after her association, with women's SHGs sponsored by SMSS, she has slowly improved her understanding of the process of development and liberation.

When her husband made arrangements for her contest, she first refused to contest, out of fear. But her husband encouraged her and assured her all help. Because of this encouragement she could engage in some activities, in addition to household and farm activities. Her opinion is that only an educated woman could be an independent women's leader. To liberate women, women must be provided with education.

CASE – 30

SUNDARAJAPURAM GRAM PANCHAYAT RAJAPALAYAM BLOCK, VIRUDHUNAGAR DISTRICT

Socio-Economic Background

Smt. Padmavathy is the President of the Sundarajapuram Village Panchayat. Sundarajapuram is one of the twelve Panchayats reserved for women among the total 36 Panchayats in Rajapalayam Union. It is a monocaste village. Except a few families of Dhobis, Cobblers and Barbers all the families belonging to the SC community. The caste is Pallar but there are two clans among them. One is the Atha Pallar and the other is the Agna Pallar. Each clan is independent in its social activities. They have separate temples, celebrations and separate community leadership and the collection of common fund is also done separately. But this segregation did not matter during the Panchayat elections. The two village headmen representing each clan jointly proposed to select one woman as the seat is reserved for SC women. They listed seven women who opted for the position. After scrutiny, the community leaders decided by lot upon Smt. Padmavathy. As the remaining women did not accept it they contested against the candidature of Padmavathy. So six women including Padmavathy were in the fray. Most of them had the support of political parties whereas Padmavathy enjoyed the community support.

The Background

Padmavathy's husband is working as a watchman in the Social Forestry programme. He used to involve himself in public activities since his youth. He served as the treasurer for a period of one year in the Village Committee. His honest activities and his fair and strightforward observations in the settling of local disputes earned the respect of Padmavathy. Though they belong to the same caste the parents of Padmavathy did not approve of their love affair. So they disowned Padmavathy. In spite of this hardship, Padmavathy and her husband are leading a successful life. This was considered as a good sign and so the majority of the villagers supported her.

The Recruitment Process

With the support of the community leaders, Padmavathy, along with the candidate who contested for Councillor's position, organised a door to door campaign. Wall posters and notices were also printed and widely displayed in all streets. The canvassing was vigorously done for more than a week. Improvement of the basic amenities and individual loans were promised during the campaign. At the end of the canvassing the community leaders, particularly males joined Padmavathy's campaign. She won by a marigin of 47 votes. Though there was a tough competition the election was held smoothly without any untoward incidents.

Now Padmavathy is the woman Gram Panchayat President. So far she had engaged in farm activities, helped in augmenting her husband's income by her farm labour. She has studied up to the 7th standard only. But she runs her family in a planned way, calculating the income and expenditure carefully. This practice now helps her in understanding the income and expenditure of the Panchayat.

Earlier she did not have the practice of reading the newspaper. But now she has started reading the Tamil newspaper

Dinathanthi. She has cultivated the habit of watching the news on the TV available at her house. Understanding the dual responsibility loaded on her shoulders, Padmavathy engages herself in the family activities and is readily available to visit government offices in connection with the Panchayat activities. Her husband and her children do not feel it a handicap when she is not able to prepare meals for them. Her son aged 19 now works as the Panchayat clerk in Sundarajapuram Panchayat itself and her daughter is studying in the local school. Both of them know cooking. They are managing the household. This is a contributing factor in her Panchayat work.

The Village Setting

The village Sundarajapuram has a small hamlet Chozhapuri. All together there are about 1,500 houses. The traditional community leadership administers the social celebrations and temple celebrations properly. It also maintains good relationship with the Panchayat President. It helps in identifying the right beneficiaries without dispute.

The village youth run an orchestra-cum-folk dance troupe and earn money occasionally. Padmavathy, with the help of the MLA, provided a playground and play materials to the youth centre for play and recreation. Now the youth are utilizing the centre properly. They organise Pongal celebrations. The Youth Committee formed by the Panchayat consists of 28 members. They help the Panchayat President during the Gram Sabha meetings.

Under the Joint Forestry Management Programme, a Village Committee was constituted. The village is situated at the foothills of the Western Ghats range of Rajapalayam sector. It is a reserved forest area. There are wild animals in the forest. Hunting of animals is prohibited here. The Panchayat helps the Forestry officials in identifying the poor and farmer families. The West Street residents are economically poor. Hence the Panchayat selected them. Under the JFM programme, a lot of activities are carried out in the village.

The Forestry officials and the village community have a conflict whenever the villagers hunt the wild animals. But the

Panchayat President maintains smooth relationship with the Forestry officials. Once, with the permission of the Revenuc officials, the President brought rubble stones from the quary which is situated on the side of the hillock. The Forestry officials complained that the Panchayat President transported the rubble stones belonging to the Forest Department. They came to the village and checked the stones. They did not believe the explanation given by the President. The officialdom exhibited by the Forest officials irritated the public. When the stones were verified and it was found that the stones did not belong to the Forest Department, the public prevented the movement of the vehicle of the Forest Department officials. The officials at last tendered their apology. This issue touched the ego of the officials. They waited for an opportunity to settle scores. When they came to know that the cousin of the President hunted a deer and cooked the meat, a team raided his house but could not find the meat. But they fixed a complaint against him and he was arrested. The case is pending in court.

Earlier there was a dispute between a few villagers and the Forest officials with regard to cutting of trees, hunting of rabbits etc. A fine of Rs. 5,000 was slapped. The villagers met the higher officials and explained the feeling of enmity shown by the local forest staff. The fine was withdrawn.

Now after the election to the State Assembly, the difference of opinion is becoming wider. A counter-complaint was made against the local forest staff pointing to their involvement in illegal cutting and selling of trees. The DMK and the AIADMK made this issue a political one. The atmosphere is problem ridden as the villagers are grouped into different groups.

The women SHGs are the other local organisations functioning in the village. One of the women, who has already served as a volunteer in the Total Literacy Mission, was interested in forming SHGs. Padmavathy joined her in SHG activities since the introduction of SGSY programme. A lady organiser of the village who is working in a NGO based in Rajapalayam met the President and discussed NGO activities and the scope of the Panchayat's involvement. After this sharing, Padmavthy is now invited to share her Panchayat experience in a forum. So far 6 SHGs have been formed and are functioning well. The women members of SHGs regularly attend the Gram Sabha meetings.

A Farmers' Committee is functioning in the village. It meets periodically in a building provided to them by the Forest Department. They discuss the irrigation management system. Padmavathy periodically shares ideas with the office bearers of the Committee.

Her Perception of Panchayati Raj

Providing basic facilities to the public is the main task of the Panchayat according to Padmavathy. Reservation for women is essential to improve the status of women. She could not say more on Panchayati Raj. After the investigator explained the concept of devolution of powers, she felt that the government officials give due recognition to the Presidents when they meet the officials and properly explained the details needed to the Presidents. With regard to the scope of Panchayati Raj she hopes that the village conditions will improve a lot.

On Development

To bring about development the villagers should come forward to do hard work. Padmavathy compared the progress of the family because of the hard working members of the family with the progress of the village. Even now there is profit in animal husbandry as a lot of land is available for grazing. What they need is hard work. The introduction of group approach for economic development is a good concept and so the government must give priority to forming and strengthening SHGs in villages.

On Village Economy

Agriculture is the main source of income to villagers. Hence the government must take necessary steps to improve the irrigation sources. The farmers subsidiary source of income is animal husbandry. The practice of keeping herds of cattle has now been discontinued as the farmers use more and more of fertilizers. But a lot of hybrid milch animals are now reared by farmers. About

120 families are involved in this avocation in Sundarajapuram Village. The construction industry is a labour intensive one in which more women are engaged. Textile mills provide employment to young girls. Illicit distillation of arrack is a good source of income to a large number of villagers in Sundarajapuram. In addition to agriculture, quite a number of farmers engage in this illegal trade. Two years ago the district authorities decided to put an end to this problem. During their raid, they sought the help of the Panchayat. The district authorities promised to help in getting government loans for these families. But the promise was not kept. Village women engage in arrack sales.

Social Justice

1. Alcoholism is a serious problem in the Panchayat. Due to police raids, most of the men engage their wives for selling the liquor. It is a menace and in spite of police raids, there is increased sales.
2. The families who are below the poverty line send their children for employment to the Rajapalayam mills. In poor families, the mothers are sick and the fathers are addicted to alcohol. Hence the children drop-out from school and work in mills to take care of the families.
3. Extra-marital relationship is prevalent in this village. Due to this there are many divorces. The divorce procedure is very simple and informal. After receiving a payment of Rs. 5,000 for seeking divorce, the community Panchayat summons the couple and their close relatives and awards the divorce after hearing the details from both parties.

In some families, to avoid the transfer of assets by marriage, two sisters are married to a single person. This issue was not considered to be serious earlier. But now-a-days it is considered a bad social custom and the women are showing their displeasure in this regard. Sometimes some families requested Padmavathy to settle their problems. After divorce, the husband visits and unnecessarily interferes in the life of a divorced woman. As she sought Padmavathy's help she, with the help of her husband, met the person and severely warned him. After that the man did not create any problem to his divorced wife. As a woman President she cannot exercise her authority over drunkards.

Political Parties

Political parties like the DMK, the AIADMK and the Puthia Thamizhagam are functioning in the village. As she is a sympathiser of the AIADMK, the DMK Party cadres join the Forest Ranger and try to trouble her. The political parties do not have a vision in their activities. The Puthia Thamizhagam shows interest in her development activities and extends support to her.

Common Property Resources

There are two *ooranis* and six tanks. The tanks are Panchayat Union tanks and there is no power to the Village Panchayat in this regard. In the *ooranis* there is adequate water for fish-cultivation. But, as per the request of the community, tender is avoided so that the water is available round the year whereby drinking water for cattle is ensured. Near the health sub-centre, there is a Panchayat poramboke. Five families have encroached upon this land and constructed huts/tiled houses. It is natham poramboke and so it can be taken for future necessity. As there is no space for a threshing floor the Village Committee purchased a site from a patta holder. The Village Panchayat constructed a threshing floor there.

The Role of Panchayat During Communal Riot

Sundarajapuram and Krishnapuram are separate Village Panchayats but located nearby. In Sundarajapuram the SC is the dominant caste and in Krishnarajapuram the Nadar community is the predominant caste. In Rajapalayam both these communities used to meet in connection with vegetable vending. Due to difference of opinion in their transaction one person belonging to SC was murdered. Hence, to take revenge, the SCs of Sundarajapuram mobilised themselves and murdered three Nadars of Krishnarajapuram. To prevent any further clashes, the Police officials came to Sundarajapuram during the night and formed a Peace Committee without any intimation to the Village

Panchayat. On the next day the District Collector visited the village and enquired about the Panchayat President. She met the Collector and informed him that the Police ignored the Panchayat President and took steps to arrest several persons without verifying the *prima face* case and that due to this the issue was getting complicated. The Collector advised that the President of Village Panchayat had a vital role in the process of peaceful settlement and he encouraged her to involve herself in this process of settlement. After this meeting with the Collector, she boldly met the Police officials when they entered the village. She stood in front of their vehicle and asked them to go back. She talked with the Tehsildhar and the Superintendent of Police in this connection. After this all the policemen camped in the village left. Another Committee was convened at the Tehsildhar's office where all agreed not to resort to any unlawful activities. If she had failed to involve herself as per the advice of the Collector, the police would have unnecessarily overstayed in the village which might have created other problems. This was managed effectively by her in her capacity as the Village Panchayat President. She feels indebted to the Collector for his encouragement. She was able to understand the nuances of various activities in this regard. During this exposure she learnt a lot about establishing and maintaining rapport with officials.

Panchayat Council Meeting

There are 9 Ward Members: 6 men and 3 women and all are SC Members. They all regularly attend the meetings. They verify the accounts, bills and vouchers. The items of work are allotted after a long discussion. During the first two years they did not understand the allocation details. Later they understood about the SFC grant, 10th Finance Commission award and JVVT allocation. After this they hoped that, in course of time, the felt needs of the people will also be fulfilled.

Gram Sabha Meetings

Around 125 persons attend the Gram Sabha meetings. Sometimes the attendance is more, particularly when the selection of beneficiaries for group housing is on the agenda.

Apart from the Panchayat related activities, people used to share other problems like eviction of encroachments in the approach path and encroachments upon agriculture lands. People expected the Panchayat to take necessary steps in all social problems, whether it is directly related to the Panchayat or not. Women demand public toilet and bathroom facilities. The parents demand school toilet and the same was provided by the Panchayat.

Once the people in the Gram Sabha demanded steps to improve the standard of the high school students as many students of 10th standard failed. The headmaster was asked to attend the Gram Sabha meeting and a special night school was proposed along with periodical monthly/weekly tests. After this sharing, the teachers took appropriate steps and, in the next year the results improved. Women generally participate actively in the Gram Sabha meetings.

Social Development Activities

After attending the SIRD training programme, Padmavathy organised a Health Committee and interacted closely with the health staff. Details regarding child birth, child death, nutritional status, immunization etc. are frequently discussed with the health staff.

With the support of the RAMCO Polytechnic, the Panchayat arranged a vocational training centre and typewriting training was provided free to the youth. The PTA was activated and the difference between a few parents and teachers due to the punishment given to some students was settled with the intervention of the Panchayat President. Padmavathy visits the *balwadi* and advises the organiser to keep the premises always clean and tidy. A drinking water tap has been provided by the Panchayat.

Other Development Activities

Thirty-three group houses have been completed. Six Jeevandhara wells have been provided to small farmers. Drainage, road, cement concrete road, 12 culverts were provided under JVVT. A

BT road was also provided under JVVT during 1997-98. With TWAD assistance a 30,000 litre capacity OHT was provided and 75 new taps were provided during 1999-2000.

The Panchayat office building and a ration shop building were constructed under JVVT in the year 1998-99. From the Panchayat Union fund 2 handpumps were provided in the year 1998-99. As 75 families did not have ration cards, the Panchayat listed their names and took efforts to provide ration cards to them.

Social Institutions

The Panchayat actively cooperates with the Farmers' Association which looks after the maintenance of the irrigation tank. There is a Youth Association which is professionally trained in playing music instruments. They stage folk dance and conduct folk music under the banner of Ilam Thendral Oyilattakkulu. The women to meet together streetwise during the celebration of village temples, namely Mariamman temple, Vinayakar temple, Ayyappan temple, Masanam temple, Muniyandi temple and Esakki temple. They are very popular temples among the people. There are twenty Christian families in the village and for them there is a church. Poor families who live in huts joined together and sought help from the Panchayat to get *pucca* houses. Under a special programme for SC/ST communities the Panchayat in trying to get them. In this connection, Padmavathy met the higher officials at the Madurai office in consultation with the AD Tehsildhar of Rajapalayam Taluk.

Removal of Encroachment

The streets in the village are becoming very narrow due to encroachment by residents who extend their houses and so the free movement on the streets is disturbed. The issue was raised several times during the Gram Sabha meetings. When Padmavathy asked the villagers whether the Panchayat could take the matter seriously and initiate necessary steps to remove all the encroachments the villagers agreeded to cooperate.

Then she met the Revenue officials, higher police officials and at last the District Collector in this regard. Funds were provided for a bulldozer to remove the encroachments. With due notice to all and with Police protection, the encroachments in seven major streets were completely removed. Rs. 9,500 per day was spent for hiring the vehicle. It took four days to complete the work.

Tax Revision

The house tax fixed earlier was very low. The maximum was Rs. 11 only. During 1997-98 the Panchayat revised it from Rs. 1.50 to Rs. 5.50, Rs. 3 to Rs. 16.60 and Rs. 11 to Rs. 22.00 and Rs. 44.00. Collection of house tax from the poor is an uphill task. Some pay only after two or three reminders. The Panchayat was not able to collect fully as every year there are some dues of the house tax.

Relationship with Officials

In general the officials assert their superiority. But Padmavathy very politely tells them her demands. She used to argue with them to get the dues to her Panchayat. In this process, she learnt a lot and she got recognition from the officials.

Social Development Activities

She associated herself with the Village Committee to upgrade the school into a higher secondary school and met the officials to take up the construction activities in the school. When there were not adequate teachers in the school, the Panchayat passed a resolution in the Panchayat meetings and met the educational authorities and ensured the posting of additional teachers. Padmavathy maintains contact with the village health nurse and discusses with her the ANC and PNC activities. After attending a training programme organised by SIRD, she started to convene health committee meetings to discuss the health of children, health of adoloscent girls and pregnant women. She tried to undertake a lot of activities through the Namakku Naame scheme. But, due to the non-availability of the *Nattanmai*, the traditional village head man, the village common fund could not be availed of as public contribution. The Panchayat office is functioning in a new building and a library has been installed in the old office building. There is no problem regarding the audit. The officials used to give necessary guidance in accounts maintenance. She used to give money to the Block officials during their audit inspection.

Her Vision

She wishs to completely eradicate arrack and its sales but the villagers are not ready to take risks in this regard. The administration of the existing milk society has to be further streamlined so as to make more profit for the members. Padmavathy is of the opinion that the reservation for SC women has brought a new respect to the SC women and hence she was able to carry out a lot of welfare activities in the village. If the Panchayat system is continued, women will learn a lot and show their ability in all dimensions. The training she received through the Social Welfare Board, RETC, SIRD and Gandhigram shaped her leadership qualities and her husband encouraged her.

CASE – 31

THAMARAIPADI GRAM PANCHAYAT DINDIGUL BLOCK, DINDIGUL DISTRICT

Socio-Economic Background

Mrs. Muthulakshmi, the President of Tamaraipadi Village Panchayat, is 29 years old. She has studied up to the 10th standard. Hailing from Pallar Scheduled Caste, she lives in a joint family with her husband, mother-in-law, father-in-law and her two children, one male and the other female. Agriculture is their major occupation. They own five acres of land of which 2 acres are garden land with well irrigation while the remaining three acres are rain-fed. This family lives in a tiled house without toilet and water tap facilities. Her husband being an unemployed M.Com. degree holder, looks after the agricultural operations and Muthulakshmi helps him in the agricultural activities. Her husband helps in her Panchayat activities during his leisure time.

Recruitment Process

People from fourteen caste groups from all the three major religions live together in this village. The Pallars are the dominant caste group in this village. There are many educated persons in this caste group. Economically, this group is sound and employment-wise, they are well placed. The other caste families include Christians, Vanniars, Parayars, Sakkiliars, Kammalars, Chettiars, Pillais, Gounders, Thevars, *Dhobis*, Ayyars and Muslims. The village people have constituted a Village Committee with eight members, of whom 6 are Pallars, one a Parayar and one a Gounder. All the activities of the village are discussed and decided upon by this Committee. The people of this village accept all the decisions of this Committee.

The ex-President of this Panchayat is also one of the members of this Committee. This Committee helps in preventing caste disputes in the village. The village festivals are also decided upon by this Committee and people accept whatever amount the Committee fixes as their contribution for the village festivals. The Committee also punishes the offenders in the village. Thus, the Village Committee exercises strong power in all the village affairs. This is applicable also to selecting proper candidates as beneficiaries. When the elections to the Panchayats was announced, the presidentship was reserved for SC women. The Village Committee decided to elect Muthulakshmi as Panchayat President for the following reasons: Muthulakshmi's family members are better educated than the members of the other families in the village. Her family members have a cordial relationship with all the other families. They mingle with the community with affection. Her father-in-law used to help the people in getting ration cards, community certificates, birth and death certificates and in getting government loans and benefits from other welfare programmes. Moreover he used to help the people financially. Muthulakshmi's brother-in-law, is a government employee, used to help the village to get benefits from government welfare programmes. All these factors made the people have a regard for all the members of Muthulakshmi family.

The number of educated women was very small in this village. So the Village Committee selected Muthulakshmi to become the President of this Panchayat and no other candidate contested against her. The Committee also selected a Vice-President from among the Pallar caste people. All the nine Ward Members were also selected by the Committee giving due representation to the major communities in the Panchayat. There are five Ward Members from the Pallar community, three from the Christian community and one from the Muslims. Thus, the President and the other Members were all elected unopposed and all the candidates for all these positions were decided upon by the Village Committee of this village.

This Village Committee often convenes a meeting of the public, discusses with the people and then decides upon things. The people are given sufficient opportunity to express their views and feelings and then the decisions are taken. The Committee analyses everything carefully and then only announces its decision. Political and economic factors were not considered in selecting the candidates for the positions, but only the qualities of the persons.

Perception about Panchayat

Muthulakshmi has undergone training in Panchayati Raj in Gandhigram Rural Institute. She feels that the present Panchayat system enables implementing development work easily with funds directly received from the Government. The present system hclps the President to fulfil the basic needs of the villages. The Gram Sabha helps in meeting the people and discussing with them their basic requirements and enables the Panchayat to plan development programmes based on their needs. At the Gram Sabha meeting the people review the work carried out.

The present system of Panchayat Raj helps in fulfilling the basic needs of the people like drinking water, streetlight, road facilities, drainage and public health. Muthulakshmi said that under the earlier system, the Presidents were to work under the guidance of the officials, but now, the Presidents can work independently.

The major drawback, according to Muthulakshmi, is that there is no organic link between the three-tiers of the New Panchayati Raj Institutions. She suggested that the Village Panchayat President should be a member of the Panchayat Union and the Panchayat Union Chairman should be a member of the District Panchayat as was in the earlier Panchayat system.

Village Economy

Paddy and sugarcane are the major crops cultivated as the lands have well irrigation. The landless families go to Kerala and work as labourers since the wage rate is very high there. The others go to nearby Dindigul and engage themselves as construction workers and labourers in industries.

Political Parties

The major political parties of the village are the DMK, the AIADMK, the TMC, the CPI, and the MDMK. The DMK is in the majority here. Since the village has more DMK members, the Panchayat is able to get more funds for development work.

Social Justice

There is no evidence of discrimination on the basis of caste or religion. The Pallars are dominant in the Panchayat. The SC groups have lived in this village for three generations with lands. This condition helps in preventing any unwanted disputes among the groups. Moreover, all these caste groups are treated equally by Muthulakshmi in all development activities and Ward Membership has been offered to all the major caste groups. The selection of the President and the Members was unanimous and it is an indicator of the prevailing unity and cooperation among the various caste groups of this Village Panchayat.

Socialisation Process

All the males of Muthulakshmi's family were in the Congress Party till 1996. Being in the Congress Party, the males of her family rendered a number of services to the people. But, in 1996, all these members joined the TMC. Muthulakshmi got married 6 months before the elections. As the elections were announced with reservation of the presidentship for SC women, she was motivated by her husband and other family members to accept the recommendation of the Village Committee to be the President of the Village Panchayat. So, though she had no political experience or experience in Panchayat affairs, she accepted the leadership only because of her husband's motivation and the Village Committee's recommendation. Her husband joins hands with her in the Panchayat activities.

She does not feel that she is the President, but during the Panchayat Council meetings, she listens to the Ward Members and allots responsibilities to all the Members at their request.

The Panchayat office is kept open from 9.00 a.m. to 12 noon and from 2.00 p.m. to 5.00 p.m. on all working days and the Panchayat clerk is available during these hours in the office. But Muthulakshmi does not visit the office regularly. She comes to the Panchayat office whenever her presence is needed. Sometimes, on her way to Dindigul to the Panchayat Union office, she may peep into the Panchayat office.

All the works of the Panchayat are carried out through proper tender system. Even during the execution of the work, the President used to inspect the quality of the work and ask the contractor to maintain the quality of the work. She also seeks and obtains the people's support in all types of developmental work. For example, in the house construction work for the SCs, she motivated the beneficiary family members to take part by giving their labour as well as supervising so that the quality of work would be ensured and also the expenditure kept down.

Panchayat Income

The Panchayat is a poor one. This Panchayat has not much income except the house tax and funds given by the government. Even with regard to the house tax collection, it is not fully collected. A perusal of the records shows that year after year, the quantum of outstanding house tax is increasing. When probbed further, it came to light that the Panchayat clerk, being an aged person, could not be very active and go to all the houses regularly and frequently to collect the house tax. Moreover, the leadership quality of the President is not high. The Panchayat is not interested in getting the matching grant for the fully collected house tax. The fact of the irregular visits of the President to the Panchayat is also one of the reasons for the failure in collecting 100 per cent house tax.

The Village Committee members as well as the Ward Members insist upon the village people to pay the house tax without any delay. But they have failed to listen to the words of these members only with regard to the payment of house tax while they are ready to accept all the other decisions of the Committee.

Panchayat Council Meetings

As for the monthly Council meetings of the Panchayat all the Members attend them regularly. In such monthly meetings the women, particularly the SC women, urge the Panchayat President to do the needful for their Wards. The women Members used to involve themselves actively in discussions and raise more questions than the males. This may be because of the fact that the President is also a woman, that too one belonging to the SC. The decisions taken in the Council meetings are discussed in the Gram Sabha meetings.

One interesting point is that the Members for the second Ward demanded a cement road in their area. But as the first Ward Member pleaded for the same, quoting the poor condition of that area, they agreed to give up their demand and they asked the Panchayat to lay the cement road in the first Ward. Thus, depending upon the conditions and also depending upon the availability of funds, these Members adjust their demands for the welfare of the entire Panchayat and for even development.

This shows that these Members have cultivated the habit of give and take. Even if they engage in serious discussion and debate, at the end, they decide to share the work depending upon the availability of funds.

Committees

As instructed by the Government, Muthulakshmi has formed seven committees, but these committees are only on paper and do not function actually. When the committees were required, the President readily stated that they had formed the committees as per Government instructions, but they are not actually functioning and she could not give any reasons for the same. It may be due to the reason that the Village Committee looks after the village activities and the committees may not have a notable role to play. But, in reality, Muthulakshmi seems to have no interest in motivating or requesting the committees to perform their roles effectively.

Gram Sabha Meetings

Muthulakshmi feels that the Gram Sabha meetings are useful to inform the people about the various items of work that are being carried out as per the demands of the people and to review the progress of such work. Based on the demands of the people, resolutions are passed and plans are prepared for the work. In the Gram Sabha meetings, 50 per cent of the participants are women. These women demand road facilities, drinking water facilities, extending the pipeline to new areas, cement concrete roads in streets, public latrines, school latrine, new buildings for school, repair of existing school buildings, compound wall for school, drinking water for school etc.

Of the participants 30 per cent are *Dalit* women and they also demand drinking water facilities to their area, drainage, streetlight, medical facilities and employment opportunity for women etc. Muthulakshmi said that even 50 per cent of these demands could not be fulfilled due to paucity of funds from the government.

It is to be noted that since the Panchayat President is an SC woman, the attendance in the Gram Sabha meetings is good with more women, especially more SC women. As for their demands, they are mostly women oriented, *i.e.* drinking water, drainage, public latrine, employment to women etc. They have demanded a school latrine which is essential for the girl students.

It is clear that the people of this Panchayat have really felt their basic needs, but, at the same time, they expect that all their needs should be fulfilled by the government. So, it is necessary to make them understand that they can fulfil some of their basic needs by their own schemes at their own efforts. Muthulakshmi said that only about half of their demands could be fulfilled with the grants of the Central and State Governments and the income of the Panchayat.

Common Property Resources

The Common Property Resources available in this Panchayat include ponds (2 acres and 06 cents), one Panchayat office building, three community centres, 13 TV rooms and three motor rooms. The ponds are used by the public for the cattle population. These ponds also yield income to the Panchayat through fishing rights. These Common Property Resources are maintained properly by the Panchayat with the support of village elders. The people also protect the roadside trees which provide good income. The people do not indulge in felling of trees or tinker with the other Common Property Resources mainly out of fear of being punished if they are involved in such activities. The Panchayat also took steps to evict the encroachers and the eviction has broadened the roads.

Auditing

Muthulakshmi felt that the present system of auditing once in three months is good because it helps in correcting mistakes if any and it prevents the difficulties involved in preserving the bills. But the BDO comes once and at another time the district officials visit for auditing. This should be avoided.

Corruption/Bribes

Muthulakshmi was strong in her view that corruption cannot be eradicated, because it starts right from the Village Panchayat and goes up to Delhi. Whenever the accounts are audited, they have to provide a minimum of Rs. 1,000 per year apart from food. If they do not bribe, the officials raise objections. Because of these factors she felt that corruption has become part and parcel of daily life in Panchayat activities. In this set-up a honest President will be punished for the good work done to the people unless she bribes the officials.

This Panchayat Presidentship was reserved for SC women. Since the members of Muthulakshmi's family are educated and are service oriented Village Committee thought of selecting a member of this family as the President of the Panchayat. So they selected her the President. The village elders, after discussion among themselves selected her as the President unanimously. Even the Ward Members were also selected without election by the village elders providing due representation to each caste and religion. The Panchayat, with the active support and cooperation of the village elders, has fulfilled about 40 per cent of the basic needs of the village like drinking water, road facilities, transport and medical facilities. The President and Members of the Village Panchayat are under control of the village elders and they believe that the Panchayat will try to fulfil the basic needs of the village without involving in corrupt activities and only with this faith they have selected this woman the President of the Panchayat. The development work is always implemented by proper tender system. Since this is a poor Panchayat, Muthulakshmi has made many efforts to augment the Panchayat income by planting trees on the roadsides by constructing a shopping complex and collecting rent from the shop owners.

CASE – 32

THUTHIPATTU GRAM PANCHAYAT
KANIYAMPADI BLOCK, VELLORE DISTRICT

Socio-Economic Background

Smt. P. Jayamalini, the President of Thuthipattu Village Panchayat, is aged 32. Her husband is an office assistant working in a Government office at Vellore.

She is a young smart woman doing business (grocery shop) in the SC colony. She has 1/2 acre of dry land, and during the agricultural season, engages in farming the land. After her schooling she wanted to continue her studies, but due to family circumstances, she was not able to continue her studies. At the age of 20 she got married. After her marriage she started a grocery shop in her colony. She has a two wheeler and she used to go to Vellore to purchase materials for sale in her shop. She has the ambition to educate her children to become doctors or engineers.

Her husband's frequent contact with the villagers, and his service to the poor for the last 15 years in getting government loans for the needy, guiding the people to go to the Government hospital to get treatment, helped her to go to the people for securing their votes. Moreover her husband is an ardent supporter of the DMK Party. When the election was declared in the year 1996, her husband approached the SC colony and Kamaraj Nagar people and asked for their opinion to make his wife contest in the Panchayat President's election. After consulting the village elders and other leaders she contested in the election.

She is the secretary of a women's group and has worked for 5 years for the group's development. This was an additional point to get support from the villagers. Jayamailini and another two candidates contested in the election. She concentrated on the SC colony, Kamaraj Nagar, and Edappalayam, because the voters are more in number in these areas. She conducted a door to door campaign, distributed notice and conducted poster campaign. She went for canvassing along with women's group members. She won the election with a difference of 400 votes.

Socio-Political Environment

The Village Panchayat consists of eight hamlets, namely Thuthipattu, Edapalayam, Gandhi Nagar, SC Colony, Sirukalambur, Kamaraj Nagar, Athisilampadi, Ambedkar Nagar and Mettupalayam. The majority community is the SC. There are also Mudaliars, Yadhavas and Arunthathiyars, Gounders, Reddiars, Barbers, and Dhobis. A total of 388 families live in this Panchayat. Of the population of 1,674, 865 are males and 829 are females. The majority of the families live in the SC Colony (137 families). The Village Panchayat has two *ooranis*, ten open wells, seventeen handpumps, three electric pumps, forty-two public taps, fourteen house tap connections, 89 streetlights, five colour TV sets, two primary schools and one ration shop. These are the basic amenities available in this Village Panchayat.

The political parties, the DMK, the AIADMK, the MDMK, the TMC, are functioning in the village. But the DMK Party is dominant in the village. Jayamalini's husband is a DMK Party man and at the time of the election the party people engaged in canvassing for her. In this Panchayat the role of the political parties is limited. Jayamalini's husband never interferes in any of the activities of the Panchayat. But he helps in execution of Panchayat activities like road work, and arrangement for Gram Sabha.

All the caste groups live together, but at the time of the festivals of the caste Hindus, the SCs are not allowed inside the temple. The Panchayat activities are carried out in all the areas and all the caste groups cooperate with the Panchayat. There are four SHGs in this Panchayat. They used to support the Panchayat at the time of conducting the Gram Sabha meetings and in work carried out in their areas. The SHGs have got a revolving fund of Rs. 25,000 and repaid it to the bank promptly.

Performance – Panchayat Activities

After occupying the Panchayat President's post Jayalamini was not able to go to the BDO's office, the District Collector's office and other offices. Her husband joined her twice or thrice to get copies of the new rules and regulations and Panchayat activity books from the Government officials. After one year, she lost her fear and moved well with the officers and the Collector.

She has carried out many items of work in the villages: in the year 1995-96 extension of drinking water pipeline at a cost of Rs. 33,830, construction of TV room at a cost of Rs. 30,700; in the year 1996-97 extension of drinking water pipeline at the cost of Rs. 5,453, in the year 1997-98 extension of drinking water pipeline at a cost of Rs. 2,736, extension of streetlights at a cost of Rs. 4,840; in the year 1998-99 extension of drinking water pipeline at a cost of Rs. 10,440; constructing a small bridge at a cost of Rs. 43,700, construction of drainage at a cost of Rs. 16,409, installing a threshing floor at a cost of Rs. 29,974; in the year 1999-2000, the Panchayat spent Rs. 14,482 for extension of drinking water pipeline, Rs. 19,985 for construction of drainage, Rs. 63,805 for construction of small bridges, Rs. 31,880 for construction of the TV rooms, Rs. 4720 for construction of household latrines, and Rs. 3,17,511 for construction of colony houses for the villagers.

Monthly Meetings

There are six Ward Members and among them two males and one female are from the BC, two males and one female are from the SC. Every month all the Ward Members, particularly the women members, particpate in the monthly meetings and ask about the income and expenditure statement and demand basic requirements like drinking water, streetlights and so on. Jayamalini used to explain the financial position, the works going to be carried out, and the work carried out so far. There is no difference of opinion among the Members in the monthly meetings. They mostly take decisions by consensus.

Gram Sabha Meetings

As for the Gram Sabha, when the government directs to conduct the Gram Sabha meetings, Jayamalini convenes the Gram Sabha meeting in front of the Panchayat office or in any public place. They prepare handbills and paste them in the tea stalls, circulate them to all the hamlets through the clerk, sweepers and Ward Members. Jayamalini invited the SHG members personally to attend the Gram Sabha meetings.

In the Gram Sabha meetings nearly 20 to 30 per cent of the females, particularly the SC women, participate and demand the income and expenditure statement and their basic needs like road, small bridges, streetlight and extension of pipelines to their streets were demanded. The Panchayat clerk reads out the work carried out by the Panchayat and gets approval in the Gram Sabha meeting. The income and expenditure statement is also read out. The work going to be carried out in future is approved by the Gram Sabha. Jayamalini invites Department officials to attend the Gram Sabha meetings, particularly the District Collector, PO(DRDA), APOs, Executive Engineer, BDO, ABDO and other officials. She invites the village elders also to attend the Gram Sabha meeting. All the Gram Sabha meetings go on well without any problem. The Ward Members are very cooperative in conducting the Gram Sabha meetings.

Tax Collection

Jayamalini said that the collection of house tax was carried out with much difficulty, because of severe drought for the past two years, *i.e.* 1996-97 and 1998-99. Due to this reason the Panchayat is not able to collect the house tax fully. Nearly 20 to 25 per cent of the people have not paid their house tax. In the remaining three years the Panchayat was to able to collect the house tax 100 per cent.

Regarding the house tax she informed to the villagers that if they do not pay the house tax promptly, the Panchayat will not be able to get the matching grant from the government and so cannot provide the basic facilities in the villages. This way she collected the house tax fully. She used the SHG members for the collection of the house tax. The professional tax was collected every year without any problem.

Accounts and Auditing System

Jayamalini knows the details of the records numbering 31, but she does not know how to write accounts. At the time of auditing done by the BDO office officials, she answers some of the questions and the remaining questions are answered by the clerk. She felt that the present system of audit is good because every three months the Panchayat has to clear the accounts, and in this process if there is any mistake it could be rectified. The major obstacle is the local audit. At the time of the audit the Panchayat takes care of the food and other expenses of the officials besides giving some amount of money. It all depends on the queries. She has completed the audit up to March 2001.

Perception about Panchayat

Jayamalini is clear about the new Panchayat system. But she does not know about the earlier system of Panchayati Raj. She pointed out that the New Panchayati Raj System there is reservation of seats for women and that because of the women reservation she has become the President of the Panchayat. The Panchayat President gets money directly from the Government on the basis of the population of the Panchayat. The Gram Sabha is a special feature. Panchayat meetings (monthly meeting) are a regular feature.

In the new system, the Panchayat must satisfy the basic needs of the people. At the time of meeting in the Collector's office, the APO pointed out that the President and Vice-President have the power to draw money by cheque and meet the expenditure on work maintenance of streetlights, public taps, electric motors, TV etc. The representatives are answerable to the people for the Panchayat administration.

Development

Jayamalini defined development as nothing but enabling the people by providing basic facilities to improve their living conditions. For the development activities in the villages, the government has to take necessary steps to allot sufficient resources to Village Panchayats. Development activities have to be carried out on the basis of the needs.

On the basis of this idea Jayamalini has established contact with the Departments of Agriculture, Education, Social Welfare, Health, PWD, Social Forestry and National Highways to get things done.

Agriculture Department

She approached Agriculture Department and they planted 300 teak wood seedlings and 200 seedlings of eucalyptus, 300 casuarina seedlings in the tank area, and a person has been appointed for watering the seedlings. The Department also supplied 2,500 saplings of different varieties to the farmers free of cost. The Department also provided sheep loan to 20 widows in the village, with one unit consisting of 20 sheep.

Educational Department

In the whole of Vellore District Development Education was introduced in Thuthipattu Village. School drop-outs in 8th, 9th and 10th standard have joined the new system. In this village nearly 30 students got benefits under this new scheme. After the examination nearly 10 students have opted for higher studies. This system is successfully going on in this village. Jayamalini approached the Education Department and got this benefit. Then she approached Duraipandi ITI and obtained tailoring training (through TRYSEM) for 2 batches (*i.e.*, 30 members) including 10 SC women. Typewriting training was given to 60 members in the village, and among the sixty, 12 got higher typewriting skills under TRYSEM.

Linkage with NGO

An NGO is also working in this village. The NGO also gave training in making small household ornaments with palm leaf to 17 self-help group members. They were given Rs. 250 as stipend at the time of training for 6 months. The NGO constructed household latrines at a cost of Rs. 2,500. The NGO took care of the construction. The beneficiaries paid Rs. 500 and the remaining Rs. 2000 was provided by the NGO. The NGO arranged a medical camp in the village and supplied medicines through a mobile medical van.

Social Welfare Board

Jayamalini approached Mr. Ramasamy Reddiar, a village VIP, and landlord, got 2 acres of land and divided it into 40 household plots. With the help of the Social Welfare Board, she obtained household pattas for 40 SC people. She got marriage loan for 10 females in this Panchayat.

District Councillor

She approached the District Councillor, and got Rs. 2,35,000 for laying a metal road and a blacktop road in the Panchayat.

Linkage with the MLA

She approached the MLA, and requested him to do some welfare activities for the village. The Tamil Nadu Government provided playground facilities in the Panchayat. The expenses were met from the MLA funds Rs. 25,000 being allotted to the Panchayat. In this District the village playground scheme was introduced first in this village. The village benefited from this scheme and one girl went to the State level sports meet and participated in a volleyball match. The tank desilting programme started first in Vellore District in this Panchayat. The District Collector inaugurated this programme first in this village.

Perception : About Panchayati Raj

When the elections were announced for Village Panchayats in the year 1996, Jayamalini's husband approached the village elders, VIPs and the people, because the Panchayat was reserved for SC women. Jayamalini was interested in serving the people in someway. She had already started a Mathar Sangam and developed small savings among the womenfolk. Being an educated woman, she was enthusiastic about doing some good to the villagers.

Her husband had also done some social work to the SC colony people in many ways. He helped many to get government loans, ration cards, and medical facilities from the government hospital and so on. This social service to the villagers was considered the qualification for public activities. These activities helped Jayamalini to win in the Panchayat election.

The opposition candidate's background did not attract the people. There was no strong background for the candidate. Jayamalini won the Panchayat election by a 400 vote difference. When she entered the Panchayat office, Jayamalini did not know anything about Panchayat activities, how to move with the Government officials, how to get programmes and schemes from the officials. From training programme conducted by the Collector's office staff and from her husbands' advice, she learned the Panchayat activities. After some time, with the help of the BDO's office staff, she learnt about the village work, how to move with Government staff, get funds, conduct monthly meetings, and Gram Sabha meetings, and so on. She does not know anything about the earlier Panchyati Raj System exactly. The New Panchayati Raj System provided opportunity for women through reservation. Similarly, reservation for SC is also available. Gram Sabha meeting is a special feature to establish direct democracy. Regarding money matters funds are given by the Government and there are means to get money from different agencies like District Councillor, MLA and NGOs and several departments. Now-a-days (*i.e.* after 6 months) Jayamalini is doing the Panchayat activities independently. She attends programmes organised by NGOs.

Regarding the gender issues, Jayamalini pointed out that there is wage discrimination against women. She is one of the members of the Mathar Sangam and acted as secretary for one group. With the help of the NGO the women are getting awareness, are motivated to engage in useful activities like making small plan leaf ornaments. Box trays, plates, flowers etc. are prepared and sent to the local market as well as to foreign countries. Women have to face the illtreatment meted out to them by alcoholic men. Another problem is women's illiteracy in the villages. The illiterate women do not act independently and must make efforts to learn through adult education or through their relatives. If the women are educated nobody can cheat the women.

Regarding common property resources Jayamalini said that the tank areas and the village porambokes are not clearly known to the Panchayat President. The government must take steps to identify the poramboke lands and hand them over to Panchayats. Only the Panchayat can plan for the Panchayat, plant trees, construct shops and prevent encroachment of the village porambokes. In this Village Panchayat social justice prevails to some extent. There is no two tumbler system. *Dalits* are allowed to walk in the streets and common places like tea stall, chavadi and ration shops. But the caste Hindus do not allow the SCs inside the temple premises.

Socialisation

When she become the President, she did not know about the Panchayat and its activities. Training programmes and the encouragement of her husband and officials (Collector's office, BDO's office and other department officials) and the villagers helped her to understand the Panchayat and its activities. She learnt about the programmes through government orders, newspaper, BDO's office, and hearing news from different places helped her to understand the Panchayat, and to get funds from different sources.

Another important help she got from a political party. Since her husband belonged to the DMK Party, she also followed the same principles. The party people gave information about the Panchayat and its activities to her.

She encouraged intercaste marriage in the village. Considerng the age at marriage for girls, she persuaded two persons to postpone their marriage by one year, and in another case by six months.

Jayamalini belonging a poor family was not able to continue her studies after +2 education. After marriage, she looked after her family. One year before she contested in the election, she involved herself in forming a Mathar Sangam in the SC Colony area. She encouraged the womenfolk in the savings habit, and helped in getting loans at low rates of interest. She helped the women to start some small trades, get profit in the business and avoid unnecessary gossiping.

After she became the president of this Panchayat with the help of her husband, officials like BDO, the Collector office, she learnt about the activities and functions of the Panchayati Raj Act. She approached different departments like, Agriculture, Education, Social Welfare Board, NGOs and MLA to get benefits for her village. Her involvement in NGO activity helped in getting a number of welfare programmes to the village. Within these five years she has learned many activities of the government and how to get the funds/programmes from the government as well as the NGO sector. The village setting is also a supportive factor for her involvement in public activities. She is brilliant and courageous to carry out the Panchayat activities in future with this experience.

CASE – 33

UCHIMALAIKUPPAM GRAM PANCHAYAT SENGAM BLOCK, THIRUVANNAMALAI DISTRICT

Socio-Economic Background

Mrs. Annapoorani is the President of Uchimalaikuppam Village Panchayat. She belongs to the SC community and is aged 27. She has studied upto the 10th standard. She has a joint family. She lives with her four brothers and she has one female child. She has two acres of dry land and there is no regular income from this land. Her husband is doing agricultural work in the local area. Her father has a two wheeler and a taxi and he is also a contractor. She has a tiled house, electrified, with toilet facility but there is no individual tap connection.

She is closely associated with local SHGs. Besides she belongs to the AIADMK Party. She has not engaged in any intense political activity. She is a party member since her father belongs to the AIADMK Party. The party helps her in certain activities in the village. She felt that village people should know the government programmes. For this reason she joined the AIADMK Party in order to know about the government programmes and carry out the same in her village.

Village Panchayat Profile

This Panchayat has a population of 738, and of them, 361 are males and 377 are females. This Panchayat has 3 hamlets and six Ward Members. Of them 3 are male, and 3 are female. One male and 2 females belong to the SC. The total households are

359, of which 30 are *pucca* houses, 151 are tiled and 178 are huts. The major caste groups are Naidus, Udayars and Scheduled Castes.

For drinking water facility there are one OHT, 13 public taps, 40 individual tap connections, 17 handpumps and 3 open wells. Drainage facility is available only for 30 metres and there is no toilet facility. Twenty houses have individual household latrines. A private clinic (RIMP) is available in this Panchayat. There is one *balwadi*, one noon-meal centre and one primary school in this Panchayat. A higher secondary school is available in Kannakurukai, which is 5 km away from this Panchayat. This Panchayat has three SHGs, one Ambedkar Sangam, two Cine Fans Associations but no youth association. There are 120 farmers and the major crops are groundnut, paddy, kambu, kelvaragu and cholam. The major source of irrigation is well.

A one acre common pond is available in this Panchayat and this pond is utilised for irrigation purposes, and for drinking water for livestock. All the farmers except a few have milch animals, goats, and poultry. Fifty people are involved in pig rearing. No veterinary centre is available in this Panchayat but one is available in Eraiyur, 4 km away. All political parties are having their units in this Panchayat and the AIADMK is the dominant unit in terms of membership. Untouchability is the major social issue in this area. The people of the SC are not able to enter the village temples in the local area.

Village Setting

The Dr. Ambedkar Sangam is the only major social institution of this Panchayat. This Sangam has been engaged in Panchayat work and Gram Sabha activities, *i.e.* conducting awareness meetings for the villagers. Besides, this Sangam has demanded basic facilities for this Panchayat.

Recruitment Process

Village people, school friends, and her parents advised Annapoorani to contest the election. Her father is doing contract work and so he is very popular in this area. Initially she was doing tailoring work in the village. In this way she was well known in the Panchayat and so contested in the election. Four candidates contested against her. But she won due her fathers' influence. During the electioneering, she promised the following facilities: drinking water, roads, streetlights and other basic amenities.

The expenditure on the election was Rs.10,000. The village traditional Panchayat maintained rivalry with her even after the election. The other defeated candidates did not develop any antagonism. In fact the caste Hindu groups supported her in the election. She was aware of a few features of the New Panchayati Raj System, namely reservation of seats for women and *Dalits* and Gram Sabha before the election.

Perception

Annapoorani does not know much about the 73rd Constitutional Amendment Act and the Tamil Nadu Panchayati Raj Act, 1994 but knows that 33 per cent reservation for women is the major feature of the New Panchayati Raj System. With the help of her father and Block officials, she came to know about the new Panchayati Raj System. Because her father had good contact with the Union office as a contractor the Block officials helped her with the Panchayat development activities. She felt that providing employment opportunity to the people and basic facilities to the community will develop society. This New Panchayati Raj System can provide the opportunity to develop infrastructure facilities.

Agriculture and animal husbandry activities will help in the improvement of the village economy. Groundnut, paddy, kambu and sugarcane are the major crops cultivated in this area. In addition most of the self-help groups are engaged in livestock rearing and poultry farming.

Annapoorani said that small scale industries which provide employment for the skills of the people are essential for the community and particularly for the women. For women, getting employment opportunities is very difficult and hence she suggested that any industry which provides jobs for the women is needed in this Panchayat. Women's participation is essential in the process of development, *i.e.* educated women must participate in the Village Panchayat development activities. Particularly SC women should participate in the Panchayat activities.

A few Panchayat Ward Members are not participating effectively in the Panchayat activities. Annapoorani stated that cooperation is essential between the Ward Members and the village people.

Politics

Annapoorani stated that the AIADMK Party members are supporting the Panchayat activities, particularly in getting old age pension, marriage assistance fund for the poor and school development activities. Gender discrimination prevails in the Panchayat. She said that it could be solved only through the SHGs. They have to sensitize people to the issues of women and only then gender discrimination could be eliminated. A great deal has to be done to establish social justice. Her father and brother were involved in AIADMK Party activities as members of the party. So she entered politics at the age of 20. She stated that since her family members followed the AIADMK line she also followed the AIADMK Party. She is a regular reader of Tamil newspapers like *Thinamani, Thinamalar, Thamilarasu* and she also watches the TV news.

Performance

Once in a month the Panchayat meeting is conducted in the Panchayat office. In the Panchayat meetings, Ward Members' cooperation is ensured and they expect some kind of benefits from the Village Panchayat. In the Gram Sabha meeting, the following major items have been discussed and resolved upon drinking water facility, streetlights, maintenance of streets. Of these water facility is not fully provided but the other items of work have been carried out. Further Annapoorani stated that the Gram Sabha resolutions have to be honoured by the officials. Otherwise there is no use in conducting Gram Sabha meetings. The Presidents find it difficult to organize Gram Sbaha meetings: 25 per cent of the SC women attend the Gram Sabha meeting and they are agricultural labourers. The *Dalit* men participate is poorly, because they are more interested in attending to their daily work. The following are the ways to improve the Gram Sabha meetings.

1. Selection of beneficiaries should be properly done in the Gram Sabha meeting;
2. Block officials should help Panchayat activities to carry out the resolutions of the Gram Sabha; and
3. Allocations have to be made only on the basis of the demands projected in the Gram Sabha.

Annapoorani felt that the basic facilities have to be provided at the grassroots level and for weaker sections. She has carried out the following items of work effectively: maintenance of streets installation of new streetlights, providing road facility getting old age pension for few eligible candidates persons, marriage assistance scheme for eligible, extension of lighting facility to the new streets. The Panchayat is not able to meet the water needs of the people. With regard to committees they have not been formed. Annapoorani did not know about the significance of the committees. Hence she is not interested in the formation of the committees for the Village Panchayat.

Panchayat Finance

The tax revisions made as follows :

	Old Rate	*New Rate*
(i) Huts	Rs. 2.20	Rs. 2.20
(ii) Tiled house	Rs. 5.50	Rs. 11.00
(iii) *Pucca* house	Rs. 22.00	Rs. 44.00

Annapoorani has no ideas for mobilisation of resources other than raising the house tax. There are about 200 tamarind trees and each tree fetches Rs. 150 as income to the Panchayat. Annapoorani did not know about the details of the government grants. But she has suggested that the government grant has to be increased from year to year. Adequate grant is needed for

Village Panchayat development activities. The government officials have to explain about the grants available for Panchayats. Officials' cooperation is essential in all aspects of the Panchayat development activities, including accounting and auditing. Four years of accounting and auditing have been completed. She does not have adequate knowledge of accounting procedures. With regard to the auditing system, every 3 months the auditing is being carried out and she feels that it is a good system because, if there is any mistake in the bills or accounts it can be rectified immediately.

Corruption prevails at every stage in the Panchayat administration. Officials are demanding money for even giving schemes to the beneficiaries. For audit also they demand money. To clear the bills also the President has to give money. Unless corruption is stopped at the official level, the Panchayat administration cannot be streamlined.

Social Development

Annapoorani is interested in tree planting activities. But there is water scarcity in this area. However individuals plant trees in their homes. For environmental activities she frequently discusses with the SHGs and village committee and other people. She maintains close relations with self-help groups and the village committee for the development of the Village Panchayat. Being a woman she has provided health information related to family welfare and child care. In addition she has helped the weaker sections of the people to get government schemes for instance old age pension and marriage assistance for women. With regard to awareness she has conducted many meetings for the youth and women for their own development.

For school development she has taken efforts in terms of maintenance of school building, providing a small OHT, extension of pipeline, whitewashing. She has held discussions with the *balwadi* teachers for improvement of the children. Sweet packets were distributed to the school students on the Republic Day and Independence Day and this amount was spent from her own money.

For sanitation purposes, she has conducted a few meetings, like Gram Sabha meetings among the village people. But the villagers do not cooperate effectively in this regard. They do not have adequate awareness due to illiteracy. Annapoorani has held discussions with Block officials for sanitation in this Panchayat. There is no health centre in this area. Hence the villagers have go to Thiruvannamalai hospital, which is 40 km from this Panchayat. The drainage system is constructed in only a few places. A health centre is essential for this Village Panchayat. The VHN is taking care of the health of the children and the womens. She visits the villages once a week. Annapoorani has gained sufficient knowledge about Panchayat during these years and has done some basic services to the people. Now she has developed an aspiration to contest in the next election also for the same post.

CASE – 34

SU. VALAVETTI GRAM PANCHAYAT THIRUVANNAMALAI BLOCK, THIRUVANNAMALAI DISTRICT

Socio-Economic Background

Mrs. Sowbakkiam is the President of Valavetti Village Panchayat in Thiruvannamalai Block. She is a retired teacher, aged 65. She served in the Panchayat Union school, and she belongs to the SC community. She lives in Valavetti Village with her husband. Their sons and daughters are married and living in Thiruvannamalai. The income from her pension is Rs. 3500 per month. She possesses one acre of dry land and the annual income is Rs. 3000 per year. Having been a teacher she is not interested in political activity.

Village Profile

This Panchayat has six Ward Members, of whom three are from the BC (two males and one female) and 3 are from the SC (two males one female). This Panchayat has only one hamlet, Madura Periyar Nagar. The total population of this Panchayat is 1,850, of which 950 are male and 973 female. Among the SC category 434 are male and 453 are female. With regard to drinking water, there are 7 open wells, 14 handpumps, 4 OHTs, 32 public taps and 67 individual tap connections in this Panchayat. The streetlights are 56 in number, including sodium vapour lights. Now only one TV is available and 2 more TVs are needed in 2 places.

Recruitment Process

Sowbakkiam herself did not have any interest, but her husband compelled her to contest in the Panchayat election. Hence she contested. Three others contested in the election against her. Among the SC community a section of the people did not support her while BC community supported her because she was a local retired teacher and had earned a good name among all the communities. Besides the school going students and her old students canvassed for her. Because of this reason she won by a margin of 34 votes.

During the canvassing she promised the following facilities to this Panchayat: water, roads, basic facility based on the various needs of the villages. She went for door to door canvassing twice. In this way, she succeeded. She spent Rs.10,000 for the election, particularly for refreshments during the canvassing.

Sowbakkiam runs a Non-Formal Education Centre in her home voluntarily and gives special coaching to students belonging to poor families of all castes. She happily spends her own money for purchasing notebooks for the poor children. She distributes gifts as incentives to poor children to encourage them to study. Her service mentality is known to the villagers and so the majority of them supported her.

Perception

Sowbakkiam at first did not have any awareness about the 73rd Constitutional Amendment Act and the features of the New Panchayati Raj System, and the Tamilnadu Panchayati Raj Act.

But she gradually learnt about Panchayat administration with the help of Block officials.

She perceives development as an opportunity provided to individuals to equip themselves to manage their lives and to lead a decent human living. After interaction with officials, she understood the important aspects of the Panchayati Raj System, particularly the significance of reservation, procedure for fund allocation, account maintenance, and availability of various schemes.

Development

As for the role of the government in the development process, Sowbakkiam insists upon the necessity of a infrastructure facility to the rural Panchayats, *i.e.* school, health facility and modern agricultural techniques should be known to the farmers. Small scale industries are essential and Village Panchayats must pay attention to industrial activities.

Common Property Resources

In every village one can see the functioning of traditional Panchayats. They actually control the activities of the community. They have community norms to resolve disputes. Village properties which are under the control of the traditional Panchayat are safe but the properties of the village formal Panchayats are not safe and they are being encroached upon as they are the properties of the government. Retrieving the property is not so easy. The traditional Panchayat is in the hands of the dominant caste. The formal Panchayat has to adjust with the traditional Panchayats. Otherwise no work can be carried out smoothly.

Gender Issues

The SHGs will be empowered by giving training and arranging loan facility to women for their business ventures. In this Panchayat SHG members are engaged in tamarind selling. The tamarind fruits are purchased from the wholesale merchants in the town areas and sold in the rural areas. There are a variety of trades that could be done by women and hence they should be encouraged.

Men always migrate from one place to another place to earn money while women cannot migrate like men. There is no second opinion that the status of women in the rural areas is poor and inferior to that of men in terms of living conditions. Awareness has to be created among the women about this condition in the society.

Social justice means "Equality and equity for all". Sowbakkiam complains that community law is in operation in the place of rule of law. The traditional Panchayat leaders are from the dominant community and they want to perpetuate the domination of the caste Hindus.

She felt that this kind of practice could be eliminated only by a mass movement for which the oppressed people should be conscientised. She said that the self-help group women are being conscientised on gender issues and on the issues of the *Dalits*. It is a long drawn struggle for which she is preparing the people. Further she created awareness among the people about their living conditions.

Performance

Once a month the Panchayat meeting is conducted but the Ward Members do not support the development work of the whole Village Panchayat. They ask questions related to their own wards and not for the development of the whole Panchayat. Every Gram Sabha meeting is conducted in the school building. Steps are taken to announce the Gram Sabha meetings. The Ward Members also spread the communication relating to Gram Sabha meetings. In this situation, the Ward Members and the President should have discussions for the Village Panchayat's development and on work based on the receiving of regular grants and income.

Since 1997 onwards, Sowbakkiam has given much importance to drinking water facility, as water supply is inadequate in the months of April, May and June in her Panchayat area. The road facilities become poor during the rainy season. People cannot walk in the streets and on the roads. So she has paid special attention to road facilitics since 1996. From 1997 the maintenance of new group houses for SC people has been attended to. Two individuals benefited through the Jeevandhara schemes for digging open wells. The following items of work were done effectively after consultation in the Gram Sabha meetings – linkage roads, library facilities and community hall. Apart from this through various schemes items of work like threshing floor, small culverts and drainage have been carried out. Seven committees have been formed but they not functioning effectively.

The village people demand more number of house tap connections but only 67 persons are having individual tap connections. For health and sanitation a public toilet is not available and only 10 houses are having individual household latrines. A graveyard shed with lighting facility is necessary in this Panchayat.

Sowbakkiam maintains that only through Panchayti Raj Institutions, a number of activities have been carried out within a short span of time. So there is scope for improvement of the infrastructure facility of the village in the near future.

The Panchayat meetings are conducted regularly in the Panchayat office. The Ward Members always demand the basic amenities, namely streetlight facility and drinking water. In the Gram Sabha meetings, the government schemes are discussed and the lists of individual beneficiaries are being decided upon. Attendance is always poor. The Panchayat Presidents some manages to show.

Panchayat Finance

House, professional and local taxes have been collected regularly. Stamp duty and SFC grants are the regular income of this Panchayat. The SFC grant is sanctioned from 1997 onwards and gradually increased year by year, *i.e.* 1997-98 Rs. 64,097, 1998-99 Rs. 66,907, 1999-2000 Rs. 1,49,452. The house tax matching grant is as follows :

1.	1995-96	Rs. 2,000
2.	1996-97	Rs. 3,000
3.	1997-98	Rs. 1,099

JVVT fund is sanctioned from 1997 to 2000 regularly, while in 2001 it is not yet sanctioned. The earmarked fund is meagre. Sowbakkiam insists on regular grant from the government every year without fail. If any income source fails the Panchayat cannot carry out development activities.

The major expenditure is on the salary of the Panchayat staff, maintenance of streets/tanks/OHT/TV rooms and construction of small bridges, extension of pipelines for water supply. The tax revision for huts house was from Rs. 5.50 to Rs. 11.00 and for tiled house from Rs. 11.00 to Rs. 22.00. But the people do not properly pay the house tax.

Those who have individual house tap connections pay Rs. 30 per month regularly. Sowbakkiam is not clear about the details of the government grant she depends upon the Panchayat clerk. Sometimes the Panchayat clerk does not tell her the information related to Panchayat works.

The relationship between the clerk and the President is a strained one. The clerk is a local youth belonging to the SC community. He accuses Sowbakkiam of not doing anything for the SC community. She feels that the caste Hindus would feel that she is always helping the SC. She asserts that she is the President of the Panchayat and not the SC community alone.

She complains that the clerk does not properly bring to her notice, the various communications received by the Panchayat. Sometimes very important information pertaining to availing of funds is not shared by the clerk with the President.

She complains that the SC families expect that the President must turn all the development work to the SC segment. There are various schemes available only with the Union and Government Departments which do not come under the power of the Village Panchayat. The clerk misleads the youth and through them he is planning to disturb the Panchayat activities.

The difference of opinion between the President and the SC community is visible. In the name board written on the wall of the Village Panchayat office, the name of the President was erased. The President took up the issue with the Union administration and the officials visited the village and explained to the villagers that this type of interference could not take place.

Then the name of the President was written again. But within a few days somebody removed the name. As the mood and temperament of the villagers are against her leadership, she doesn't want to spend her energy on taking this issue again to the officials. She has decided to complete her period without any serious disputes with the SC community members. In the SC community, a few members behave rudely with her and spoil her name.

Social Development

Among the three opponents who contested in the election two women took their defeat as a very serious affair. They do not meet or talk with Sowbakkiam even now but otherwise there is no problem in this Panchayat. The basic facilities have been provided according to her capacity. For total community development she has taken various steps but the village people do not understand, particularly the fund allocations to the Gram Panchayat. She has taken sincere and serious efforts for women's development in two areas. One is family welfare, the another is age at marriage.

An OHT and toilet facilities were provided and a school building has been constructed. These facilities are very useful to the students and staff of the school.

Conclusion

The BC communities and few people belong to the SC community appreciate the Panchayat activities. They also support the development work of the Panchayat. They regard Sowbakkiam as a suitable person as she is a retired teacher and has good character and an aptitude for social work. Some of them have asked her to contest in the next election but she has refused. She wants to take rest in her daughter's house. Besides she explained that Panchayat administration is a new system which she could not understand fully. Sometimes the Village Committee also plays an interfering role in the welfare of the people with the help of the party people, without consulting the Panchayat President.

CASE – 35

VANDUVANCHERI GRAM PANCHAYAT VEDARANYAM BLOCK, NAGAPATTINAM DISTRICT

Socio-Economic Background

Mrs. Rani Muniyakannu, aged 39, is the President of Vaduvancheri Village Panchayat. She belongs to the most Backward community. She has studied upto higher secondary course. Her family is a nuclear one consisting of her husband, one son and one daughter. Both are studying in school.

Her husband is the former secretary of the local unit of the DMK Party and the President of the Cooperative Society. The family has 10 acres of wet land and 10 acres of coconut plantation. They live in a tiled house but have decided now to construct a new house this year. The present house is having all facilities like electricity, toilet and drinking water tap connection.

Rani is an active member in the federation of women leaders. She is the secretary of the eastern region covering four districts, namely Pudukkottai, Thanjavur, Nagapattinam and Thiruvarur. She is also an active woman leader in the DMK since 1996, serving as the union level women's wing convener. She used to deliver speeches effectively during the DMK Party's public meetings.

Recruitment

A cousin of Rani was a former member of the Gram Panchayat. Her husband wished to contest in the election but unfortunately the position was reserved for women. The DMK Party proposed Rani for the post as their family is a reputed family and their affluence and honesty is known to all.

Moreover Rani is an educated woman. Earlier she served as a *balwadi* teacher in her native village before her marriage. She used to show her boldness in dealing with family issues. Since her husband was involved in settling disputes in the village, she also participated in the conflict resolution process and through these incidents she earned a name among the public. Against this backdrop she was fielded in the Panchayat elections.

There were five candidates in the fray including Rani. Except Rani all the rest had political backing. Though Rani's family belongs to the DMK Party, the DMK partymen supported the candidate fielded by the Congress Party. Even the lone SC candidate in the fray was supported by the Communist Party of India. But except Rani, the rest were less educated, older than her and economically weak.

During the election campaign Rani promised all essential services to the needy. Individuals who belong to the Tamilar Bhoomi Party, close relatives, both men and women, and the labourers who were working on her farm accompanied her during the campaign.

The expenditure was less than Rs. 10,000 as only notice and wall posters were printed. Rani won the election by a margin of 300 votes. Her husband's social involvement, her caste and her family reputation, in addition to her education and age were the contributing factors for her success. There was no untoward incident but the defeated persons did not continue their friendship with her. But she used to visit their houses to attend social functions.

Village Setting

Vanduvancheri is a multi-caste village where Ambalam, Thevar, Konar, Reddiar, SC, Naicker, Muslim and Nadar communities are living. The Ambalams are the majority caste. The village has six hamlets, namely Sarubojaramapuram, Dulasiapattinam, Vanduvancheri, Periya Thidal, Panchankulam and Vellikkidangu. The Panchayat is situated along the costal area and the backwaters flow through it.

Village Temples

Avvaiyar, Kollathu Mariamman, Sivan and Ayyanar temples are considered common to all, but the SC people cannot enter them. Vandurai Mariamman temple belongs to the Ambalams. Now-a-days the SC men come to this Mariamman temple and offer the

Kavadi during the festivals. The Thevars will not come to the Amman Kovil and the SC women cannot come into the Mariamman temple. But they are permitted upto the statue of the Nandhi in the Sivan temple. The village temple celebration is organised by the Village Committee consisting of representatives from the major castes. People donate money to the Village Committee to conduct the celebration.

The committee members are mostly involved in other public activities including the Panchayat's. Usually the Ambalam community's decision is upheld by the others. A Muthirayar caste association once functioned actively. But after its transformation into a political party, namely Thamilar Bhoomi Party, the caste association lost its significance. Moreover the Ambalam allies of the Muthirayars switched over to the then ruling party, the DMK. There is one mosque in the Muslim street.

Political Parties

The DMK is the dominant party and the AIADMK is almost equally strong. Other parties like the CPI, CPI(M), BJP, Tamilar Bhoomi, Makkal Tamil Desam are also present in village. The office bearers of all the political parties used to meet and share their concerns and opinions on the Village Panchayat activities. Mostly the men belonging to the DMK evince keen interest and enthusiasm in public issues. The youth wing of the DMK Party is an active body. The members show their involvement whenever needed to tackle issues. At the time of the issue of silicon sand misuse, the youth mobilised themselves and participated in programmes like *dharna*, demonstration and fasting, to protect the environment.

Women's Association

With the guidance of an NGO, a women's association is functioning in the village for the past six years. About 15 SHGs are functioning in this Panchayat out of which seven have got the revolving fund. Obtaining land for lease, obtaining fishing rights by tender, extending micro credit among themselves are the prime activities of the SHGs. Handicrafts training-cum-production is also organised for one group. The NGO, the President of Village Panchayat and the SHGs maintain good relationship among themselves. The SHG women attend the Gram Sabha meetings. They extended their support during the mass action in connection with the misuse of silicon sand. A retired headmistress is engaged in organising the women's association and awakening the womenfolk. The SHGs are picking up well as the women show interest in public activities and come out boldly to criticise the mistakes in the government's activities.

Village Economy

The village land is mostly sandy and so trees like coconut, mango, palm, casuarina, and cashewnut are growing. Most of the land is owned by Muslim farmers. The other castes get these lands for lease from the Muslims. Near the backwaters area, the drainage canal brings flood water and upto a depth of 12 feet. The water is good for irrigation and so paddy crop is being cultivated. The paddy variety is a good and traditional one and it can withstand floods also. The paddy is liked by Kerala people and so it is being sent to Kerala. There are around 50 acres of common land lying on the two sides of the backwaters canal. The poor farmers are cultivating paddy in those lands.

As the village is a remote one, the Agriculture Department officials do not visit and provide guidance. Due to lack of professional guidance in agriculture, the yield in cashewnut is now-a-days reduced. The Department of Horticulture has a scheme but it is not suited to the local farmers. To improve the agriculture, the government sectoral departments must visit and interact with the farmers and help them in farming activities. There is potential for inland fishing for which the farmers need orientation as for about five months, from July to November, it is a good season for fish culture in the backwaters. During the rest of the year, the native fishermen community has the right to catch fish. During this season fish is available in plenty. Farmers and fishermen have maintained this agreement traditionally. Due to non-availability of cold storage and market access, most of the fish caught by the fishermen goes waste or is used as manure in groves. So the government must come forward to properly help both the farmers and the fishermen community.

Due to non-availability of adequate grazing land, the cattle population has been reduced now. The poor who availed of government loans misused the loan assistance but those who availed of them from the society regularly repaid the loan. To improve the village economy, modernisation of fish farming and proper marketing access is necessary. Value added production from mango, coconut and cashewnut will also improve the economy of this area. There should be a provision to give a large sum to develop the land by mortgaging as the farmers mortgage the land to individuals and waste the money on non-productive items of expenditure. To avoid any default in repayment, the registered document can be in the possession of the lending institution.

Social Problems

Suspicion and mistrust between Hindus and Muslims resulted in a communal dispute during 1999-2000. Muslims youth hailing from other areas pasted posters in the streets where Hindus are living. Usually the Muslim never entertain any advertisement in their street. And so there was a dispute between the Hindu and Muslim youth in which two Hindu young men suffered injury. Cases were registered and a Peace Committee was formed. As the two communities usually never entertain any ill-will, they wanted to settle it amicably. The Hindus advised the Muslims not to encourage outsiders in the village as they do not understand the relationship among the various communities. At last, the Muslims sent away the youth who had come from other areas to this village for jobs. The Panchayat played an active role in this peace process.

Alcoholism is now-a-days increasing and toddy is freely available as the distillers are not controlled by the Police in spite of complaints made against them. The Panchayat could not do anything against the culprits as the Police do not support the Panchayat.

Perception on Panchayati Raj

New Panchayati Raj is getting popularity as provisions like reservation for women, Gram Sabha, three-tier system and decentralisation of power to Panchayats are very much useful for village development.

On Development

Individual development in the Panchayat will be possible only through land and through land the basic need of food will be met. After this fulfilment only development can be possible. The women can be given training in skills to get employment opportunity in the non-farming sector also. Loan and technical guidance have to be given to farmers.

On Polity

If their role is effectively performed by the people's representatives most of the people's issues and problems could be solved. At present political parties do not have an ideological background and they are not effective in addressing the problems of the people.

Due to this understanding, as a leader belonging to the DMK, Rani gives importance to women. She has organised sports and cultural events exclusively for women during the Independence Day celebration. This was possible as the woman President of Vedaranyam suggested this idea of sports and cultural events for women. The DMK Party oriented her in this perception.

On Gender

The mindset of society is getting changed regarding women's liberation but still there is some hesitation among menfolk. Women are treated as a commodity and an object. It is true that women are not treated on par with men. Women should be awakened to meet the challenges in the society. Education plays a vital role in eliminating discrimination on gender basis. Men should also be conscientised on gender and then only gender discrimination could be eliminated.

On Common Property Resources

In the Vanduvancheri Panchayat and in two nearby Panchayats, silicon, the rare earth, is available in plenty. The silicon sand is fit for export to foreign countries as raw material used in glass and software industries.

Three companies established near Vanduvancheri own four acres, two acres and five acres respectively and have got licence to quarry the silicon. But they take the silicon even outside their land and cause damage to the sub-soil and soil-erosion takes place. When the farmers complained to the Panchayat, a resolution was passed to refer the issue to the Government's Pollution Control Board. As nothing happened, the people decided to stage a demonstration and to prevent the transportation of the silicon. The Police came and arrested Rani with other women and the youth. All the people mobilised and sat in front of the Police station. By evening all were released as the Superintendent of Police ordered to do so. When the matter was brought to the notice of the District Collector, he felt unhappy over the activities of the Panchayat President.

The matter was further refered to the Additional Collector of Mines. Then fasting was observed by the villagers. When the problem became serious the President met the Rural Development Minister and asked for his intervention. He told that the licence is issued by the Central Government. A high level official visited from Chennai and inspected the site and verified the complaint against the Panchayat. The sites belonging to the companies were marked and they were advised not to quarry sand in other areas. The NGO SNEKA rendered counselling, guidance and assistance in this regard. Moreover the media blow up this issue.

The MLA, when contacted and asked to extend his support but advised Rani that it was not possible to prevent quarrying as the companies had got licences. After the struggle, when Rani had succeeded in regularising the activities of the companies, the MLA himself paid a visit to the village and felicitated her.

There is a garden site of 57 acres belonging to the Panchayat, with 200 mango trees, 300 cashewnut trees, 100 coconut trees and casuarina trees. There are also 30 small ponds in the site. The garden is properly maintained as two watchmen are employed by the Panchayat. The Panchayat President in the previous period took no action when the villagers cut the trees. Even now his family members cut trees and sell them without the knowledge of the Panchayat. The incident was reported to the Union officials and the Police. None of them came and took action. Once a villager stole a cashewnut tree. He was caught and punished by the Panchayat and after that such theft has declined.

The garden could be fenced with barbed wire if the government permits the Panchayat to utilise the seed money from the income. But only 10 per cent of the total income is allowed to be spent by the government. There are about 36 palm trees, 27 ponds and 2 acres of poramboke where individuals grow coconut trees. A sum of Rs. 8 per tree is collected by the VAO and paid to the Panchayat. Earlier the amount was Rs. 50 per tree but the government reduced the rate. About Rs. 50,000 is earned from the garden. From the auction of ponds Rs. 15,000 is received and from the palm trees Rs. 250 is received. About Rs. 4,000 is the income from the 2 trees. There is enough scope for planting more trees, particularly mango, and the Panchayat is planning to plant new saplings in the garden year by year.

Government Officials *vs.* Panchayat

Provision of drinking water is an essential activity in the Village Panchayat but any repair to the motor pump could not be immediately attended to as there is a rule that the work estimate has to be approved by the TWAD engineer. Due to this unnecessary delay is experienced and the public get angry with the Panchayat. Due to unexpected transfer of engineers and other officials, the work sanctioned by them or monitored by them are put to unnecessary scrutiny by the new staff. The work is being executed anticipating settlement after sanction is accorded for the same but due to the transfers it is delayed. There are 27 electric posts in a damaged condition and so fitting of lights on these posts is not safe. When the same was informed several times to the officials of the Electricity Board, they failed to take action. Usually, most of the officials give oral instructions and refer to other officials. So there is unnecessary misunderstanding. The Forest Department officials expect personal benefits when the Panchayat approaches them for getting permission to cut and sell the casuarina trees grown in the garden.

Gram Sabha

Usually the public do not come to the Gram Sabha in large numbers. About 100 men and two hundred women attend the Gram Sabha meetings. The NGOs create awareness among the people in respect of the Gram Sabha. As the communication regarding SGSY/SHG is received from the Chief Minister it is important to invite the women to the Gram Sabha.

Issues like bringing the VAO's office nearer to the Panchayat and his shortcomings, alcoholism and desilting of tanks are discussed. The public take the opportunity to comment all activities during the Gram Sabha meetings. Once in the very presence of the VAO, they demanded the passing of a resolution to transfer the VAO for his shortcomings. The Ward Members regularly attend the Gram Sabha meetings.

When the problem of alcoholism was discussed in the Gram Sabha, the public suggested forming a committee and accordingly a committee was formed with 25 members from all hamlets. In spite of this, the people expected the President to take a leading role. When the Youth Sports and Recreation Committee was formed as per the suggestion of SHG women, four women members were enrolled in the committee. If proper orientation is given to the public, they will improve their participation.

Panchayat Meeting

Once a month the meeting of the Panchayat is convened. All the members attend regularly. The members give more attention to drinking water supply and proper functioning of streetlights. A few members used to take care of the EB staff and ensure the replacement of old bulbs promptly. When one member was absent for two meetings, he was pulled up and then he attended regularly. He explained that as he had gone out on business he could not attend and requested to be excused. The fund available is informed to the members and they suggest the work. The priority is also determined by them. Accordingly the resolutions are passed. The Muslim and *Dalit* members are very serious in their activities to do service to their areas and are always dominating the discussions. There are nine members, six male and three female. Only one SC male represents the SC community, but he is an active person.

Works Carried Out

In the year 1996-97, there were no major expenses other than the maintenance of drinking water source from the Panchayat fund. In the year 1997-98 from the Common Property Resources the Panchayat got an income of about of Rs. 47,000 and so a lot of activities were carried out towards handpump maintenance, streetlight maintenance, TV maintenance, and repair work in the Village Panchayat office. Under the scheme fund, materials for the TV room were purchased. During the period 1998-99 the major expense was the electricity bill of Rs. 23,000. Maintenance of OHT and handpumps and streetlights were undertaken from the Panchayat fund at a cost of Rs. 34,000. Under JVVT, during 1998-99, TV room, road improvement, CRSP, retaining wall were provided. Two group houses were also constructed. Under the earmarked fund a new hand pump was provided at an estimate of Rs. 20,000.

In the year 1999-2000 sanitation was given due attention. Dustbins were provided to streets to collect waste. Bathing ghats were provided at the village tanks. Under the 10th Finance Commission allocation drinking water pipeline extension was undertaken at a cost of around Rs.40,000. During 2000-2001 maintenance expenses for handpumps, streetlights, passenger shelter, pipeline extension (IInd phase) were carried out from the Panchayat fund.

More money is needed for maintenance of streetlights and handpumps who functioning is frequently disturbed. If only the

Panchayat has its own source of income maintenance will be possible of the drinking water system and streetlights. Otherwise it is really a problem. During 2000-2001 under JGSY, a culvert, a bus shelter and a cement road were provided at a cost of Rs.1,68,000. Graveyard approach road maintenance in all hamlets, hamlet approach road maintenance, construction of culverts in the approach road leading to the graveyards, establishment of library and sports and recreation centre for youth were the other activities carried out in the Village Panchayat. Most of the work was executed by the contractors who were very prompt in their work as they did not need to give any commission to the Panchayat. But there was undue delay in the settlement of the bills in the Union discouraged them.

Social Development Activities

School building, *balwadis* building, laboratory in Government High School, toilet in school, borewell in school were provided from the Union as well as the MP area development fund. From the allocation under the MLA constituency development fund, bridge, five sodium vapour lights, BT road and PDS building were provided. Twelve biogas plants were provided to eligible farmers. Rani is the honarary Chairperson of the Parent-Teacher Associations. She actively engages in the activities of the PTA and students are encouraged to improve their standard of education. Prizes and trophies are awarded to the best students for which she used to mobilise resources. As the residents of the Muslim street demanded proper sanitation, dustbins were provided and the waste is stacked for manure. Under CRSP 20 toilets were provided to 20 families.

Rani maintains good relationship with the VHN and helps her in her activities. The nurse used to provide details of the communicable diseases like cholera to the public. The higher secondary school is far away from this village and so most of the girl students discontinue their studies after school final due to the distance. As most of the SC families do not possess pattas, the Panchayat is taking efforts to get pattas for all SCs. About 120 persons got pattas last year due to the initiative of the Panchayat.

Conclusion

The position of the Village Panchayat President is very significant and needs full time attention. So Rani and her husband spend a lot of time improving the Village Panchayat. As their time is spent on public activities they cannot spare adequate time for agriculture which has resulted is a heavy loss. Being a honest person she has to face a lot of problems in the Panchayat administration. She has to incur the displeasure of the officials and the high caste elite. She will not contest again in the Panchayat but, in consultation with the NGO, she plans to work for women's development.

CASE – 36

VAZHAKKARAI GRAM PANCHAYAT KEELAYUR BLOCK, NAGAPPATTINAM DISTRICT

Socio-Economic Background

Sri V. Kannaiyan, aged 49, is the President of the Vazhakkarai Village Panchayat. He belong to the SC community. He is literate but has failed to continue his writing practice. His family is a nuclear one. He lives in a hut with electricity facility. He has two sons and one daughter. The daughter has completed her school final and the sons are still studying. He is a member of the CPI(M) and an office bearer of an agricultural labourer's association at the Union level.

Political Orientation

Kannaiyan said that the functions of their Village leader attracted him even in his youth. He was very keen to understand the process of empowerment of the village leader and hence he developed interest in public activities. He volunteered before the CPI(M) leaders of his village and gradually took up the responsibility of meeting the Government officials with regard to solving the village problems. His main role during his younger days was to get government loans to eligible individuals who belong to the SC community.

He closely observed the leaders of his party so that he could learn their way of approach, interaction with people and officials and their understanding of people's issues. His thirst for leadership was fulfilled in the year 1986 when the Panchayat election was announced. During that Panchayat election, he faced stiff competition from the ex-President. The opponent also belonged to his own party but refused to obey the party's instruction. He was confident of winning the election. But people supported Kannaiyan and he won the election. Since 1986-91, Kannaiyan has served as the President of Vazhakkaai Panchayat. In spite of his poverty, he spends much more time for the public welfare. He used to engage in agricultural labour activities to a minimum for his livelihood. After that he spent all this time for his party and public work.

His smooth and cordial relationship with even the caste Hindus and his sustained spirit of public service earned a good name for him among the people. So the party chose him as its candidate in the Panchayat elections in 1996 also. Under the New Panchayati Raj System when the elections were held in 1996, Kannaiyan was opposed by a strong candidate with the united support of the CPI and the DMK. The opponent and his team worked hard. But Kannaiyan was confident that he would win as he could get more votes from the BC community even though most of the BC people were the supporters of the DMK. As he expected he won the election and became the President for the second time also.

Kannaiyan or his party did not spend any money apart from the printing of posters and handbills. The BC supported him as he is a very approachable candidate to them and he could understand the problems of the BCs also. The opponent mustered strength by establishing an understanding with the AIADMK and the DMK Party cadres. He hired a taxi and spent a lot of money for canvassing. He holds a high position in the CPI and is also educated. But the CPI(M) Party functions as a socially responsible party. It intervenes in personal and group problems when the situation demands and ensures the welfare of all.

Moreover Kannaiyan is a straightforward person. His honesty and straightforwardness were considered by the public as good qualities and so they supported him.

Village Setting

Vazhakkarai is just like the other villages of East Tanjore belt where the SC community is organised. Including the main village of Vazhakkarai there are five hamlets. The others are Melakakkattalai, Therkkuveli, Soorachuvali and Ayyanarpathu.

Village Temples

Chokkanathar temple, Vinayagar temple, Thoondikaran temple, Kaliamman temple and Mariamman temple are the common temples for the worship of all communities. Among the SCs the Pallars have the Kathavarayan temple exclusively under their control. The Parayars have the Kaliamman temple as their heriditary temple. There is no problem with regard to temple celebration among the different communities.

Village Committee

Kannaiyan meets the representatives of all the political parties whenever need arises to discuss with them the activities like temple celebration, fixing of wages for agricultural labourers, farmers' problems and the functioning of the paddy procurement centre.

Farmers Federation

To exclusively discuss the problems pertaining to farms an institution is constituted in Vazhakkarai Village over which an eleven member committee holds responsibility. The meeting of the committee is usually scheduled at the Village Panchayat office.

Youth Wing of Political Parties

The youth affiliated to various political parties have their own party units. They meet whenever necessary and carry out their party assignments.

Women Self-Help Group

There are 12 SHGs sponsored by the NGO Sevalaya. Apart from this there are two women's Sangams functioning independently.

Cine Star Association

Vijayakanth Fans Association and Rajinikanth Fans Association are the two associations functioning in the village. The Rajinikanth Fans are backed by DMK Party cadres.

Democratic Youth Federation of India

Democratic Youth Federation of India (DYFI) is the youth wing of the CPI(M) Party in which the party youth are carrying out activities like organising demonstration to influence the government with respect to employment assurance, problems of school going youth and other common issues. Ammavasai Day meet is organised by the communist parties. The activities of the Panchayat, the government and the concerned political party are discussed in the Ammavasai Day meeting. All the social institutions are closely working with the Panchayat. The office bearers of the institutions have established good relationship with the President of the Village Panchayat and share their feelings and perceptions of the Village Panchayat.

Other Facilities

One noon-meal centre and one *balwadi* function in this Panchayat. The primary school is located at Mela Vazhakkarai, 3 km from the village. A secondary and a higher secondary school are in Thirukkuavalai at a distance of three kilometres. A PDS is available. The community hall is an old one. There are 3 TV rooms. An animal husbandry sub-centre is located at Thirukkuvalai.

Common Property Resource Management

There are 11 ponds out of which three are big in size. Rs. 12000 is earned out of the auction. There are nine coconut trees and

Rs. 1000 is earned as income from these trees. In two ponds, 27 coconut saplings are planted to augment income. Two persons are engaged unofficially to look after the ponds and the trees. There is only one tamarind tree giving a meagre income of Rs. 100.

There is scope for planting 500 coconut trees on the banks of the ponds as well as the roadsides. The investment cost for planting of a coconut sapling would be around Rs. 150 and if the total amount for planting of 500 saplings and a considerable amount for maintenance are provided by the government, after 5 years the grown coconut trees would give income. The Panchayat could make its own arrangement for further protection and maintenance.

Caste Association

There is no caste association in the village. But the youth belonging to the Padayachi community have mobilised themselves under the banner of the PMK.

Political Parties

The political parties functioning in the village are the CPI(M), the DMK, the PMK, the CPI, the AIADMK and the TMC. Among them only the CPI(M) and the CPI have offices for their party activities. The political party leaders of Vazhakkarai do not have any quarrel. They used to meet informally at the Village Panchayat office and share the village problems and Panchayat activities also. The political parties work together if necessary. The development activities were more in number during the period of the DMK than in the period of the AIADMK.

The Union Chairperson who belongs to the DMK shows partiality when allocating funds to Village Panchayats. When there is a necessity for a bus shelter in Vazhakkarai, instead of allocating money for the same, he sanctions a bus shelter for Meenamanallur, where already bus shelters were there. The President has informed his party higher-ups of this.

Village Economy

Agriculture and animal husbandry are the two main avenues of economic activities in the village. The SC community people are landless labourers. Among them only 20 persons have land to the extent of only one acre each, but about 50 persons possess leased lands. There are very poor in backward caste people also. They are all landless agricultural labourers. Construction in the new source of income to both men and women. As the wages are given in paddy, most of the poor maintain their families with this meagre income.

More infrastructure facilities are needed for successful farming. Threshing floor, pump set and timely maintenance of irrigation channels are essential to protect the farmers. Around 200 families own milch animals and goats. For want of employment, the poor landless agriculture labourers are going to other districts like Coimbatore and Erode.

Perception on Panchayati Raj

Kannaiyan served as the President in the old system and hence he easily distinguishes the salient features of the New Panchayati Raj System. The present day Village Panchayats are functioning more or less independently; the reservation for women and *Dalits* is a good sign for their empowerment; the guarantee of regular election is really a boon to the Village Panchayat; fund allocation has been increased; and the Gram Sabha is a good arrangement for people's participation. The Panchayati Raj System in Kerala is better than that in Tamil Nadu as more fund is allocated to the Panchayat with power, according to Kannaiyan.

On Development

Prompt implementation of Land Ceiling Act and new employment opportunities to women are needed for development in villages. The Government's role is that of a provider of adequate infrastructure facilities for agriculture and small scale industries. Alcoholism is the major issue in poor families.

Political parties who work for development fail to understand this issue. Around Rs. 5,000 is spent on alcohol by every poor person every year and if it could be saved, the amount would substantially help the poor during distress.

Gender Issues

Personal hygiene, cleanliness, proper and adequate dressing, education and improvement in housing are the major issues influenced by women now-a-days. Women show eagerness to understand politics and they are courageously participating in the Gram Sabha meetings. The women members demand facilities to their ward. Only women belonging to employed families and well to do families are continuing their higher education. The rest discontinue after high school studies.

Achievement in Assigned Duties

The Panchayat has three wards. There are 6 Ward Members, four men and two women. Only one male is a caste Hindu and all the rest belong to the SC community. Kannaiyan said that convening the Panchayat meeting is never a problem. Every month the meeting is promptly organised and all the members attend the meeting.

The members know the available finance and so unnecessary disputes are avoided. The women members stress the importance of drinking water supply and road maintenance. As the Panchayat income is very poor (only Rs. 18,000 to Rs. 20,000) the basic needs are fulfilled only from the JVVT allocations.

Bathing ghat and retaining wall at a cost of Rs. 70,000 were provided from JVVT allocation in the year 1996-97. The Pipeline repair work was carried out from the 10th Finance Commission allocation and the Panchayat fund. The Union undertook road maintenance and the construction of a culvert at a cost of Rs. 1,15,000 in the year 1997-98.

Maintenance of approach road to graveyard, handpump, streetlight and Panchayat building were the major activities carried out during the period 1997-98. Around Rs.1 lakh was spent on these items of work. During 1998-99, under JVVT, another bathing ghat was provided. A PDS shop was constructed from the Union allocation. Desilting of big tank at a cost of Rs. 1,10,000 was undertaken from the Union allocation. A school building and a BT road were also provided by the Union.

From the Panchayat fund, the SC colony approach road maintenance work was done. As water became scare from the month of January to March, rainwater was harvested in a small pond where a new hand-pump was provided. The existing handpump was removed and refixed in the river belt to manage the water crisis. New streetlights, new public taps, construction of steps in the pond were carried out in the year 1999-2000. In 2001, 11 group houses were allotted and the eligible beneficiaries were selected in the Gram Sabha. The fund allocation is not sufficient. Political intervention is really a handicap to development. The revision of house tax is not encouraged by the political parties.

Kannaiyan never demands any commission from the contractors. He wants the completion of work to the satisfaction of the common people. The contractors used to give donation to the Party. But, at the same time, the quality is never compromised. A contractor who constructed the PDS was asked to discontinue the construction due to poor standards. The defect was rectified. The Councillor is helping to avail of Union schemes, provided her or his benami is given the contract.

The Gram Sabha

The Gram Sabha meeting is periodically organised. Kannaiyan presents the activities carried out. The BC members are more in attendance. They want to know the available funds and individual benefits given by the government and so the BCs show interest in attending the Gram Sabha whereas the majority, belonging to the SC, do not give importance to the Gram Sabha. The political party office bearers used to verify the accounts during the Gram Sabha meeting. On an average 120 persons attend the Gram Sabha meetings. Among women, mostly SHG members participate in the Gram Sabha meetings. The members who participate in Gram Sabha used to criticise the contractors as all the contractors are sons of the soil.

Relationship with Official

The Union officials are helpful and explain the procedures and rules under the New Panchayati Raj System. But all government orders are not distributed by the officials. The officials explain all procedures and periodically inspect the records and advice to keep the accounts properly. As the President is honest, the officials are not demanding commission for the work sanctioned.

Assumed Activities

Kannaiyan gives importance to land related activities and infrastructure facilities like roads and streetlights. He maintains that only with more money more activities could be carried out. He could not get Namakku Naame Thittam. The people prefer him for his honesty and simplicity. He is still a poor man engaged in agricultural labour. He is plain but needs higher qualities of leadership to develop his Panchayat.

CASE – 37

VEERANAM GRAM PANCHAYAT THANDARAMPATTU BLOCK, THIRUVANNAMALAI DISTRICT

Socio-Economic Background

Mr. Munusamy is the President of the Veeranam Village Panchayat and he belongs to the SC community. He is aged 49, and has studied upto the 5th standard. He is an agricultural labourer. He has 40 cents of wet land but there is no regular income from the land. Before 1996 he worked as an OHT operator in this Panchayat. At present he is living with his wife, son and daughter who are studying 7th standard and 8th standard respectively. He has his own tiled house, electrified but with no toilet facility and no individual house tap connection. He has association with a caste organisation and is also a member of the DMK Party.

Village Profile

The people of SC are more in number than those of any other caste. The total population is 1,585. There are 6 Ward Members of whom 4 are males and 2 are females and in the SC category 3 are males and 1 is female. The following community people are living in this Panchayat: SC Sakkiliyars, Arunthathiyars, Gounders, Konars, Barbears, Oodayars and Muslims. Adequate water supply facility is available in this Panchayat. For health and sanitation there is no public toilet facility and health centre. For hospital, people should go to Thandarampattu or Sathanoor located 10 km. away. A few houses are having individual household latrines.

For education there is one *balwadi*, one noon-meal centre, and one primary school. A Higher Secondary school is in Sathanoor and it is 10 km. away from this Panchayat. The Ayyan Library is available but no body is interested to come to the library. A bus shelter is available in this Panchayat on the main road. There is no TV facility for this Panchayat but a TV is kept in Munusamy's house in a state of disrepair. The following facilities are absent: market, butchery shed, community hall and post office. All these facilities are available in Thandarampattu 10 km. from this Panchayat. There are a farmers sangam and an Ambedkar Sangam but they are not functioning effectively. Every year Mariamman Koil celeberation is observed very well with the cooperation of all communities.

The majority (more than 50%) of the people are agricultural labourers and they are not having any lands. About 150 families engage in rearing milch animals and goats. These activities improve their standard of living through milk vending and sale of animals every year. The DMK and the AIADMK parties are functioning in the village. The DMK Party is dominant. The AIADMK is the next in the village. Besides these caste associations are also functioning in this village.

Recruitment Process

Before 1996, Munusamy worked as an OHT operator in the same Village Panchayat. At that time he earned a good name from the people. He did his duties sincerely, and obeyed the public and gave respect to the village elders. When announcement came for the elections the village elders asked him to contest in the elections in 1996. Three candidates contested against him. He defeated the other three candidates by a margin of 87 votes. The other communities extended support to him. The SC community also supported him because they saw him as a better worker than the other three candidates. During the electioneering he projected the work to be done in this Panchayat, and pointed out that all the work would be carried out if he was elected Panchayat President. He met every individual in this Panchayat. In addition his relatives and his brothers were involved in the election work. He spent Rs. 5,000 for printing of notice and issued the same to the people. At present his brother has joined as OHT operator and he is also interested in Panchayat activities.

Perception

Munusamy has highlighted the following as the salient features of the New Panchayati Raj System: Gram Sabha, reservation of seats for *Dalits* and women and planning at the village level. He is not fully aware of the implications of the 73rd Amendment to the Constitution of India, and the details of the Tamil Nadu Panchayat Act of 1994.

To him development means increasing the capacity of the people. By improving the skills of the people development could be achieved. Infrastructure facilities are essential for development. It is all the more important that people should know-how to make use of the infrastructure facilities for development. For developing the village economy agriculture and allied activities are essential. Highly deepened borewells in the rural areas is a major problem. A veterinary centre is needed for maintenance of livestock. Further he wants housing facility for the poor.

With regard to politics, he underscores the role of the rich people in local politics. People speak about politics. But rich people won't speak but will play politics. Politics is for development but now it is not so. People are joining politics for personal gain and not out of attachment to ideology. At present he is not involved in the activities of political parties. People affiliated to political party are helping only the partymen in the village and not the deserving families. Politics is nothing but development of partymen.

On gender issues Munusamy says now-a-days various schemes are being implemented for women's development. Self-help groups are emerging as a movement in the rural areas and the members are attending Gram Sabha meetings regularly. In these ways women are empowered. He admitted that women are discriminated against. But women have accepted it. Among women SC women are further discriminated against. Women should be empowered economically first and it could be achieved through self-help groups.

As for Common Property Resources (CPR), Munusamy said that the CPRs have to be identified properly, through the VAO and Block officials. Even today they are not having close association with the Village Panchayat. For improving the CPR, Munusamy has an idea of the planting fruit yielding trees.

For social justice, Munusamy said that only on record one can say there is no discrimination. Only through struggle social justice could be achieved in the rural areas. At the house level, and the heart level there is discrimination. To some extent economic empowerment would help the deprived to gain justice.

Performance

For effective performance Munusamy emphasised that training is needed periodically, and without training there will be no good performance. The following items of work were carried out in the Veeranam Panchayat: construction of two threshing floors and nine culverts under the JVVT fund, electricity facility to 20 houses and blacktop road under Union Councillor's fund and PDS building constructed under Councillor's fund. For school development, the Panchayat President has helped in two ways one maintenance of school building and another water supply facility to the school. From the MLA fund 2 OHT tanks have been constructed with a capacity of 30,000 litres of water.

Munusamy has close association with all the sectoral departments, namely Electricity Board, TWAD, Police, Agriculture and other departments. Generally has a close association with the people, because he was working as an OHT operator previously in the same Panchayat. He has completed two important items of work based on the people's demands; namely desilting of ponds and a new building for the Panchayat.

Tax collection is a difficult work and tax is the only income source of this Panchayat. For huts tax revision was effected from Rs. 1.50 to 5.50 and for tiled houses it was from Rs. 5.50 to 11.00 during the year 1998.

Panchayat Meetings

The Ward Members are interested in the Panchayat meetings. They participate in the meeting and ask for basic facilities to their wards. Similarly in the Gram Sabha meetings the villagers are interested while SHGs attend the meetings and demand loan facility to organise small trades to develop their economy.

Social Development

With regard to social development Munusamy compares the old Panchayat with the new Panchayat system. In old Panchayat system, there was no transparency in Panchayat activities and in the new Panchayat system transparency is maintained. Gram Sabha meeting is convened and fund allocations are made directly. Hence he stated that the New Panchayati Raj System is the indicator for social development.

This Panchayat has got more number of people belonging to SC community and they emphasise that housing facility is essential for all the SC people. Only one graveyard is available in this Panchayat and all the community people utilize that graveyard without any discrimination. The following three

Sangams have been functioning in this Panchayat and they participate in the village development activities :

(*i*) Farmers' Association,
(*ii*) Ambedkar Association, and
(*iii*) Indian Democratic Youth Federation.

They also participate in Gram Sabha meetings and temple festivals.

Some of the women groups are engaged in palm leaf work. They manufacture small household articles. In Gram Sabha meetings, all the villagers passed a special resolution that toilets should be available in every house but only 10 persons have constructed toilets in their houses. A veterinary centre is essential for this Panchayat.

Future Plan

Munusamy has a vision for this Panchayat.

(*i*) Road facilities are needed for this Village Panchayat, particularly in the graveyard area.
(*ii*) The local ponds should be maintained periodically and desilted yearly. They are essential for this Panchayat.

Munusamy is not interested in the contesting in the next election, because he has inadequate capacity in Panchayat administration. Sometimes officials are not helping the Village Panchayat. The village people have not clearly understood about Panchayat finance, conducting Gram Sabha meetings, accounting and auditing procedures. However, Munusamy is very popular and a sincere hard worker and has earned a good name in this Panchayat area.

CASE – 38

VILANGUDI GRAM PANCHAYAT
ARIYALUR BLOCK, ARIYALUR DISTRICT

Socio-Economic Background

Sri V. Manivel, aged 47, is the President of the Vilangudi Village Panchayat. He belongs to the SC community. He is married. His family consists of his wife and two sons. His sons are studying +2 and 9th standard respectively. He posseses one acre of land with borewell facility in which trees like coconut, mango and teakwood are growing. In the dry land which he additionally owns, eucalyptus trees are grown to the extent of around 5 acres. He has studied up to the eighth standard only.

Since his boyhood days he was a fan of MGR and so, after his schooling, he joined the AIADMK Party. The leadership of MGR and his concern for the poor are the guiding principles in his life. Since 1972, he has been associating with the AIADMK Party and involved in its agitations, meetings and other programmes and he was even in prison.

Within this political orientation he understood the public needs, government's functioning and various welfare programmes pertaining to the SC.

Along with the political activities, Manivel is associated with the social institutions like Village Committee also. He is one of the eight office bearers of the Village Committee as *Nattanmai*. The committee is meant for the SC community and about 500 SC families come under the purview of this committee. Issues among SC families are settled through this committee.

Village Setting

Vilangudi is reputed for its Sivan temple known as Sorneeswar. It is a central place for ten villages and many marriages are being conducted. Apart from SCs, there are Vellalars, Padayachis, Asaris, Chettiars and Boraians. About one thousand families are non-SC families. A car festival is conducted during the temple celebration. The temple is under the control of the Hindu Religious and Endowment Board, but the SCs are not permitted inside the temple. Ayyappa Pooja alone is permitted to the SCs inside the temple. Now-a-days the caste Hindus feel that the SCs are getting into power and so they fear from the SCs.

Village Economy

The villagers are engaged in farming. Around 30 per cent SCs hold land and the source of irrigation is well water.

Groundnut, sugarcane and paddy are the major crops. The landless labourers used to migrate to other states like Kerala and cities like Mumbai and Chennai for employment, particularly in the construction industry as there is no rain.

Caste Association

Vanniar Sangam, Vellalar Sangam and Viduthalai Siruthiagal are the three caste based organisations functioning. Each of the above mentioned institutions works for its own caste people's welfare and self-respect. There is no youth association in this Panchayat but there is a Sports and Recreation Committee organised by the Panchayat. The youth enrolled as members of this committee are now requesting to provide a site for them. Women's associations are five in number.

Educational Institution

Primary and secondary schools are available in the Panchayat area. Children are coming from hamlets like Keela Vilangudi, Mela Vilangudi, Urathur and Colony. There is scope for a high school and efforts have been taken by the Panchayat. But the caste Hindus are not supporting the efforts. They do not want the educational progress of the SCs.

Watershed Association and CPR

At Urathur and Vilangudi the farmers joined and formed a watershed association. There are three irrigation tanks from which 40 acres, 20 acres and 4 acres of land are getting water. There are 15 ponds. The income from the auction of these ponds is very meagre as the tanks are not filled due to drought. There are two open wells. One is not in use and the other is functioning. The PDS shop is newly built. Efforts to build a community hall have not yet borne fruit.

The Kamatchi tank has an area of 2 acres and 44 cents. Families belonging to all communities have encroached upon it and around 20 houses are built on it. One encroacher has dug a well and enjoys the same. Any attempt to remove all these would become an issue and it is not possible for the President to do anything. Income from selling the trees grown in the ponds is Rs. 43,000.

Political Parties

The AIADMK and the DMK are the major parties. Other parties like the TMC, the Viduthalai Siruthaigal, the MDMK and the PMK are also functioning in the Panchayat.

The office bearers of the political parties used to visit the Panchayat office and the President maintains rapport with them by maintaining harmony and thereby he utilises their services for the Panchayat.

The office bearers of political parties help the Panchayat to avail of funds for additional school building and deepening of tanks.

The Issue of Untouchability

In the Perumal temple and Mariamman temple the SCs are not permitted to enter. The use and throw plastic tumblers are given to the SC and glass tumblers are provided to the BC community. The SC youth protested against this to the Panchayat. But the Panchayat President advised them not to precipitate the issue and promised to deal with the issue. It is told by the SC youth that Manivel does not have the leadership quality to tackle this issue as the caste Hindus never fear him. They charge that he is not a honest and sincere administrator and so he is not ready to face the challenge from the caste Hindus.

So, the SCs themselves do not give due recognition to him. The approach road to the Colony area is encroached upon by SCs themselves. Once formation of a road was initiated, but two house owners belonging to the SC threatened to prevent the work at a turning as their property would suffer. The case was reported to the Police and survey was undertaken. The site was verified as per the record and there is sufficient space for the curve but it is encroached upon by the persons concerned. Only after the intervention of the Police they gave in.

The issue of SC *vs.* BC is always there but not in the open. The majority members in the Village Panchayat are belonging to caste Hindus. Out of the total 6, only 2 are from the SC. The Vice-President belongs to the BC. He does all the Panchayat work. Otherwise obtaining signature from him would be a problem. As the Vice-President is living in the hamlet of Orathur, the Panchayat work earmarked for Orathur is entrusted to him. The SCs have a separate Mariamman temple. The residential area of the SCs is situated away from the main village. There are no proper facilities there. Only after the introduction of the New Panchayati Raj System the welfare work pertaining to the SCs are properly implemented. The Mariamman temple belonging to the SCs is now under renovation. Manivel is spending his own money in the construction whereas it is said that the common fund collected for the temple is not properly utilised by the committee for which the President is also held responsible. It is said that Manivel is a weak person: he does not openly oppose or challenge the practice of untouchability in the village.

Manivel denies these allegations and says that in the earlier period of the AIADMK, he served as the trustee of the Sorneeswar temple and did a lot of good work in the temple. The car, once available, is now not available.

Manivel explained that the caste Hindus felt his presence necessary and hence he served as the trustee of the temple. And hence the SCs tried to prevent his service. When he sold a tree and from the sale amount he made a car for the festival, constructed a building for a shop and prepared for the renovation the caste Hindus levelled a false complaint that he was misusing the fund. This issue was handled successfully after the intervention of a Minister.

Irrespective of caste, officials helped him in this issue as they knew that there was no misappropriation of funds in the temple administration. But since then the caste Hindus have tried to dominate the SCs.

Recruitment Process

There were two opponents, one from TMC and another from the Congress. The opponents did not have much experience in public life and so people in general preferred Manivel. He spent a week for electioneering. About 50 persons, mostly family members and AIADMK party cadres, accompanied Manivel during the canvassing. He is an AIADMK Party activist. His service as a trustee and his traditional leadership were the major attractions. Moreover, in spite of the ill-feeling among the caste Hindus, since Manivel used to maintain tolerance and open sharing, there were supporters among the caste Hindus also. He spent Rs. 30,000 for the election for various activities including the food and maintenance expenses for his supporters.

One SC hamlet is situated aloof. The families residing in this area demanded road facilities when they were contacted during the election. The efforts to lay at least a mud road to this area could not be accomplished. The road has to go *via* patta land. The owners refused to give their land. So the residents suffer a lot by having to move *via* streams and brooks. People expected the supply of protected water by the Panchayat. It was done. The SCs proposed to protest against the illegal weekly market run by the BC community. Every Sunday, near the tank site, truck loads of sheep are brought and sold. The business is carried on by the BC community and the trading is handled by the BCs alone. But Manivel pacified the SC youth as there should not be any untoward incident due to this problem. The Panchayat has the power to stop or regulate the unauthorised marketing of sheep by the BC community. But the President does not make any serious effort in this regard. A few individuals assembled in the Panchayat office made this complaint.

His Perception of Panchayati Raj

It is an opportunity to serve the people and as President, Manivel felt that the needs of the people could be met. The Panchayati Raj became significant due to Prime Minister Rajiv Gandhi. Now the official control is less and work is executed immediately and the people have a say in the Panchayats.

On Development

Education and credit facilities are two important aspects in the development of the poor. Providing necessary infrastructure will bring about a change in the socio-economic life of the poor. The water sources and the supply channels need proper maintenance. A lot of money is needed. So the MLA and the MP fund allocation has to be earmarked for this type of capital intensive work. The skill of the people has to be enhanced.

On Women

Women do not come forward to arrest the sale of arrack. But they expect that others will do the work. Wage discrimination issue is present in the village. But women never consider these as topics for discussion during the women's meetings. The women are ignorant of the development process.

On Social Justice

Revolution will not come just by protest but only by a process of individual empowerment. Unnecessary disputes or agitations are meaningless but steady and concerted solidarity among the SCs will do wonders. Moreover the minority population of the SCs cannot agitate against the caste Hindus who are the majority in the village. The Panchayat President alone could not effect social justice.

His Panchayat Activities

Manivel said that the increase in the cost of rice in the public distribution system or increase in the house tax is anti-social.

There has been no change in the house tax since the New Panchayati Raj System was introduced.

Panchayat Meeting

The members regularly attend the meetings, but the majority members are caste Hindus and most of the decisions are taken according to them. The women members do not show interest in any activity other than the drinking water issue. Work is allocated to all streets including the SC one. Otherwise the public would create problems.

Gram Sabha Meeting

People attend the Gram Sabha meetings. To encourage their attendance food packets are distributed to the participants. The majority of the participants used to highlight the problems in the agricultural sector. Deepening of the tank, cleaning of bushes and weeds in the tank, maintaining of inlet channel are major activities of the Panchayat. Cement concrete road, new approach road, colony houses, individual loan assistance are the other demands of the public.

Schemes Implemented

Road improvement, realignment of drinking water supply system to prevent frequent damages, construction of TV room are the major activities in the year 1997-98. The major expenditure was for pipeline as Rs. 1.00 lakh was spent towards this work. In the year 1999-2000, culverts were constructed. The village is situated on a slope and so, there are small streams and drainways at several places. For an easy transportation, necessary culverts are provided. More than 10 culverts were constructed at a cost of Rs. 23,000 each. To improve the water supply, 30 public taps and 26 individual tap connections were provided.

From the TWAD allocation 3 OHTs were provided. To avail of the fund from TWAD, the MLA was contacted and he discussed this problem with the concerned officials. That is how the work was sanctioned. From the Union fund, house repair fund was given to 25 poor people at the rate of Rs.5,000 each and 15 group houses were provided to 15 families. After the community meeting the eligible beneficiaries were selected without any dispute. When single light connection was given, the President enlisted 120 beneficiaries and helped them to get the electricity connection without any corruption.

Retaining wall construction, *balwadi* and primary school repair work were done. Union fund of Rs. 14,000 was spent for repair work. In 1999-2000, 15 group houses were provided from the District Panchayat fund, 15 streetlights were provided Rs. 75,000 was spent towards this work. The MLA sanctioned Rs. 75,000 for desilting/deepening the tank. The MP does not provide anything in spite of requests made to him. Under NNT one and half kilometre of road work is executed at a cost of Rs. 1.00 lakh.

There are 115 streetlights of which 18 are sodium vapour lamps. People see the Panchayat work only in the provision of water supply and streetlights. But the EB does not realise the felt needs of the people and so, for quick service, a separate worker is employed for streetlight maintenance and Rs. 300 per month is given to him. The EB bill is heavy as the meter and its accessories are not showing proper readings. In spite of repeated complaints, the EB staff do not take any efforts to repair. Rs. 1.50 lakh is pending towards electricity charges. From the Union Councillor's fund activities like bathing ghat construction, retaining walls, cement concrete road, metal road were executed. But none of these activities were discussed with the Panchayat. From the Panchayat fund, 2 new motor pumps were purchased as the old motors became defunct.

Maintenance of Panchayat Office

The office building is maintained well after undertaking necessary repair work. It is situated on the roadside. Whenever Manivel opens the office, ordinary people, village leaders and known persons used to enter and spend their time uselessly.

Accounts/Auditing

The Panchayat accounts are maintained by the clerk who is a young person belonging to the SC community. If problems were reported, Manivel used to personally meet the officials and offer clarifications. The officials used to expect money and he had to give. The officials are treating the President well. But the activities can go on only if the President meets the officials frequently and explains the position in the village. The Rajiv Gandhi Water Mission Scheme is implemented in the village and Rs. 24,000 has been paid from the Panchayat fund as 10 per cent contribution for the sinking of a borewell. As per the instruction of the officials separate records and registers are maintained in respect of the water supply scheme. A separate committee is formed as per the guidelines of the officials.

The Finance

JVVT allocation has now increased from Rs. 40,000 to Rs. 69,000 and so it is helping the Panchayat to undertake welfare activities. The SFC quarterly grant is around Rs. 40,000. The 10th Finance Commission grant is only Rs. 19,904. In spite of these sources and the Panchayat's own sources of Rs. 3.50 lakh by way of stamp duty, professional tax etc., still the expectations of the people in respect of water supply are not yet fulfilled.

Manivel is an activist of the AIADMK Party. Since the formation of the AIADMK he is in the party and is known to party higher-ups at the district level. During the AIADMK period, he registered himself as a contractor and executed a work like deepening of tanks, road work, school building and he is now a professional contractor. Manivel says that he will be in politics and again try to contest in the Panchayat election if the seat is reserved for the SC. Otherwise he proposes to contest for the Union council ward. He is a moderate in his outlook but the SC youth want an active Panchayat President who will recognise the *Dalit* rights.

3

ANALYSIS AND CONCLUSION

DUTIES AND POWERS OF VILLAGE PANCHAYAT (TAMIL NADU PANCHAYAT ACT, 1994)

Sl. No	Name of the Panchayat	Mandatory Functions															Discretionary Functions									
		Construction, Maintenance and Repair Works					Light-ing		Construction of Drainage/Sewage	Public Latrines		Measures for Improvement of Sanitary Condition	Burial/ Burning Ground Activity	Water Works			Aforestation Measures	Public/Private Markets	Public Slaughter House	Reading Rooms/Centre for Formal Education	Recreation Centre	Centre for Physical Culture	Eviction of Encroachment	Maintenance of CPR		
		Road	Bridge	Culvert	Road Dams	Cross Ways	Public Road	Built-up Areas		Provision	Maintenance of Public/Private			Repairing Wells	Tank Pond Desiltation	Supply of Water								Communal Property	Irrigation Works	Poramboke
1	2	3	4	5	6	7	8	9	10	11	12	13	14	15	16	17	18	19	20	21	22	23	24	25	26	27
1.	Balamuthur	✓	✓							✓	✓				✓	✓							✓		✓	✓
2.	Bodithasan-patti	✓					✓	✓					✓			✓						✓			✓	

(Contd.)

(*Contd.*)

1	2	3	4	5	6	7	8	9	10	11	12	13	14	15	16	17	18	19	20	21	22	23	24	25	26	27
3.	Eechampoo-ndi	✓	✓												✓	✓				✓						
4.	Eramanaick-anpatti	✓							✓														✓			
5.	Guruvappan-pettai	✓					✓						✓			✓							✓			
6.	Kalaiyur			✓			✓			✓			✓			✓	✓									✓
7.	Vittaneri	✓											✓		✓	✓										
8.	Kandratheer-tham	✓		✓			✓						✓							✓						
9.	Kondacheri											✓				✓										
10.	Kottur	✓		✓						✓						✓	✓							✓		✓
11.	Kunthala-patti	✓							✓	✓			✓			✓	✓									✓
12.	Kuppampa-layam	✓					✓									✓										
13.	Kuppinaick-anpatti						✓		✓							✓	✓									
14.	Maamandur																									✓

(*Contd.*)

(Contd.)

1	2	3	4	5	6	7	8	9	10	11	12	13	14	15	16	17	18	19	20	21	22	23	24	25	26	27
15.	Manjampati																									
16.	Mathiyanur	✓					✓			✓						✓							✓			✓
17.	Melanettur	✓					✓		✓	✓			✓		✓	✓										
18.	Mudikanda-nallor	✓		✓						✓			✓			✓							✓			
19.	Kakkoor	✓		✓											✓	✓										
20.	Pali	✓				✓							✓			✓				✓						
21.	Perumalaga-ram	✓								✓						✓										
22.	Polukurichi	✓	✓				✓			✓						✓				✓						
23.	Ramarpuram																									
24.	Sarukkalai																									
25.	Saruthupatti	✓	✓				✓									✓										
26.	Sekkanur	✓	✓												✓	✓	✓							✓		✓
27.	Sengipatti	✓		✓			✓									✓										

(Contd.)

(*Contd.*)

1	2	3	4	5	6	7	8	9	10	11	12	13	14	15	16	17	18	19	20	21	22	23	24	25	26	27
28.	Sivagana-puram	✓	✓				✓				✓		✓			✓				✓						
29.	Soodiyur						✓				✓		✓			✓								✓		
30.	Sundarajapu-ram															✓								✓		✓
31.	Thamarai-padi																							✓		
32.	Thuthipattu		✓				✓									✓										
33.	Uchimalai-kuppam															✓										
34.	Su.Valavetti	✓		✓					✓							✓										
35.	Vanduvan-cheri	✓		✓				✓		✓			✓			✓						✓	✓			
36.	Vazhakkarai	✓		✓											✓	✓										
37.	Veeranam														✓	✓										
38.	Vilangudi						✓		✓						✓	✓										

(*Contd.*)

POWERS, FUNCTIONS AND RESPONSIBILITIES ENTRUSTED TO THE VILLAGE PANCHAYAT ON 29 SUBJECTS

Sl. No.	Name of the Panchayat	1. Agriculture including Agricultural Extension			2. Land Improvement & Soil Conservation		3. Water Management			4. Animal Husbandry, Dairying and Poultry		5. Fisheries	
		Assist in identification of beneficiaries under various agriculture related schemes (*e.g.* seeds, minor irrigation facilities, DPAP, etc.)	Advice in setting up godown/cold storage facilities	Contact marketing officers of benefit farmers	Land ceiling	Reallocation to landless labour	Desilting tank	Reconstruction of supply channel	Implementation of Watershed devt.	Assist in identification of beneficiaries for various schemes scheduled in this head	Facilities created for cooperative societies & financial ssistance	Identification of beneficiaries for various schemes under this head	Prevention of sea erosion projects
1	2	3	4	5	6	7	8	9	10	11	12	13	14
1.	Balamuthur						✓						
2.	Bodithasanpatti												
3.	Eechampoondi							✓					
4.	Eramanaickanpatti												
5.	Guruvappanpettai												
6.	Kalaiyur						✓			✓			
7.	Vittaneri	(Minor irrigation facility) ✓							✓				
8.	Kandratheertham												
9.	Kondacheri												
10.	Kottur												
11.	Kunthalapatti												

(*Contd.*)

(*Contd.*)

1	2	3	4	5	6	7	8	9	10	11	12	13	14
12.	Kuppampalayam												
13.	Kuppinaickanpatti												
14.	Maamandur												
15.	Manjampati												
16.	Mathiyanur												
17.	Melanettur												
18.	Mudikandanallor												
19.	Kakkoor												
20.	Pali												
21.	Perumalagaram												
22.	Polukurichi						✓						
23.	Ramarpuram												
24.	Sarukkalai												
25.	Saruthupatti												
26.	Sekkanur												
27.	Sengipatti												
28.	Sivaganapuram												
29.	Soodiyur												
30.	Sundarajapuram	✓											
31.	Thamaraipadi												
32.	Thuthipattu	✓											
33.	Uchimalaikuppam												
34.	Su.Valavetti												
35.	Vanduvancheri												
36.	Vazhakkarai												
37.	Veeranam												
38.	Vilangudi												

(*Contd.*)

(*Contd.*)

Sl. No.	Name of the Panchayat	6. Agriculture including Agricultural Extension			7. Minor Forest Produce	8. Small Scale Industries	9. Khadi, Village and Cottage Industries		10. Rural Housing	
		Coordination with forest department	Establishment of social forestry	Farm forestry scheme	Got permission to collect minor forest produce for villagers	Identification of beneficiaries for various schemes under this head	Identification of potential activities and formulation of projects	Formulate schemes for artisans/craftsmen, others	Identification of beneficiaries for various schemes under this head	Assist coop societies for house construction
1	2	15	16	17	18	19	20	21	22	23
1.	Balamuthur					✓			✓	
2.	Bodithasanpatti									
3.	Eechampoondi								✓	
4.	Eramanaickanpatti		✓						✓	
5.	Guruvappanpettai								✓	
6.	Kalaiyur					✓	✓			
7.	Vittaneri									
8.	Kandratheertham								✓	

(*Contd.*)

(*Contd.*)

1	2	15	16	17	18	19	20	21	22	23
9.	Kondacheri									
10.	Kottur									
11.	Kunthalapatti									
12.	Kuppampalayam									
13.	Kuppinaickanpatti									
14.	Maamandur									
15.	Manjampati									
16.	Mathiyanur									
17.	Melanettur									
18.	Mudikandanallor									
19.	Kakkoor									
20.	Pali								✓	
21.	Perumalagaram								✓	
22.	Polukurichi									
23.	Ramarpuram									
24.	Sarukkalai									

(*Contd.*)

(*Contd.*)

1	2	15	16	17	18	19	20	21	22	23
25.	Saruthupatti								✓	
26.	Sekkanur								✓	
27.	Sengipatti									
28.	Sivaganapuram									
29.	Soodiyur								✓	
30.	Sundarajapuram								✓	
31.	Thamaraipadi								✓	
32.	Thuthipattu								✓	
33.	Uchimalaikuppam		✓							
34.	Su.Valavetti									
35.	Vanduvancheri									
36.	Vazhakkarai									
37.	Veeranam								✓	
38.	Vilangudi								✓	

(*Contd.*)

(*Contd.*)

Sl. No.	Name of the Panchayat	11. Drinking Water		12. Fuel & Fodder			13. Roads, Culverts, Bridges, Water-ways & other Means of Communication		14. Rural Electrification		15. Non-conventional Energy Sources		16. Poverty Alleviation		
		Maintenance & Supervision of water sources & supply	implementation of distant water supply scheme	Encourage public using non-conventional energy source	Firewood & fodder plantation	Execution of TNADP	Formation & maintenance of roads, culverts	Removal of encroachment & impose penalty	Maintenance of street lights	Identifying the theft of electricity	Creating awareness	Identification of beneficiaries under this head	Identification of beneficiaries for various schemes under this head	Informed authorities misuse of funds/grant by beneficiary	Preparation of Plan
1	2	24	25	26	27	28	29	30	31	32	33	34	35	36	37
1.	Balamuthur														
2.	Bodithasan-patti														
3.	Kattuma-nnarkoil														
4.	Eramanaic-kanpatti														

(*Contd.*)

(*Contd.*)

1	2	24	25	26	27	28	29	30	31	32	33	34	35	36	37
5.	Guruvap-panpettai														
6.	Kalaiyur														
7.	Vittaneri														
8.	Kandra-theertham														
9.	Kondacheri														
10.	Kottur														
11.	Kunthala-patti														
12.	Kuppam-palayam														
13.	Kuppinaic-kanpatti														
14.	Maamandur														
15.	Manjampati														
16.	Mathiyanur														

(*Contd.*)

(*Contd.*)

1	2	24	25	26	27	28	29	30	31	32	33	34	35	36	37
17.	Melanettur														
18.	Mudikan-danallor														
19.	Kakkoor														
20.	Pali														
21.	Perumala-garam														
22.	Polukurichi														
23.	Ramar-puram														
24.	Sarukkalai														
25.	Saruthupatti														
26.	Sekkanur														
27.	Sengipatti														
28.	Sivagana-puram														

(*Contd.*)

(Contd.)

1	2	24	25	26	27	28	29	30	31	32	33	34	35	36	37
29.	Soodiyur														
30.	Sundaraja-puram														
31.	Thamarai-padi														
32.	Thuthipattu														
33.	Uchimalai-kuppam														
34.	Su.Valavetti														
35.	Vanduvan-cheri														
36.	Vazhakkarai														
37.	Veeranam														
38.	Vilangudi														

(Contd.)

(*Contd.*)

Sl. No.	Name of the Panchayat	17. Education			18. Technical Training & Vocational Education		19. Adult & Non-formal Education	20. Libraries	21. Cultural Activities		22. Markets and Fairs		23. Health and Sanitation		
		Create infrastructure facilities for schools	Recommend opening of new schools	Setup education committee	Dissemination of information regarding	Recommend necessary steps	Select beneficiaries and implement programmes	No reading rooms & Libraries	Take necessary steps to avoid social evils	Financial contribution to sports development authority	Issue of license to shops	Coordinate coop. marketing society	Identification of beneficiaries implementation of various schemes under this head	Regular health appraisal of school children/health camp	Provision of drainage, sanitation and disposal of waste
1	2	38	39	40	41	42	43	44	45	46	47	48	49	50	51
1.	Balamuthur	✓													
2.	Bodithasanpatti	✓											✓		
3.	Kattumannar-koil														
4.	Eramanaickan-patti												✓		

(*Contd.*)

(Contd.)

1	2	38	39	40	41	42	43	44	45	46	47	48	49	50	51
5.	Guruvappan-pettai														
6.	Kalaiyur	✓											✓	✓	
7.	Vittaneri	✓													
8.	Kandratheer-tham			✓									✓		
9.	Kondacheri	✓													
10.	Kottur														
11.	Kunthalapatti												✓		
12.	Kuppampala-yam														
13.	Kuppinaickan-patti														
14.	Maamandur	✓													
15.	Manjampati	✓													
16.	Mathiyanur												✓		

(Contd.)

(Contd.)

1	2	38	39	40	41	42	43	44	45	46	47	48	49	50	51
17.	Melanettur														
18.	Mudikanda-nallor	✓											✓		
19.	Kakkoor				✓										
20.	Pali													✓	
21.	Perumalagaram	✓											✓		
22.	Polukurichi														
23.	Ramarpuram												✓		
24.	Sarukkalai	✓													
25.	Saruthupatti														
26.	Sekkanur												✓		
27.	Sengipatti			✓											
28.	Sivaganapuram														
29.	Soodiyur														

(Contd.)

(*Contd.*)

1	2	38	39	40	41	42	43	44	45	46	47	48	49	50	51
30.	Sundaraja-puram														
31.	Thamaraipadi	✓													
32.	Thuthipattu														
33.	Uchimalai-kuppam														
34.	Su.Valavetti												✓		
35.	Vanduvancheri														
36.	Vazhakkarai														
37.	Veeranam														
38.	Vilangudi	✓													

(*Contd.*)

(*Contd.*)

Sl. No.	Name of the Panchayat	24. Family Welfare			25. Women & Child Development	26. Social Welfare	27. Welfare of Weaker Sections			28. P.D.S.	29. Maintenance of Community assets
		Village health committee	Asst.in identification of beneficiaries/implementation of various schemes under this head	Awareness campaign for benefit of pregnant women and others	Asst.in identification of beneficiaries/implementation of various schemes under this head	Asst.in identification of beneficiaries/implementation of various schemes under this head	Asst.in identification of beneficiaries/implementation of various schemes under this head	Action taken on bonded labourers	Civil Rights protection	Inspection of ration shops/action taken	Protection of community assets from misuse
1	2	52	53	54	55	56	57	58	59	60	61
1.	Balamuthur					✓					
2.	Bodithasanpatti										
3.	Kattumannarkoil										
4.	Eramanaickanpatti										✓
5.	Guruvappanpettai										
6.	Kalaiyur										
7.	Vittaneri										
8.	Kandratheertham										
9.	Kondacheri										
10.	Kottur										
11.	Kunthalapatti										
12.	Kuppampalayam										

(*Contd.*)

(*Contd.*)

1	2	52	53	54	55	56	57	58	59	60	61
13.	Kuppinaickanpatti										
14.	Maamandur										
15.	Manjampati										
16.	Mathiyanur										
17.	Melanettur										
18.	Mudikandanallor										
19.	Kakkoor										
20.	Pali										
21.	Perumalagaram										
22.	Polukurichi										
23.	Ramarpuram					✓					
24.	Sarukkalai										
25.	Saruthupatti										✓
26.	Sekkanur										
27.	Sengipatti										
28.	Sivaganapuram										
29.	Soodiyur										
30.	Sundarajapuram										
31.	Thamaraipadi										
32.	Thuthipattu										
33.	Uchimalaikuppam										
34.	Su. Valavetti										
35.	Vanduvancheri										
36.	Vazhakkarai										
37.	Veeranam										
38.	Vilangudi										

(*Contd.*)

Focus is always on two marginalised sections, namely women and *Dalits* in the New Panchayat Raj System in two dimensions: first, how the elected women representatives and the elected *Dalit* representatives who assumed responsibilities have performed their roles and responsibilities by making use of the opportunities provided to them constitutionally and secondly, to what extent the women and *Dalit* elected representatives have taken cognizance of the issues of women and *Dalit* while performing their functions in Panchayats. No doubt, the task before them is stupendous and the conditions prevailing in the society at the grassroots are not quite conducive. Yet they have to perform their roles since they have come to occupy the position legitimately. It is a common perception while looking at the scenario that the women and *Dalit* representatives cannot deliver goods as they have to struggle a lot even to stabilize their position in the system. To take up the issues of women and *Dalits* in the Panchayat administration they have to crucify themselves in the system. Hence it is a curiosity at all levels to understand the struggle of the elected women and *Dalit* representatives in the Panchayat Raj System. It is against this background that this study has been undertaken. Cases have been selected on the basis of information provided by the Project Officer, DRDA, of the respective Districts and the NGO functioning very near to the Panchayat. The elected women and *Dalit* representatives have proved their worth in their performance. They have established the fact that they are second to none provided opportunity is given to them legitimately. It is inferred from the study that their recruitment to the office is an outcome of a combination of factors such as the respondents' public contact, their family reputation, party affiliation, parents' status in the community and so on. But the process is not so easy. It involves a struggle. It is the reality that the existing social order does not relish this special arrangement of reservation of seats for *Dalit* and women. First the Caste Hindus deliberately made attempts to thwart the new arrangement. Since they could not succeed, they found a new way by fixing proxies both for *Dalits* and women. Whenever the community is mature, they understand the process of social transformation and look for good candidates from *Dalits* and women. The moment *Dalits* and women are elected to Panchayats, sensitized and conscientized citizens the elected representatives will take up the issues of women and *Dalits*. In many places the community Panchayats have posed a volley of problems to the elected women and *Dalit* representatives. The elected women and *Dalit* representatives could not take up the sensitive issues of women and *Dalits* as they are being challenged by the community Panchayats. Community Panchayats are very powerful as they have established a hold over the community and powers a corpus fund larger than that of the formal Panchayat. Common properties are still with the community Panchayats and they mobilize resources from them as they are auctioned by Panchayats and the reauctioned by the Community Panchayats.

To overcome the problems posed by the Community Panchayats, the elected representatives expect the support of the State Government. But the machinery of the State Government does not extend any help to the formal Panchayats. As a result they have to confront the traditional Panchayats on their own. It is beyond doubt that the reservation of seats for women and *Dalit* provides new opportunities for these two sections to improve their conditions. While taking up their responsibility, they develop a vision which, however, cannot be realized in the Panchayat system as they have to face a volley of problems and obstacles.

It is true that real democracy is nurtured at the grassroots only by the women and *Dalit* leaders as they never behave in an authoritarian fashion. Having been subjugated for long they never indulge in the authoritarian way of looking at things. They are transparent and non-corrupt. But the administrative system which handles Panchayati Raj affairs is deeply entrenched in corrupt practices. One cannot expect corruption free administration in Panchayat as corruption prevails above the Panchayat. Since the Panchayat is working in a corrupt environment, no Panchayat President is willing to be transparent on certain matters.

The Gram Sabha is convened but, without understanding the spirit of Gram Sabha, both the leaders and the people participate in Gram Sabha meetings. Gram Panchayat Presidents collects petitions and demands from the people on the day of the Gram

Sabha meeting and send the same to the District Collector. In the next Gram Sabha meeting, members ask what has happened to the petitions given at the previous Gram Sabha meeting. When there is no positive reply people feel that it is a waste of time and hence people do not evince interest in Gram Sabha meetings. Politically influential individuals consider the Gram Sabha meeting an opportunity to browbeat and shame the President by asking questions as to why the Panchayati President is not able to solve the problems of the people.

Ward members, without knowing their powers, ask for works to be carried out directly by themselves in their wards. They have both personal and public demands. In the event of not meeting their demands the President has to earn the displeasure of the ward members and they begin to disassociate themselves from the activities of the Panchayats and to act as opposition party members. The Vice-President of the Gram Panchayat either demands a share in the works to be carried out by the Panchayat or some amount of money as the Vice-President has to sign the cheque in the Panchayat administration. The Panchayat clerk is another individual disturbing the Panchayats as they are novices in administration. Sometimes Panchayat Presidents are held responsible for the mistakes committed by the clerk.

Wherever the Gram Panchayat Presidents are trained, they are able to understand the administrative procedure and they establish a grip over Panchayat administration and management. Keeping in view the poor capacity and skill of the Panchayat Presidents and the clerks, officials at higher level tend to dominate the Panchayat system. Officials want to establish their control over the Panchayat system. They expect the Panchayat to function in accordance with the directions of the officials.

The elected Gram Panchayat women and *Dalit* Presidents are aware of the problems of women and *Dalit* and they act on those issues subtly and not openly as otherwise they will face opposition.

Caste discrimination is yet another serious problem that the Panchayats face. No President from the SC has said that the village is free from caste discrimination. Barring a few many of the Gram Panchayats have this practice though not openly.

The Community Panchayats not only control common properties and corpus funds but also the temples. As a result they do not allow the *Dalits* to enter the temple. In some areas the traditional leaders have realized the on going social transformation and are not so strict in prohibiting the *Dalits* to enter the temples of the Caste Hindus. In some places, they are still strict and hence the youth of the *Dalit* community agitate against this practice. This trend has disturbed the peaceful atmosphere of the villages.

In many places, caste associations are vibrant and they look at Panchayat activities only from the caste perspective. They spend money for the activities of their association. Cine Fans' Associations have been formed and they organise cultural activities in the villages. It is a kind of identity perpetuated at the grassroots level by the youth. Beyond that they do not engaging in any useful work. Only the self help group women organize themselves for socio-cconomic activities and help the Panchayat also in its activities.

Political parties are very active only during the time of election. They do not create any problem for the Panchayats but they exert pressure on Panchayats to include the party men in the Below Poverty Line (BPL) list to get the benefits of the government through various schemes. If the Panchayat leaders refuse to do so, they approach officials through MLAs and MPs and get the names included. As a result the real BPL list is not maintained in the Panchayats. The really poor are left out as they are not party card holders. Panchayat leaders who have got trained in Panchayat administration do well in their job and they are able to manage the officials. They get almost all the schemes to their Panchayats as they have established contact with the officers who operate rural development schemes and programmes. Normally the traditional Panchayats spend money for temple festivals or repairing of tanks and ponds only. Able Panchayat Presidents establish good rapport with the traditional Panchayat and get money from them for paying the matching grant to the government for availing of government scheme.

Sectoral departments do not cooperate with the Panchayat as a system. Individual officials help Panchayats in them individual capacity as the Panchayat leaders have developed familiarity with them.

There is yet another problem in the Panchayat administration, namely, the non-payment of tax and yet expecting more services, that too quality service, from the Panchayat. The government gives incentives to the Panchayats which collect cent-per-cent house tax and that money can be used for Panchayat development activities. As MLAs and MPs give promises, local body leaders also give promises during the election. But, after the election, the defeated candidates unitedly instigate the people not to contribute anything to the Panchayat but ask for more free service. People are thus oriented not to pay any tax. Now Panchayat leaders have to revise the tax and collect the tax. It is a very big hurdle and barrier for the smooth functioning of the Panchayats.

Removal of encroachment is a threat to the life of the leaders. It is the duty of the Panchayat to remove the encroachments on the commons as per the provisions of the Panchayat Act. But the Panchayats have to rely on the support of the police as they have no police power. The police normally do not come to the support of the Panchayats. The defeated candidates work along with the encroachers to baulk the Panchayat leaders if Panchayats take steps to remove encroachment.

Yet another vital issue which affects the Panchayat administration is the menace of alcohol in the rural areas. Women leaders are conscious of the implications of alcohol in the rural society. Women and children are the most affected by the prevalence of alcohol in the villages. SHG women are sensitive towards this issue. When they take up this issue, the women leaders have to face volley of problems posted by the liquor mafia with the support of the police. Only in certain pockets they are being controlled.

All these problems are being faced by the women leaders for which the leadership quality of the Gram Panchayat Presidents and their capability and skill matter much. They have acquired the needed skill and capability within a short period of time as they had the urge, motivation and commitment to do things for the people. Further the women and *Dalit* leaders found the

Panchayat a space meant or development. To perform better and bring more schemes to the village they mend and amend themselves in terms of attitude and behaviour.

The elected women and *Dalit* leaders are interested in taking up the issues of women, *Dalits* and children. To some extent they have in this succeeded. They will show the way to others. But it is all through a prolonged struggle. Apart from the assigned responsibilities and functions the Panchayat leaders who found the Panchayat a space for development activities assume several responsibilities and work on them to bring development to their Panchayat areas.

It has been proved beyond doubt that an ordinary woman and a *Dalit* from a very poor family can come to a public space and do service to the people honestly. They can improve their skill, capacity and capability to manage the affairs of the Panchayats. Of course, the Panchayat administration will face a lot of challenges as there are several forces working against the devolution of powers.

It is their perception that by providing needed infrastructure facilities and creating awareness and opportunities people can be empowered to develop on their own. Even though the *Dalits* and women are in positions, social justice can not be ensured fully. They struggle a lot to sensitize the people on this issue. They need a support structure and cooperation from the government. But they perpetuate the hope that the Panchayat can achieve development and social justice. Since the Panchayat has come as a system it will stay despite government changes at State and Central level. For the Panchayat to perform its functions effectively a movement has to be built up from the bottom as the system has been created from above.

4

RECOMMENDATIONS

In Tamil Nadu, unlike in Kerala, West Bengal, Karnataka and Madhya Pradesh, there is no conscious effort on the part of the State Government to put the Panchayat institutions in perspective. Tamil Nadu still gives the impression that Panchayats are under the control of the State Government. The Panchayat leaders have to swim against the current. Whatever achievements are recorded in Panchayats, they are the sole contribution of the Panchayat leaders. Even the political climate is also not favourable to the devolution of powers. Rural development and Panchayati Raj issues do not figure frequently in the Legislative Assembly debates. It is against this background that the Panchayati institutions are functioning in Tamil Nadu. One noteworthy feature is that the Panchayati leaders are spearheading the movement for grassroots democracy for which they organise conferences and workshops through their associations and federations. In Tamil Nadu Panchayati Raj System, the District Panchayat Presidents, Block Panchayat Chairpersons, Gram Panchayat Presidents, *Dalit* Gram Panchayat Presidents and Women Gram Panchayat Presidents have formed their associations separately for each category. Periodically they organise conferences and workshops and discuss their issues. They submit their memoranda to the Ministers of the State Government, Central Government and appropriate officials. They invite State and Central Government Ministers to their programmes. In a totally negative atmosphere they are working positively with a sense of hope. They need support services on various fronts.

First they need training. Only through capacity building they can understand their role and function and perform effectively. Further they require the information needed for Panchayat administration from the State Government whenever orders are passed by the Government. Updated State Panchayat Act, rules, schemes available for rural development and administrative manual have to be supplied to the Panchayats.

Without the sectoral departments, the Panchayat cannot fulfil its obligation to the people. As such there is no linkage between the Panchayats and the sectoral departments. It was expected that, after the establishment of the Panchayati Raj System, the development activities would be carried out in a demand driven mode and not in supply driven mode. As the sectoral departments continue to function independently without having linkage with Panchayats, rural development activities are still carried out in a supply driven mode.

Micro level planning is an essential exercise to be undertaken in every village, every block and every district as it is included in the Constitution itself. But there is no effort on the part of the State Government to initiate this exercise. Yet, sporadic exercises have been carried out by Gram Panchayats with the support of some development organisations.

To overcome the problem of encroachment, the State Government has to initiate a massive drive against encroachment through the district administration. After the removal of encroachments, the commons can be handed over to the Panchayats for effective management.

Panchayat leaders can be sensitized on social development issues. Social development indicators can be fixed and Panchayats can be asked to work on the issues to achieve the target for which incentives could be given as in the case of house tax collection.

Special training could be given to the Gram Panchayat leaders in auditing and accounting with regard to Panchayat administration. Periodical refresher courses could be given to Panchayat leaders. Interface meetings between officials and the Gram Panchayat leaders could be arranged under the leadership of the District Collector with the assistance of the Project Officer, DRDA. Interface could be organised for Panchayat leaders by taking them to various other states where Panchayats are working for social development.

Problems in Panchayat administration are of different dimensions and nature. Some of the problems could be tackled at the Block level, many of them could be resolved at the District level, a few of them could be sorted out at the State level and still a few could be solved only through amending the existing law. Problems could be projected at the appropriate level for which Panchayat leaders could approach the appropriate institutions. For many of the problems, officials are the big hurdles. Their attitude has to be changed. Training programmes could be organised for the Panchayat officials also.

Well administered Panchayats could be projected as models for emulation through the media. An Ombudsman could be created to redress the grievances of the public against Panchayats. Annual Panchayat conferences can be organised by the State Government. A State Development Council could be formed with the representatives of the Local Bodies.

APPENDIX

Sl. No.	*Gram Panchayat*	*Panchayat Union*	*District*	*Educa-tion*	*Comm-unity*	*Sex*	*Age*
1.	Balamuthur	Orathanadu	Thanjavur	12th	BC	Female	28
2.	Bodithasanpatti	Andipatti	Theni	9th	SC	Female	70
3.	Eechampoondi	Kattumannarkoil	Cuddalore	8th	SC	Female	39
4.	Eramanaickanpatti	Palani	Dindigul	11th	SC	Female	55
5.	Guruvappanpettai	Kurinjipadi	Cuddalore	No Educn	MBC	Female	50
6.	Kalaiyur	Paramakkudi	Ramanatha-puram	12th	SC	Male	31
7.	Vittaneri	Kalayarkoil	Sivagangai	10th	MBC	Female	38
8.	Kandratheertham	Thirumanur	Ariyalur	5th	SC	Female	35
9.	Kondacheri	Kadambathur	Thirvallur	11th	SC	Female	45
10.	Kottur	Theni	Theni	10th	SC	Female	42
11.	Kunthalapatti	Virudhunagar	Virudhunagar	7th	BC	Female	35
12.	Kuppampalayam	Kudimangalam	Coimbatore	11th	SC	Male	33
13.	Kuppinaickenpatti	Theni	Theni	5th	SC	Male	35
14.	Maamandur	Kaveripakkam	Vellore	9th	SC	Female	36
15.	Manjampatti	Madurai West	Madurai	M.A.B.L	SC	Male	39
16.	Mathiyanur	Thirunavalur	Villupuram	B.A.	SC	Male	33
17.	Melanettur	Manamadurai	Sivangangai	8th	SC	Female	38
18.	Mudikandanallor	Keerapalayam	Cuddalore	9th	SC	Female	48
19.	Kakkoor	Muthukulathoor	Ramanatha-puram	9th	SC	Female	38
20.	Pali	Ulundurpet	Villupuram	10th	SC	Male	35
21.	Perumalagaram	Koradacheri	Thiruvarur	10th	BC	Female	42
22.	Polukurichi	Chentha-mangalam	Namakkal	9th	SC	Female	47
23.	Ramarpuram	Agasthees-waram	Kanyakumari	PUC	BC	Female	40
24.	Sarukkalai	Paramathi	Namakkal	Nil	SC	Female	35
25.	Saruthupatti	Periyakulam	Then	7th	SC	Male	63
26.	Sekkanur	Vellore	Vellore	8th	SC	Male	62
27.	Sengipatti	Thanjavur	Thanjavur	M.Phil	SC	Female	30
28.	Sivagnanapuram	Nilakkottai	Dindigul	10th	SC	Male	68
29.	Soodiyur	Paramakkudi	Ramanatha-puram	3rd	MBC	Female	42
30.	Sundarajapuram	Rajapalayam	Virudhunagar	7th	SC	Female	37
31.	Thamaraipadi	Dindigul	Dindigul	10th	SC	Female	29
32.	Thuthipattu	Kaniyampadi	Vellore	5th	SC	Female	32
33.	Uchimalai-kuppam	Sengam	Thiruvanna-malai	10th	SC	Female	27
34.	Sn.Valavetti	Thiruvanna-malai	Thiruvanna-malai	11th	SC	Female	65
35.	Vanduvancheri	Vedaranyam	Nagapattinam	10th	MBC	Female	39
36.	Vazhakkarai	Keevalur	Nagapattinam	3rd	SC	Male	49
37.	Veeranam	Thandarampatu	Thiruvanna-malai	5th	SC	Male	49
38.	Vilangudi	Ariyalur	Ariyalur	8th	SC	Male	47

BIBLIOGRAPHY

Arthreya, V.B. and Rajeshwari, K.S., *Women Participation in Panchayat Raj : A Case Study from Tamil Nadu,* Chennai : M.S. Swaminathan Foundation, 1998.

Aram, M., and G. Palanithurai, "Tamil Nadu," in George Mathew, (ed.)., *Status of Panchayati Raj in the States and Union Territories of India 2000,* New Delhi : Concept Publishing Company, 2000.

Celine Rani, A., *Emerging Pattern of Rural Women Leadership in India,* New Delhi : Kalpaz Publications, 2002.

Comparative Politics : System, Proess and Policy, Boston : Little Brown, 1978.

Dharampal, *The Madras Panchayat System II : A General Assessment,* Delhi : Impex India, 1972.

Eckstein, H., "Authority Relations and Governmental Performance" in *Comparative Political Studies,* 2 (Oct., 1969).

Eckstein, H., *The Ealuation of Political Performance : Problems and Dimensions,* California : Sage Publications, 1971.

Gananaprakasam, C., *Local Government in Tamil Nadu (in Tamil),* Madurai : Madurai Kamaraj University Publication Division, 1986.

Gurr, T.R., and McCleveland, M., *Political Performance : A Twelve Nations Study,* California : Sage Publications, 1971.

Jeyabal, P., and Dravidamani, K., "Women Panchayat Presidents," *Social Welfare* Vol. 44, No. 1 April 1997.

Kothari, Rajni, "Political Performance and the Policy Process" in *Survey of Research in Political Science : Political System,* Vol. I, ICSSR, New Delhi : Allied Publishers Private Ltd., 1979.

MIDS, *An Evaluation of Functions and Finances of Rural Local Bodies in Tamil Nadu,* Chennai : Madras Institute of Development Studies, 1999.

Palanithurai G., "Glittering Women Leadership" (in Tamil), *Thittam,* Vol. 30: No. 10 June, 1999.

Palanithurai G., *New Panchayati Raj System at Work : An Evaluation,* New Delhi : Concept Publishing Company, 1999.

Palanithurai, G. (ed) *Caste, Politics and Society in Tamil Nadu,* New Delhi : Kanishka Publishers and Distributors, 1994.

Palanithurai, G. (ed.), *New Panchayat Raj System Status and Prospects,* New Delhi : Kanishka Publishers and Distributors, 1996.

Palanithurai, G., (ed) *Dynamics of New Panchayat Raj System in India,* Vol. I, New Delhi : Concept Publishing Company, 2002.

Palanithurai, G., (ed) *Dynamics of New Panchayat Raj System in India,* Vol. II, New Delhi : Concept Publishing Company, 2002.

Palanithurai, G., "Capacity Building Exercise for Elected Representatives in Tamil Nadu," *Journal of Rural Development,* Vol. 16 : No. 4 Oct-Dec. 1997.

Palanithurai, G., "Capacity Building for Women Local Body Leaders" (in Tamil), *Thittam,* Vol. 31 : No. 9 May, 1998.

Palanithurai, G., "Corruption at Micro Level and Ways to Contain" in N. Narayanasamy, M. P. Boraian and M.A. Jeyaraju, (eds.), *Corruption at the Grassroots : The Shades and Shadows,* New Delhi : Concept Publishing Company, 2000.

Palanithurai, G., "Empowering People : An Agenda for Immediate Action," *Gandhigram Golden Jubilee 1947-1997,* Gandhigram : Gandhigram Trust, 1997.

Palanithurai, G., "Empowerment of Women – A Novel Exercise," *Kurukshetra*, Vol. XLII : No. 9 June 1994.

Palanithurai, G., "Evaluation Political Performance of Party in Power" in *Caste, Politics and Society in Tamil Nadu,* (ed) G. Palanithurai, New Delhi : Kanishka Publishers and Distributors, 1994.

Palanithurai, G., "Gram Sabha : A Civil Society at the Bottom," in R.C. Choudhury and S.P. Jain (eds.), *Strenghtening Village Democracy,* Hyderabad : National Institute of Rural Development, 1999.

Palanithurai, G., "Impediments to Empowerment of Women : Experience of Elected Women Representatives in Panchayats in Tamil Nadu," *The Indian Journal of Political Science,* Vol. 63 : No. 1 (March 2002).

Palanithurai, G., "Need for Revitalizing Panchayati Raj Institutions in Tamil Nadu," *Southern Economist,* Vol. 32 ; No 7 August, 1993.

Palanithurai, G., "Needing Social Action for Effective Panchayati Raj Functioning," *Kurukshetra* Vol. XLV : No. 9 June 1993.

Palanithurai, G., "New Panchayati Raj System in the Development Process" (in Tamil), *Thittam,* Vol. 29, No. 11 July, 1998.

Palanithurai, G., "New Panchayati Raj and Rural Economy" (in Tamil), *Thittam,* Vol. 29 : No. 2 Oct., 1997.

Palanithurai, G., "Plan Preparation with the Participation of People in Tamil Nadu" (in Tamil), *Thittam,* Vol. 32 : No. 3 Nov. 2000.

Palanithurai, G., "Planning for Village Development" (in Tamil), *Thittam,* Vol. 28 ; No. 18 June, 1998.

Palanithurai, G., "Planning in Peoples Panchayat" (in Tamil), *Thittam,* Vol. 30 : No. 3 Nov. 1998.

Palanithurai, G., "Role of Women in New Panchayati Raj System" (in Tamil), *Thittam,* Vol. 27 : No. 3, Nov., 1995.

Palanithurai, G., "State of the Art : A Status Report on a New Panchayati Raj System in Tamil Nadu," *Anubhav* Vol. 1 No. 2, 1997.

Palanithurai, G., "Synergization of Institutional Arrangement for Development and Social Jusice at the Grassroots : A Case Analysis," in S.P. Jain, (ed.), *Emerging Institutions for Decentralized Rural Development,* Vol. II, Hyderabad : National Institute of Rural Development, 2001.

Palanithurai, G., "The Genre of Women Leaders in Local Bodies : Experience from Tamil Nadu," *The Indian Journal of Public Administration,* Vol. XLVII : No. 1 (Jan-Mar 2001).

Palanithurai, G., "Women Leadership and Women Empowerment," *Thittam,* Vol. 32 : No. 12 August 2001.

Palanithurai, G., and Ragupathy, V., *Empowering People through Panchayats : Problems Faced by the Elected Panchayat Leaders in Tamil Nadu,* Gandhigram : Rajiv Gandhi Chair of Panchayati Raj Studies, 2001.

Palanithurai, G., *Capacity Building for Local Body Leaders,* New Delhi : Concept Publishing Company, 2001.

Palanithurai, G., *Dimensions of New Panchayati Raj System (in Tamil),* Gandhigram : Rajiv Gandhi Chair for Panchayati Raj Studies, 1997.

Palanithurai, G., Dwaraki, B.R., and Narayanasamy, S., (eds.), *Major Issus in New Panchayati Raj System,* New Delhi : Kanishika Publishers and Distributors, 1997.

Palanithurai, G., *Empowering People : Issues and Solutions,* New Delhi : Kanishka Publishers and Distributors, 1996.

Palanithurai, G., *Empowering People for Prosperity : A Study in New Panchayat Raj System,* New Delhi : Kanishka Publishers and Distributors, 1994.

Palanithurai, G., *Empowerment of Women : Emperience of the Elected Women Representatives in Grassroots Institutions,* Gandhigram : Rajiv Gandhi Chair for Panchayati Raj Studies, 2002.

Palanithurai, G., *Empowerment of Women : Problems Faced by the Elected Women Representatives – Experience from Tamil Nadu,* Gandhigram : Rajiv Gandhi Chair for Panchayati Raj Studies, 2001.

Palanithurai, G., *Good Governance at the Grassroots,* Gandhigram : Rajiv Gandhi Chair for Panchayati Raj Studies, 1998.

Palanithurai, G., *Grassroots Democracy in Indian Society,* New Delhi : Concept Publishing Company, 2000.

Palanithurai, G., *New Panchayati Raj System in Tamil Nadu (Tamil),* Chennai : South Vision, 2000.

Palanithurai, G., *Panchayati Raj in Tamil Nadu : Act, Rule, and Schemes (in Tamil)* Chennai : South Vision, 2002.

Palanithurai, G., *Panchayati System in Tamil Nadu* (in Tamil), Chennai : South Vision, 1998.

Palanithurai, G., *Perception of Grassroots Democracy and Political Performance,* New Delhi : MD Publications Pvt. Ltd., 1999.

Palanithurai, G., *Recommendations for Effective Functioning of Panchayati Raj System in Tamil Nadu,* Gandhigram : Rajiv Gandhi Chair for Panchayati Raj Studies, 1998.

Palanithurai, G., *Towards Decentralizing of Powers,* Gandhigram : Rajiv Gandhi Chair for Panchayati Raj Studies, 2000.

Palanithurai, G., "Empowering People or Bureaucracy", *Southern Economist,* Vol. 33 : No. 13, Nov. 1994.

Rajiv Gandhi Chair, *Management of Gram Panchayat* (in Tamil) Gandhigram : Rajiv Gandhi Chair for Panchayati Raj Studies, 2003.

Rajiv Gandhi Chair, *Manual for Capacity Building Exercise to the Local Body Leaders* (in Tamil), Gandhigram : Rajiv Gandhi Chair for Panchayati Raj Studies, 1997.

Rajiv Gandhi Chair, *Manual for Leadership Training for Women,* Gandhigram : Rajiv Gandhi Chair for Panchayati Raj Studies, 2002.

Rural Development Department, *Compilation of Government Orders for Development Activities* (in Tamil), Chennai : Directorate of Rural Development, 2000.

Rural Development Department, *Compilation of Government Orders Relating to Panchayati Structure* (in Tamil), Chennai : Directorate of Rural Development, 2000.

Rural Development Department, *Rules Relating to Tamil Nadu Panchayati Raj Act* (in Tamil), Chennai : Directorate of Rural Development, 2000.

Santha, E.K., *Political Participation of Women in Panchayati Raj : Haryana, Kerala and Tamil Nadu,* (OCC Paper Services), New Delhi : Institute of Social Sciences, 1999.

Saraswathi, S., *The Madras Panchayat System,* Vol. I, New Delhi : Impex India, 1973.

State Planning Commission, *District Development Plan : Guide Book* (in Tamil), Chennai : State Planning Commission, 2001.

State Planning Commission, *Entrustment of Responsibilities of Panchayati Institutions,* Chennai : State Planning Commission, 1997.

State Planning Commission, *Report of the Working Group in Decentralized Planning and Panchayati Raj,* Chennai : Government of Tamil Nadu, 1997.

Subramanian, S., "Tamil Nadu," in G. Reddy, *Patterns of Panchayati Raj in India,* Delhi : Macmillan Company of India, 1997.

Teekathir, *Special Supplement for Local Bodies,* Madurai : Theekathir Publications. 1999.

INDEX